Pakistan

After 9/11

Pakistan

After 9/11

Edited By
Sreedhar

Manas Publications
New Delhi-110 002 (INDIA)

Manas Publications
(We Convert Fighters into Writers)
(Publishers, Library Suppliers, Importers & Exporters)
4402/5-A, Ansari Road (Opp. HDFC Bank)
Darya Ganj, New Delhi-110 002 (India)
Off. 011-23260783, 23265523, Res. 011-23842660
Fax: 011-23272766
E-mail: manaspublications@gmail.com
manaspublications@yahoo.com
Website: www. manaspublications.in

2nd Impression 2015 (FP - 2003)

ISBN: 81-7049-112-6

₹ 795/-

Printed in India at
Rajdhani Printers, Delhi
and published by Mrs Suman Lata for
Manas Publications,
4402/5-A, Ansari Road, (Opp HDFC Bank),
Darya Ganj, New Delhi-110 002 (INDIA)

About The Contributors

Sreedhar was associated in various capacities with the Institute for Defence Studies and Analyses (IDSA), New Delhi, for more than three decades. A graduate from National Defence College, New Delhi, he was a visiting Fellow at Princeton University, USA, 1978-79; Australian National University, Canberra, (1982); and Middle East Technical University, Turkey, (1998 and 2001). He has written extensively on South and South West Asian security issues. His latest book, Afghan Buzkashi, co-authored with Mahendra Ved, is considered as one of the definitive works on the Taliban. Currently he is a Visiting Professor, School of International Studies, Jawaharlal Nehru University (JNU), New Delhi.

Air Commodre Prashant Dikshit (Retd.), after distinguished service in Indian Air Force, is specializing on proliferation of small arms in South Asia. He was a Senior Fellow, Institute for Defence Studies Analysis, New Delhi (1993-95). Currently he is a Deputy Director at the Institute of Peace and Conflict Studies, New Delhi.

M. K. Dhar had spent long years in the Intelligence Bureau of the Ministry of Home Affairs, Government of India. His recent book, Mission to Pakistan, is a fictionalized account of a real life story.

Pinaki Bhattarcharya, a special correspondent of Mathroobhoomi, a Malayalam daily, is based in Kolkata. He has been a keen watcher of developments in Pakistan.

Prof. Kalim Bahadur, who specializes on Pakistan, recently retired from the School of International Studies, Jawaharlal Nehru University, New Delhi.

Smruti Pattanaik is a Research Officer at the Institute for Defence Studies and Analyses, New Delhi. She specialises on security related issues pertaining to South Asia. She was a recipient of Kodikara Fellowship (1999) RCSS, Colombo.

Mahendra Ved is with the Times of India, New Delhi. He specializes on South Asia and has written extensively on developments in the region. He co-authored with Sreedhar the book, Afghan Turmoil: Changing Equations and Afghan Buzkashi.

Kapil Kaul, who was educated at Jawaharlal Nehru University, New Delhi, had worked with IDSA, New Delhi. He is currently one of the leading defence analysts in India.

Preface

The Western world has always looked upon Pakistan today as a single geographical unit. However, a look at the history of the Indian subcontinent tells us that birth of Pakistan state is one of those accidents of history. A close look at the map of Pakistan shows that Pakistan comprises four provinces–Punjab, Sindh, North West Frontier Provinces and Baluchistan; Northern Areas which were part of the princely state of Jammu and Kashmir prior to 1947 and acceded to Pakistan without the consent of the then ruler of J&K in 1947; and Pakistan occupied Kashmir. Geography apart, there are imbalances in the political and economic clout that various population groups wield. The Punjabi elite, who constitute the power center, have been trying to govern the other three regions for the past 55 years. Has Pakistan evolved as a cohesive nation state, as the rest of the world understands the concept of nationhood? The answer is a definite 'No'. The reasons are many and varied. The various contributors in this book have explained some of them.

After 9/11, with the epicentre of terrorism in Afghanistan decimated, Pakistan has become a new risk to the entire neighbourhood. But the Western media is telling us that Pakistan's ruling elite is a changed lot. The high and mighty in the international security arena are rubbing shoulders with the General in Islamabad. In fact, some of them have parked themselves in Pakistan and with the General's help, have been trying to capture the culprits of the 9/11 tragedy for the past one and half years. The December 2002 clashes between the US and Pakistan troops have shaken them. But there is little to show that their enthusiasm has dampened.

One is tempted to draw an unsavoury comparison: the modern-day Lord Chamberlains have yet to, and may take a very long time to understand the real General in Islamabad. The 1930s had seen an appeasement of the mighty Corporal. What we witness now, very ironically, is appeasement of the weak.

The people responsible for 9/11 are still roaming around, either in Pakistan or in Afghanistan, drawing logistic support from Pakistan. The rulers in Islamabad are making policy statements at regular intervals about their change of heart. However, the ground realities tell us that these are violated even before the ink is dry on those statements. The Pakistani armed forces played what ever games they want for the last 55 years, always with a helping hand from external powers. These games were endorsed some times by extra regional powers like the USA and Saudi Arabia and some times by neighbours like China. The developments since 1998 in and around Pakistan became cause of concern to all these countries.

What happened on 9/11 became a wake up call to them. What happened on 13 December, 2001, in New Delhi is but an example of how India is bearing the brunt of global terrorism in all its ugly forms. And all the while, amidst verbal gymnastic of calling Pakistan the perpetrator of terrorism, India is asked to hold a dialogue with it. In this new situation how Pakistan is looked upon from New Delhi–is examined in this book. It is really an Indian-eyeview of Pakistan. As a nation that is most affected by the shenanigan and being the most valiant fighter against global terrorism, India is at least entitled to have its say—and be heard.

India has dealt with Pakistan in its own way by making a subtle difference between Pakistani rulers and people. I think that is the only policy that can be adopted with a neighbour like Pakistan. In one of my chance encounters with late Murtaza Bhutto, in mid 1980's in south east Asia, he said, "sir we are made prisoners by people like Gen. Zia in our own country in the name of independence. It is not a homeland for muslims but grave yard of muslims. ... How happy are the people in India as compared to us. We have no visionaries like Nehrus and Indirafis and people like Shastre are nonexistent. ... Because of India's benovolence, we remained still today as a nation. If it was any other country, we would have ceased to exist as a seperate nation". Even in the changed situation after 9/11, India has no option but continue this policy.

I am grateful to all the contributors for responding to my request and sharing their views on the subject. We all try to cover the events up to October 2002; and look into future. Nothing dramatic has happened since then to alter our assessment. My thanks are to Dr. K. Santhanam, Director, IDSA, New Delhi, for his continuous encouragement throughout the making of this book. Special thanks to Raju and Situ, my wife and daughter, for allowing me to pursue my work in our little home.

Sreedhar

Introduction

If there is one country that has borne the maximum brunt of nearly three decades of turmoil in Afghanistan, it is Pakistan.

And if there is one country that has befooled the world, and benefitted from being the "frontline" state—earlier against communism and now against terrorism—it is, again, ironically, Pakistan.

For, it is Pakistan alone that does a U-turn in its Afghanistan policy displays a changed heart to the world, but can carry on with its support to the remnants of its erstwhile proteges, and hoodwink the world. It is a classic case of hunting with the hound and running with the hare.

After being a "frontline" state for more than one year in the US war against the Taliban and al-Qaida, Pakistani strategy appears to be similar to the one that it pursued during the US-led proxy war against the former Soviet Union in Afghanistan in the 1980s. By a coincidence, on both the occasions Pakistan was ruled by military dictators –in the 1980s it was General Zia-ul-Haq and now it is

General Pervez Musharraf. Both of them lacked legitimacy to govern and were desperate to cooperate with the West to gain the much needed acceptability of their rule. Their attitude was that if the lone superpower accepted them, then others would automatically follow suit. The economy was in a bad shape in the beginning of the war in the 1980s, and was in much worse shape in 2001 as compared to the early 1980s. On both the occasions the US and its allies provided a lifeline to Pakistan for the services rendered and have helped it to recuperate.

These similarities apart, one can notice some commonalities in Pakistan's strategic objectives. In the early 1980s, when Pakistan agreed to become a frontline state it had three objectives. First, the vexed problem of its western frontiers, the Durand Line between Pakistan and Afghanistan could be resolved; second, if the US-led campaign succeeded, Pakistan could legitimately demand installation of a pro-Pakistani government in Kabul, and lastly, by remaining an ally of the West, it could pursue its clandestine nuclear programme.

On two counts—Durand Line and nuclear programme—Pakistan succeeded. But due to some over-ambitious and corrupt generals, plans of installing a pro-Pakistani regime in Kabul ran into problems. The Mujahideen it had nurtured were too independent for Islamabad's comfort. Pakistan was able to divide them, but not rule them. So, it opted for the Afghan students in the seminaries that dot the Pakistan-Afghanistan border. By all accounts it was Pakistan that installed the Taliban regime in Kabul in 1996. When things were going in its favour, the ambitious generals enlarged their agenda to become leaders of the Islamic world through the Taliban and Osama bin Laden. By about 1998, the initiative was lost to Osama and the rest is a matter of history. Pakistan had total success in its nuclear programme. Pakistan pursued its nuclear weapons programme throughout the 1980s and by 1987-88 it acquired the needed technological capability. This time it pursued its missile programme and succeeded in procuring missiles in completely knocked down state from North Korea.

In 1989, the US, having achieved its own strategic objectives, gave Afghanistan as a war booty to Pakistan and left the region. Once the US left the region, its allies too followed suit. What happened subsequently is Pakistan's search for new allies and friends to finance its programme of manufacturing weapons of mass destruction (WMD). In this new search, Pakistan claimed to have had help from a number of Islamic countries. Whether this help is for the pan-Islamic cause as articulated by jehadis or Pakistan is acting as a proxy to another power in confronting the West is not known as yet. This also means WMD proliferation, which was started by China through Pakistan in mid 1970s, is on the way. This is inspite of the international community's concerns about this proliferation. By projecting itself as a state aligned to the US, Pakistan thus made a mockery of the nuclear non-proliferation treaty. In fact if the reports coming in December 2002, and January 2003, are to be believed, A.Q. Khan Laboratory in Pakistan was marketing nuclear technology as Western multinationals sell chocolate making.

The American friends of Pakistan tell the rest of the world that they will not commit the mistakes they did in 1989; and after 9/11 Pakistan is a changed state. The General talked to another General (Colin Powell) in the Bush Administration and they 'gel' well with each other. A General's word to another General is honoured, the world was told. General Musharraf's swift changes, disowning the Taliban, to discontinue violence and terrorism etc., are to be taken seriously; and he will need time to implement them, the world was repeatedly told by the security managers in Washington D.C. Now it is an open secret that Mutahida Majlis-e-Amal (MMA), the founders of Taliban and al-Qaida, came to power in October 2002 elections through a clear manipulation at ground level, on instructions from GHQ in Rawalpindi. One may argue privately like the Americans and to a certain extent the Chinese too, that General Musharraf can never feel comfortable with people like Maulana Fazlur Rehman and the electoral victory is one of the accidents of the democratic process. To overcome the embrassment created by the MMA's Victory, Gen. Musharaf cleverly manipulated the elected representatives and installed a government headed by Zafarulah Jamali in November 2002. However, in no time it became clear that Jamali's government is a front organisation of Gen. Musharraf and is providing a civilian facade to an army rule. In fact, an Indian Army officer who studied with Musharraf for an year in England told me that the American assessment is right, but the Americans must also note that Musharraf is a great survivor. "To survive he will not hesitate to sleep even with the devil", the officer said. Therefore, General Musharraf allowed the entire top brass of Baluchistan to attend the funeral of Mir Aimal Kansi, who was executed on 14 November, 2002, in the US for killing two US CIA agents way back in 1993. Kansi became a martyr according to people who attended his funeral on 19 November in Quetta. What is amazing about the entire event is that the local corps commander, Lt. Gen. Abdul Qaidir Baloch attended the funeral. Whether the wreath he placed on the coffin was on behalf of the Pakistani Army or State or of his tribe is not known.

All these developments enabled the General in Islamabad to tell his allies in the Bush Administration that he was doing what all he could do for the past one and half years and get away with it. The only concrete thing, he seems to have done after 9/11 is to demonstrate to the US, that he will not allow of the Jehadis to attack western targets from Pakistan soil; and succeeded in it. The US seems to be happy with this decelopment. After the 10 October, 2002, elections, he even acquired a pressure point (some would call it justification of what he is doing vis-à-vis the US). Since the men who matter in the Bush Administration are listening to his arguments and tacitly accepting them, one can safely assume that Pakistan has succeeded till now and may succeed in future. If one goes by the arguements of a section of Pakistan intelligentsia, Bush Administration has no choice but to fall in line with his arguements. It appears the lone super power became a hostage to a tin pot dictator.

However, these developments unleashed two sets of new forces. The ideologies of radical groups, who first succeeded against the Soviet Union and now with the US, have become a force to reckon with in Pakistan politics. Their network is spreading far and wide. The developments of the past one year have shown the amazing ease with which they can shift their base of operations—first from Afghanistan to Pakistan and now partly to Bangladesh. They have extraordinary organizational capabilities!

For a group of radicals to acquire such capabilities, they invariably need a state's support. Here the Pakistan factor comes in. The nexus between radicals on one side and intelligence agencies and the armed forces in Pakistan on the other now became open. By all credible accounts the Pakistan state is providing such support. As has been proved in the case of other countries like Sudan, once the radicals establish such a relationship, they first penetrate deep into the security apparatus, and as and when opportunity arises they will try to enter other organs of the state.

This is exactly what appears to be happening in Pakistan. Initially the radical Islamists cooperated with the intelligence-armed forces nexus for about two decades (from Zia-ul-Haq assuming power in 1977), and penetrated deep into the security apparatus. As the price of cooperation they also got fringe benefits like getting some concessions–the now infamous blasphemy law and Shariat implementation. With the arrival of the Taliban on the scene in 1994, the relationship between the two groups got further cemented. Throughout the rule of popular government from 1987 to 1999, Pakistani armed forces even ensured that these radical Islamist groups were not disturbed by people wielding political power in Islamabad.

With the military coming back to power in October 1999, the relationship once again flourished. One can notice on innumerable occasions Pakistan government supporting the radical Islamists' cause in the name of

Taliban at international fora. Even after 9/11, though people in Islamabad made policy shifts in terms of relationship with the Taliban and al-Qaida, we find the latter finding safe havens in Pakistan. This cannot happen without active support from the Pakistani state apparatus. The US may claim that rogue elements in the ISI and armed forces are doing it. But did these rogue elements do anything in the past without the GHQ's approval? If the answer is yes, then General Musharraf is taking the US for a ride; and if the answer is no, the much talked about command structure in the Pakistani armed forces has broken down. The US game plan is going wrong. Therefore, New Delhi needs to take the US assessment of Pakistan with a pinch of salt.

By clever manipulation of the electoral process, after the 10 October, 2002, elections, most of the known sympathizers and supporters of radical Islamists captured political power in NWFP and a large voice in the National Assembly. The world may be witnessing in the coming months a systematic penetration of these people in the entire Pakistani socio-political systems and consolidation of their position. This means, whether one likes it or not, the theocrats getting firmly entrenched in the system; weeding them out now from mainstream politics will not be as easy as some people hope.

The second force that has been unleashed is the role of the drug mafia. Now it is an established fact that narcotics were the prime source of financial support in the war against the Soviet Union in the 1980s. The same drug barons are now being used to track down the Taliban and al-Qaida for the US, and the Pakistani state apparatus is to protect their interests in the process. If we go by the latest estimates, the opium production level in the Golden crescent which was brought down to less than 2000 metric tons in 2000 has zoomed to about 3500 metric tons in 2002.

A number of reasons are attributed for this increase. The US and its allies who are operating in the Pakistan-Afghanistan region are taking the help of the narcotics mafia to track down the Taliban and al-Qaida cadres and leadership. Therefore, the US is looking the other way. Since the drug mafia is patronized by the Taliban and al-Qaida, they get the needed support. The narcotics mafia is working for both sides.

The way MMA won the elections makes one suspect that the narcotics mafia is making its own independent political power base as well. They brought about an understanding among the various radical Islamist groups, and even proposed a person like Maulana Fazlur Rehman as a primeministerial candidate. It is a different matter, in the end, it is PML (Q) candidate who became the Prime Minister.

Therefore, having gained the requisite political legitimacy through popular mandate, now a confrontation between the policies of the ruling Junta in Islamabad and the MMA can happen any time. Already "Americans go back," and "Americans leave Pakistan" can be heard in places like Peshawar and Quetta. A section of the intelligentsia thinks that except nuisance value, MMA, has no relevance in Pakistan. They ignore the fact, it is the MMA which produced more than 100 suicide bombers, and it is MMA constituents which created Taliban and assited al-Quida. If the US thinks in terms of cheque book diplomacy, it will find it hard to succeed. If the

MMA is removed from power, under the special powers acquired by the President just on the eve of the elections, the MMA can make things difficult for General Musharraf. Now the entire region has to live with this element of uncertainty in Pakistan.

As we go to the press, the war on Iraq is looming large on the horizon; and al-Quida leadership has already announced that leadership of the Islamic countries who support US war on Iraq, have no right to rule. If this is true and the MMA takes this sermon seriously, Pakistan is heading towards an explosive situation.

Contents

I

An Overview

Kapil Kaul

Pakistan, today, finds itself at a crossroad. After fifty-four years of its existence as an independent sovereign state, the only identity it could create for itself amongst the international community is that of a country which breeds, nurtures and promotes Muslim radicals. It is a country torn within by sectarian violence and increasingly identified with jehadi groups engaged in violence and terrorist activities outside its territorial boundaries. The roots of this tragic journey of violence can be traced back to the narrow and weak foundations on which Pakistan was established on 14 August, 1947. The common religious identity on which Pakistan was created failed to deliver to its people the fruits of economic prosperity and political power which they had thought were being denied to them in undivided India. The glue of Islamic brotherhood proved a weak ingredient to hold together a country dominated by feudal values, sectarian pulls and pressures of regional aspirations.

The failure of consecutive political regimes in Pakistan to deliver the goods provided the opportunity to Pakistan's military establishment to step in, beginning with General Ayub Khan's tenure in 1958, to provide an alternative system of governance. Thus started Pakistan's journey towards becoming a praetorian state. The omnipresence of the Pakistan Army in the governance of Pakistan, even during the short civilian governments under the leadership of Zulfiqar Ali Bhutto, Benazir Bhutto and Nawaz Sharif ensured that these regimes were weak and short-lived. The end result of this dispensation was that the key socio-political and economic institutions were left to degenerate or, at best, could only manage a stunted growth.

It was the failure of both, the political as well as the military governance, which left the Pakistani stage wide open for radical Muslim organisations like the Jamaat-e-Islami to step in, and to present before the frustrated and impoverished people of Pakistan a political and economic alternative of Islamic rule. A rule that condemned the 'jahiliya' culture of decaying Islamic values and promoted the hardline puritanical Wahabi culture. One must not forget that the late seventies saw the emergence of neo-Islamic revivalism, at the core of which was a common hatred of the West and western values. The impact in the region of the Islamic revolution in Iran was buttressed by the United States when it deliberately encouraged the growth of Muslim radicalism to combat the presence of the Soviet Union in Afghanistan. Pakistan, as the base for anti-Soviet operations, became a recipient of American largesse in cash as well as in arms. Infused by the jehadi doctrine and flush with monies and arms from the US and Gulf countries, Pakistan became a breeding ground for jehadis. Thousands of madarsas cropped up across the country.[1] Most of them were funded from outside agencies, churning out highly motivated individuals, fired by the zeal to liberate all Muslim lands and to kill or die in the name of jehad.

It was not surprising that the Pakistani power elite tried to cash in on this new Islamic resurgence; General Zia-ul-Haq played a crucial role in the Islamization of the Pakistani civil and military society. He had realised the economic benefits of the approach (financial encouragement from Saudi Arabia, Kuwait and the United Arab Emirates) as also the usefulness of Islam as an effective instrument of social control.[2] It was during Zia's tenure that the Jamaat-e-Islami was able to successfully penetrate key educational, administrative, military and political institutions in Pakistan.[3] These developments were to have grave consequences for future direction of the country and for the peace and security of the region as well as distant lands. Within Pakistan, the trend to support and promote jehadi activities continued through the regime of Nawaz Sharif and, after his deposition from power, has become the hallmark of General Pervez Musharraf's regime. By encouraging the jehadi groups, Pakistani rulers have successfully diverted the attention of the masses away from local issues and helped them vent their pent-up frustrations for a greater Islamic cause spread across Asia and Africa.

By the time the tragedy of 11 September, 2001, unfolded in New York, Washington and Pennsylvania before a shocked world, the tentacles of groups professing militancy in the name of Islam had spread deep and wide. While the international community went about seeking solutions on Palestine, Afghanistan and Kashmir they ignored repeated warnings from countries like India, Russia and Iran that Pakistan had for all practical purposes become a terrorist state keen on destabilising South West Asia through the Taliban.

A factor which has gone unexplored so far or perhaps been underplayed by the United States is the possibility or direct linkage of Pakistan with those involved in executing the dastardly acts of 9/11. By mid-2001, Pakistan was a country on the verge of collapse. For all practical purposes the foreign as well as the domestic policies of Pakistan were being guided by the shadowy Inter-Services Intelligence Agency (ISI) whose linkages with the Taliban and larger terror groups i.e. al-Qaida, Lashkar-e-Toyaba, Harkat-ul-Mujahideen and Jaish-e-Mohammad, are well known. It is also well-known that these groups are constituted of not only the fanatics from Pakistan and Afghanistan, but have recruits from across the globe. The most dangerous aspect of all was that after having tasted success in Afghanistan in 1979-89, these jehadi groups were refusing to listen to their own mentor-the Pakistani Government. They were now looking up to the likes of al-Qaida and the Taliban leadership for guidance and help in achieving their goals beyond the regional boundaries of Pakistan.

Sensing the visible shift of power and popularity towards the jehadi groups within Pakistan, and a growing alienation of the international community, it became imperative for the military regime of General Musharraf to act fast. The ruling military elite had to seek a quick and 'honourable' way of de-linking themselves publicly from the jehadi groups, cut them down to size in order to control them and, once again re-assert the rule of army in the country. Given the circumstances, the best option for Pakistan was to seek assistance from the US to achieve this goal. The example of Iraqis having successfully drawn the US into the Gulf war (with Iran) by carrying out an Exocet missile strike on *USS Stark* in 1987 was already there.[4] If Pakistan, could somehow manage to force the US to seek its help, then the former's task would become easier. Pakistan's long politico-military relationship with the US had given it an opportunity to understand the American psyche. They knew that the Americans at that point of time were fixated on al-Qaida and its elusive leader Osama bin Laden. They also knew that the best way to engage the Americans directly was to hit them where it hurt most-the American people. The agency which carried out the 9/11 attacks, al-Qaida, was also within reach of the ISI through its Taliban connection. What happened next is history. Following the terrorist attacks in the US on 11 September, 2001, Pakistan, curiously, was first off the block in offering its services to the United States in the latter's war against terrorism. It offered bases and support facilities within Pakistan to facilitate the American strike against Taliban and al-Qaida targets in Afghanistan, an offer which was readily accepted. Pakistan had finally succeeded in getting qualified US attention.

Management of Terror

The choice of the US to focus on Pakistan for its anti-al-Qaida/Taliban operations was based on hardcore information that Pakistan was directly involved in Taliban operations in Afghanistan. It is estimated that at the time the World Trade Centre was attacked on 9/11, there were about 3000-4000 jehadis from Pakistan fighting along with the Taliban which had been trained, equipped and advised by the ISI and Pakistani generals. The ISI is also credited with having brought about the marriage of convenience between the Taliban and al-Qaida.[5] An example of the depth of Pakistani involvement was the capture of Taloqan in Afghanistan where more than 60 Pakistani military officers and a unit of the Special Services Group had actively participated in an "advisory and support role". They had full knowledge of the Taliban's military machine, supply lines, storage facilities and the organizational hierarchy.[6] The US now wanted full cooperation of the Pakistanis in fighting the same forces the latter had bred, and the latter's options were limited. They had to show their willingness to cooperate in order to escape the same fate which awaited Afghanistan. The US threat had been subtly put across in President George Bush's statement that "We will give the Pakistani Government a chance to cooperate and to participate as we hunt down those people."[7]

However, Musharraf and his hard-line generals were playing a game of their own. In declaring their support for the US's war against terror they had secured for themselves, atleast initially, Pakistan's safety, future economic benefits and an ally on their Kashmir agenda. At the same time they were careful to keep their terror squads safe from maximum possible harm. They openly declared that they would not participate in any military action beyond their borders and tried to convince the US that the Taliban was not a terrorist movement.[8] They sent a high-level delegation to Kandhar to presumably convince Mullah Omar to hand over Osama bin Laden and his cohorts. In reality, the ISI chief Lt. General Mehmood Ahmad was convincing the Taliban leadership to reject the US demand and stick to their guns.[9] Having declared that the Afghan border was being sealed by deployment of troops to prevent the Taliban and al-Qaida from crossing over to Pakistan, they, in fact, facilitated the evacuation of the jehadi forces and Taliban supporters through the 1,560-mile border with Afghanistan and by airlifting them from Kunduz with the help of Pakistan Air Force transport aircraft.[10]

The prevailing mindset in the Pakistani military elite was best reflected in the view of ex-ISI chief Hamid Gul who declared that the US chances of finding Osama bin-Laden were remote and that they would come out of Afghanistan bloodied and empty handed.[11] In other words, he was hinting that the US could hope for little help in their fight against terror from Pakistan's official machinery including the ISI. Keeping in view the international scenario at that time, it was not in Pakistan's economic or security interest to openly support the activities of either the Taliban or the jehadis operating from its territories. Therefore, they started to follow the next best option of turning a blind eye to their activities and feigned ignorance as to their whereabouts. Warnings on Pakistan's doublespeak and continued interest in Afghanistan and the Taliban came from the newly installed interim Afghan government's chief of intelligence, General Niamullah Jalili who believed that Pakistan was still engaged in supporting the Taliban which had established itself in Quetta.[12]

Musharraf's jehadi jugglery could not last for long. The daring attack by the fidayeen of Jaish-e-Mohammed and Lashkar-e-Toyaba in Jammu and Kashmir (J&K) and other places were on the increase. Following attacks on the J&K Assembly on 1 October, 2001, and the Indian Parliament on 13 December, 2001, tremendous pressure was brought on Musharraf both by India and the international coalition against terror. India's mobilization of its troops and the Pakistani utterances of using 'all means at its disposal' (hinting at the use of nuclear weapons) against India raised the concerns of the US and its allies. The coercive pressure brought upon Pakistan resulted in Musharraf banning seven major militant organizations and introducing reforms for regulating the politico-religious groups so that they operated only within acceptable parameters. Similarly, measures were initiated to eliminate the militant character of the thousands of madarsas operating in Pakistan. All madarsas were to be de-militarised and registered with special education boards being set up by the government. Foreign aid to these madarsas was banned and each madarsa was required to submit annual accounts for inspection by the respective board.[13] All foreign students and teachers wishing to join these madarsas were required to get clearance from the Pakistani Ministry of Interior. The process of effective management and control of the jehadi organizations had begun.

In order to legitimise his control over the groups engaged in the jehad cause, Musharraf took recourse to the teachings of the Koran. Addressing the State Assembly of Pakistan Occupied Kashmir (POK) on 5 February, 2002, he stated that those who think that they know all about Islam must know that it is Allah who bestows (or withdraws) position and respect to an individual. Since this honour had been bestowed upon him, the people

(Muslims) should respect him and have faith upon him as their leader. By this statement, General Musharraf was reminding the jehadis that, according to the Koran, the head of the State should command absolute obedience amongst the Muslim people. The Koran states that the believers must "obey Allah and the Apostle and those in authority among you".[14] Furthermore, as only the State can order a jehad against non-believers, the declaration and direction of waging a jehad to the people of Pakistan can only come from General Musharraf as head of the State.

The overt banning of militant organizations and sealing of their financial assets by Musharraf should be seen in the context of his desire to command absolute control over these groups. Those groups who reached an understanding with him were left to operate freely though under different identities. Some called this exercise by General Musharraf as a move to mend fences with the clergy. In quick succession, leaders like Maulana Fazlur Rehman of the Jamiat-ul-Ulema-e-Islam and Qazi Hussain Ahmad of Jamaat-e-Islami were released after a short detention. No criminal charges were pressed against the leadership of Lashkar-e-Toyaba and Jaish-e-Mohammed and more than 1,000 activists belonging to the five militant organizations banned by him earlier were allowed to go scot free 'for lack of evidence'. Even the Human Rights Commission of Pakistan noted that they had not seen any comprehensive measures to root out extremism.[15]

The fears expressed by many, including some officials in the US administration, that General Musharraf was not being sincere in his approach towards tackling terrorist forces within Pakistan, proved true with a series of suicide bombings in Karachi in May and June 2002, which targeted French naval technicians and the US Consulate staff.[16] The attacks came in the wake of the brutal murder of Daniel Pearl, a *Wall Street Journal* correspondent by jehadis in Karachi in January 2002. It was clearly evident that an effective network of terrorists was still operational in Pakistan in spite of official claims of a "focussed" crackdown on the jehadis.[17] Then came the attack on a church and a Christian hospital near Islamabad taking more innocent lives. It appears that inspite of having a tacit understanding with the jehadi organizations, Musharraf's writ was being challenged by some groups whose hatred of the West precluded any arrangement with Musharraf's game plan. In fact, the fear of these loose cannons forced Musharraf to take extra security precautions, even going to the extent of hoisting the Pakistani flag behind closed doors on the occasion of Pakistan's Independence Day celebrations on 14 August, 2002!

The terror bombings highlighted the fact that al-Qaida was now directly challenging the US interests on Pakistani soil. An ex-Taliban commander, Fazul Rabi Said-Rehman, is supposed to have claimed that these attacks would continue. "The Muslim Brothers will do this, but the leaders will be al-Qaida."[18] Pakistani, as well as the French authorities, had hinted at the involvement of al-Qaida in these attacks. The suspicion was based on the fact that none of the Pakistani militant groups had the tradition of carrying out suicide attacks, and that this phenomenon was usually associated with Arab militant groups.[19] However, one must point out that organizations such as Lashkar-e-Toyaba and Jaish-e-Mohammed have in 2001-02 also earned notoriety by carrying out fidayeen attacks on Indian Army establishments in Kashmir and on high profile targets such as the Indian Parliament.

One fact which emerged from the terrorist bombings in Pakistan was that the administration was at a loss to effectively control these terrorist groups scattered all over the country. According to Hussain Haqqani, former Advisor to Benazir Bhutto, "Pakistan's involvement with the jehadi groups and its tolerance of armed extremist religious groups has contributed to ineffective law enforcement ... Resources of the police and intelligence gathering agencies are overstretched ... The terrorists know that and take advantage of the State's weakness."[20] Haqqani presumes that the Musharraf regime is indeed serious about tackling terrorism and has not taken into consideration the not so secret fact that there are elements within the army and police which overtly and covertly support the activities of these terrorist groups. How is it that inspite of General Musharraf's assurances to the US that the al-Qaida will not be allowed to enter Pakistan, most of the top-rung leadership of the organization has found refuge in the country? Osama bin Laden is supposed to be hiding in one of the fortified villages in Waziristan. Abu Zubaidah was caught by the FBI from a Lashkar-e-Toyaba safe house in Faisalabad. Khalid Sheikh Mohammad, the "Pakistani brain" behind the logistical support for 9/11 attacks, and Bilal bin Marwan, the Saudi planner behind the attack on *USS Cole* in Yemen, are also believed to be hiding in Pakistan.[21] Ramzi bin al-Shib, a key planner of the 9/11 attacks, was finally caught in Karachi in September 2002, from his hideout barely 11 kilometres away from the US Consulate.[22]

According to several reports, the former Taliban finance minister, Maulvi Abdul Kabir, and the group's deputy chief of intelligence, Qari Obaidullah, have been seen in Peshawar. It has been reported that for almost a month during April and May 2002, hordes of Taliban and al-Qaida activists passed unchecked through Wana, Tank and Dera Ismail Khan en route to Punjab and Karachi.[23] How come such a large number of people moving in a steady train of pick-up and cargo trucks went unnoticed by the police or intelligence units? The explanation comes in various forms. Some within the Pakistani military have termed these terrorists in transit as local smugglers, while others tolerate them or sympathise with them.[24] The US forces hunting al-Qaida and Taliban were on several occasions deliberately led astray by local police and military commanders. The US success in getting prize catches were mostly due to the electronic surveillance and investigations by the US FBI and during raids of which the local administration, police or military officials had no knowledge about.[25]

In order to bring about effective management of the terrorist groups and militant religious organizations General Musharraf sought to bring about a form of coalition of these groups under one umbrella. This attempt came to light during the meeting of the 'Defence Council of Pakistan and Afghanistan' organised by Maulana Sami-ul-Haq of Jamiat-e-Ulema-e-Islami in Islamabad on 10 June, 2002. Among those present at the meeting were Hafiz Abdul Rehman Makki of the Lashkar-e-Toyaba re-incarnated as Jamaat-al-Dawa, and a curious mix of representatives from the Tehreek-e-Jaffriya, Hizbul Mujahideen, Jamaat-e-Islami, Sipah-e-Sahaba, Harkat-ul-Mujahideen and Jaish-e-Mohammed.

What made this meeting more intriguing was the presence of General Zaheer-ul-Islam Abbasi, former Pakistani Army Chief, General Mirza Aslam Beg and former head of the ISI, General Hamid Gul.[26] in all probability it was during this meeting that an understanding was developed between the regime of General Musharraf and the jehadi organisations. It appears that the trade-off called for the jehadis to go slow with their activities in Afghanistan and within Pakistan, especially against the Western targets. In exchange they were to be allowed a stake in the future 'democratic' government and would have a free hand in Kashmir–provided they operated within the Indian territory. As far as Kashmir was concerned there was a convergence of interests between the Pakistani military and the jehadis.

Benefitting from Terror

President Musharraf never ceases to pat himself on the back for having brought about a turnaround in the Pakistani economy. Speaking from various forums while lobbying for himself in the run-up to the referendum, as well as bringing up this issue in his various 'addresses' to the nation, the General has tried to impress the people of Pakistan by claiming that good times lie ahead. He proudly claimed that Pakistani foreign exchange reserves were in excess of $6 billion and debt rescheduling of nearly $12.5 billion had been achieved. Trade balance had improved by nearly $ 1 billion and the remittances from Pakistani expatriates had jumped from previous annual average of $1.1 billion to $2.2 billion. This economic euphoria was also sold to the Pakistani public in Finance Minister Shaukat Aziz's budget for 2002-03: "Today the economy of Pakistan is in more comfortable and stable position than at another time in at least the last three decades."[27] Inspite of all the spin created around the economic comeback, the fact remains that the only economic gains Pakistan achieved in the post 9/11 scenario came about due to "massive cash grants from international anti-terrorism coalition allies, rescheduling of outstanding foreign debts and conversion of high interest carrying loans to lower interest bearing loans (which) brought invaluable foreign exchange on one hand, and saved a considerable amount of foreign exchange on the other."[28] It may be recalled that during US Secretary of State Colin Powell's visit to Pakistan shortly after the 9/11 tragedy, General Musharraf was quick off the block to ask for enhanced quotas for the faltering Pakistani textile industry.

However, according to Pakistani journalist Najam Sethi, this optimistic feeling of the Pakistani administration does not coincide with the feelings of the common man and neither it is reflected in the industrial hubs of Karachi, Lahore and Faisalabad, etc. He finds that the Government has failed to explain as to why the prices of domestic oil and electricity had not gone down despite falling oil prices in the international market (prior to the US scare to wage war on Iraq). He also questions this Pakistani exuberance in the face of a downturn in the domestic market. By May 2002, Pakistan's imports had fallen and exports had not increased. Agricultural growth in Pakistan was down by one percent, industrial growth was down by two percent and private sector borrowing for industrial development was down by 40 percent compared to 2001.[29] To top it all, there was a revenue deficit of Rupees(P) 126.6 billion.

Notwithstanding General Musharraf's claim of engineering an economic turnaround by introduction of corrective measures, the economy of Pakistan is currently sustained by the large handouts he is receiving in exchange for his support in the US-led war against terror. In addition to the US aid of more than $1 billion, the Japanese have promised him a package of $3.8 billion. In fact, he gave a lecture on 'roots of terrorism' to an audience in Tokyo on 13 March, 2002, hoping that the Japanese would appreciate the crucial role his country was playing in the fight against terror and in return, would agree to write off Pakistan's $5 billion debt[30*]. The World Bank and the Asian Development Bank have already given $500 million to Pakistan and have pledged an additional $1 billion.[31]

The big question is that will Pakistan utilise its internal revenues and the generous aid being given to it to improve the lot of its people or is it going to utilise the external aid for development of infrastructure and divert internal revenues for procurement of military hardware and in support of its covert activities in Kashmir? Pakistan has a dubious record of forsaking the country's development for pursuing its 'interests' in the neighbourhood. Again to quote Najam Sethi, even the government of General Musharraf had prior to 11 September, 2001, "ploughed ahead with regional and national security policies designed to keep Pakistan in splendid isolation. The dividend from peace and trade with India was spurned in favour of sponsoring jehad in

* As we were going to the press, Pakistani collaboration with North Korean nuclear programme came to light, and now Japan is reported to be reconsidering its aid to Pakistan

Kashmir. The dividend from oil and gas pipelines from Iran and Central Asia was wrecked on the altar of the Taliban in Afghanistan."[32] Indications are that despite his new found role as a crusader against terror, General Musharraf will continue with his earlier policy of strengthening himself and the institutions, like the Army and the ISI to help him survive the ruthless power politics of Pakistan. Kashmir is still in his blood and no amount of economic transfusion is going to cleanse him of this self-induced haemophilia.

In all likelihood Pakistan's defence spending is expected to go up once again after touching an all time low of 4.5 percent of its GDP in 2000-2001.[33] It has again forwarded a list of military hardware it wants to purchase, including the stalled supply of 28 F-16 fighter aircraft from the US. This is in addition to the US offer of six C 130 Hercules Transport aircraft at a throwaway price of $90 million.[34] There are also plans to build four F-22 frigates with Chinese help. These are supposed to boost Pakistan's naval power which has recently developed two Agosta B90 submarines with French help and expects one more by 2003 end. These naval acquisitions, according to General Musharraf, are going to have far reaching positive effects on the economy of the country.

What is of utmost concern for India is the renewed cooperation within the US and the Pakistani military establishment. By 'catching' al-Qaida operatives hiding in Pakistan in instalments, General Musharraf has been able to keep alive the US interest in his country. The US is now keen to "enhance security and foster the rule of law" in Pakistan for which a Joint Working Group on

Counter-terrorism has been established. In addition to modernising and strengthening Pakistan's law enforcement capabilities, the US is addressing President Musharraf's critical priorities of economic and social reforms by bilateral efforts and support through International Financial Institutions.[35] In August 2002, the US and Pakistan signed an agreement for rescheduling the latter's debt of $3 billion of which $2.3 billion was declared as official development assistance that will be repayable over a period of 38 years. The remaining $700 million will be treated as a non-official development assistance, to be repaid over a period of 23 years.[36]

The interesting, and also alarming part of this entire US-Pak romance is that the US is again choosing to ignore the Pakistani nuclear capabilities and intentions as it had done earlier. Neither the open threat of nuclear weapons used by Pakistan following heightened tensions and troop deployments on the border by both India and Pakistan in early 2002, nor the recent disclosures of the British intelligence agency M15 uncovering a Pakistani undercover purchase of nuclear weapons material from a Blackburn-based company, have deterred the US in its support of General Musharraf.[37]

The growth of militant organisations in Pakistan has resulted in a growing clandestine arms market in the country. The industrious people of Dera Adamkhel who have been traditionally known as small arms manufacturers have seen a growth of their business as well as in the quality of their weapons. According to a recent survey carried out by *Dawn* in Dera Adamkhel, Khyber Agency and Khurram Agency, this market provides a large variety of lethal weapons including US M-16 (Rs.1,80,000), Bulgarian and Czechoslovakian Kalakov

(Rs.20,000 to 35,000), Israeli Uzi machine pistol (Rs.1,30,000), MP assault rifle (Rs.60,000) and other US military equipment i.e. laser designators, binoculars and pistols.[38] Who says that terror doesn't pay?

Foreign Relations

The path on which Pakistan progressed in the wake of 9/11 should not have come as a surprise to the world at large and neither to the Indian establishment. As early as 1998, the Indian Foreign Office assessment of General Pervez Musharraf dubbed him as "an ambitious and scheming individual" and a hardliner on India. Bruce Reidel, the special assistant to President Bill Clinton, was more specific when he observed that the General was "determined to humble India once and for all."[39] Following 9/11, the shrewd dictator had realised that the Pakistani linkages with the Taliban and other jehadi groups would soon make the country a prime target for the US who was bent upon smoking out and destroying the terrorists. The best option available for Pakistan's survival was to play ball with the US. But it was easier said than done.

In his televised address to the nation on 19 September, 2001, General Musharraf used the Kashmir and India card to sell his collaboration with the US in the latter's fight against terror. The contents of his speech were filled with bravado and he warned India to 'lay off'. He extensively quoted the Quran to justify his decision. "This is a moment for strategic thinking" and "when faced with two problems choose the lesser one." He placated the hardliners by saying that "all we are doing is in consonance with Islam and for the benefit of

Muslims. He quoted how Prophet Mohammed (PBUH) had entered into a Treaty with the Jews which had contributed towards his victories over the non-believers. While he was explaining strategic nuances of Islam to his people, General Musharraf started to portray himself as a new Attaturk to the Western world. All of a sudden he became aware of how radical the Pakistani society had become.

Till the incidents of 9/11, Pakistan had been more or less pursuing a successful foreign policy, especially in the context of its immediate strategic interests. It had successfully manoeuvred a subtle takeover of Afghanistan through the Taliban and, given time, would have consolidated this newly acquired strategic depth. It had flourishing business and defence ties with China which fulfilled its military requirements, assisted Islamabad to consolidate its position in Kabul, and helped tie down India. It unabashedly used its Islamic card to woo the Muslim countries of the OIC and the ASEAN. As far as India was concerned, Pakistan had continued with fervour to bleed the former through terrorist acts and its policy in Kashmir - where it encouraged insurgency under the garb of extending "moral, political and diplomatic support" to anti-India forces.

Following 9/11, Pakistani's image did come unstuck in the eyes of its former supporters. The biggest ally Pakistan had ever had, after China, was the US. This relationship had soured over a long period following Pakistan losing its importance as a strategic frontline state, following the withdrawal of the Soviet Union from Afghanistan and the final collapse of the former in 1990, and Pakistani involvement in Afghanistan through the

Taliban. Pakistani relations with the US got a further jolt after the former conducted nuclear tests in 1998. The US concerns had been heightened by the fact that while Pakistan had acquired nuclear weapons capability, it was actively pursuing a multiple-range missile development plan with North Korea. News reports in October 2002, revealed that this cooperation was a two-way traffic. While North Korea supplied missile technology to Pakistan, the latter provided nuclear weapons technology to North Korea.[40]

During the past one year, Pakistan has been desperately playing the Islamic card to garner support to boost its economy and, vis-à-vis India on the Kashmir issue. In June 2002, General Musharraf visited Saudi Arabia and the UAE and tried to generate a fear psychosis amongst his hosts about the fallout in the region due to increasing cooperation between India and Israel. However, the changed geo-political environment following the 9/11 incidents has necessitated a re-think among Arab nations, including those in the Persian Gulf, in giving blank support to Pakistan as a brother Muslim country. The changed approach of the Gulf countries was indicated by the statement of Sheikh Mohammad Sabah al-Salim al-Sabah, Kuwait's Minister of State for Foreign Affairs, who expressed that "We refuse to view India-Pakistan disputes in Islamic terms ... Our policy towards India is not influenced by the factor of Pakistan."[41]

Though agreeing to help Pakistan with economic aid to tide over its financial problems, the Gulf countries have maintained that in spite of being Islamic, they disavow Islamic fundamentalism as an instrument of any country's foreign policy. The reason for this attitude is simple. There are pockets of Muslim radicals within each Islamic State – be it a monarchy, democracy or a military dictatorship. The ruling regimes fear that Pakistan's influence and support to these elements would unleash forces that would challenge their authority. These countries have faced violent political unrest in the past and similar fundamentalist uprisings cannot be ruled out in the future. Therefore, it is in the interest of each regime to curb this new wave of militant Islamic revivalism.

Notwithstanding the lukewarm response to his appeals to the Muslim countries of West and South-East Asia, President Musharraf is hardly going to let go off his hostility against India. In order to strategically encircle India, he has an old trusted friend in China with whom relations are being expanded – including a joint venture of building a deep-water naval facility in Gwadar capable of handling heavy freight. The facility, to be developed in three phases, is being linked via an all weather road with Karachi. This facility is going to provide direct access to the Chinese, to the Gulf waters which will have both economic and military implications for India. For long, the Pakistanis have nursed a desire to control the sea-lanes through which India conducts 70 percent of its commercial trade, including its vital supply of oil. The Pakistani presence is also being increasingly felt in Nepal, Bangladesh and Sri Lanka. Nepal and Bangladesh have become major hubs of anti-India activity of Pakistan. The ISI has developed strong links with the local underworld and extremists groups of these countries which facilitate anti-India operations (such as the hijacking of Indian Airlines aircraft IC-814 to Kandhar in December 1999) and provide safe houses from which terrorists and subversives carry out repeated strikes in the bordering regions of India.

Pursuant to his anti-India strategy, Musharraf made a historic visit to Bangladesh on 29 July, 2002, where he expressed 'regrets' over Pakistani excesses on Bengali Muslims. For Musharraf, swallowing this bitter pill was a prerequisite to ensure full cooperation from Begum Khalida Zia who has gone into overdrive to "de-Mujibise" Bangladesh. The visit saw the opening of "a new chapter in bilateral trade" between the two countries. There is apprehension amongst Indian security officials that the ISI will utilise this opportunity of growing bilateral relations to revive contacts with the Bangladeshi jehadis. This concern is not unfounded. Bangladesh has, in recent times, shown a growing propensity to support insurgent activity in India. According to a report in *India Today*, Dhaka has softened its attitude towards the ULFA, BODO, NSCN and Tripura Tiger Force insurgents operating in India from Bangladeshi territory. It has provided these groups with legal aid and is taking steps to 'facilitate their extended stay.'[42]

Post 9-11, there has been no basic change in Pakistan's policy towards India and Kashmir. The attacks on Indian Parliament, Kaluchak massacre of civilians in Jammu and other similar incidents had generated a lot of concern within India as well as in the international community.[43] To some analysts it appears that the Pakistani military establishment is still working in collusion with the jehadis, while others feel that General Musharraf has lost control over these mercenaries. In order to avoid further international condemnation by such 'loose' acts of terrorism, the General and his team went into a damage control exercise. They did not want the Kashmir issue to mar Pakistan's newly acquired image of a soldier against terror. It was, therefore, essential that all jehadi outfits operating from PoK in Kashmir were brought directly under General Musharraf's control. According to General Talat Masood, "There has been no basic change in the Kashmir policy, but the emphasis has shifted to the political, diplomatic and human rights aspect. The military instrument has been downgraded and militant groups will not be allowed to operate as they are undermining the cause of Kashmir and creating serious problems for Pakistan both at the domestic and international level."[44]

Addressing the PoK Assembly in Muzzafarabad on the occasion of 'Kashmir Day' on 5 February, 2002, General Musharraf reassured the legislators that the Kashmir issue remained central to Pakistan's relations with India and that he would not compromise with any situation not favourable to them. He, however, made it clear that the Pakistani Government was now going to take over the direct control of anti-India activity. "No party has a right to follow its own agenda in the external affairs of the country ... Government alone has the right to deal with India, Kashmir or Palestinian issues", he said.[45]

General Musharraf followed up his new Kashmir policy by coming to an agreement with the jehadi groups operating from Pakistan. The *quid pro quo* was that while the jehadis would restrain from making irresponsible statements, stop terrorist actions within Pakistan, they would be allowed a free hand in Kashmir. According to Lashkar-e-Toyaba operative Yahya Mujahid, they were told that if they kept quiet about the Afghan situation, then they would be left alone to do what they wanted in Kashmir.[46] It may be recalled that even while General Musharraf was trying to impress the West by banning various fundamentalist outfits, he had done nothing to ban the Harkat-ul-Mujahideen. This group comprising Pakistanis and Kashmiris from PoK is linked with the Jamaat-e-Islami of Pakistan. According to Rory McCarthy and Hasan Zaidi, "exclusion from the ban may indicate an attempt by Islamabad to focus the campaign on Kashmiri Groups."[47]

To present a 'softer' face of Pakistan on the Kashmir issue, General Musharraf constituted a National Kashmir Committee in January 2002, and appointed the supposedly moderate Mohammad Abdul Qayyum Khan as its chairman. The Kashmir Committee was to ensure an image change for Pakistani involvement in Kashmir from a militant movement to a political one. In order to bring about this image change it became necessary to bring the 6000-8000 Mujahideen under a 'political command.'[48]

Simultaneously, Pakistan went on a diplomatic offensive to win the international community over to their point of view that the resolution of the Kashmir problem (in Pakistan's favour) was the only way to end militancy in the region. Addressing a press conference in Tokyo, Japan, on 13 March, 2002, General Musharraf urged the world community to assist in bringing peace to the region. "Kashmir is the core issue that cannot be denied by anyone. We have fought three wars on it, we have killings along the line of control, so anybody who thinks there are other issues to be dealt with and not Kashmir is being totally unrealistic."[49] Pakistan also convinced a few members of the European Union to call for a special hearing on Kashmir in April 2002. It also tried to play a diplomatic game with India by offering to sign an agreement to check misuse of territory and showed a readiness for an extradition territory between the two countries.

But even as these diplomatic moves were being played by Pakistan, it refused to hand over 20 terrorists wanted for crimes committed in India. This snub was further aggravated by Pakistan's aggressive moves on its borders with India. It may be recalled that following numerous fidayeen strikes on civilian and institutional targets in the country, the government of India had deployed its forces along its borders to check cross border terrorism and to pressurise Pakistan to reign in the jehadi groups operating from its territory.[50]

Instead of putting a stop to cross-border terrorism by checking infiltration of jehadis into India, Pakistan chose to follow the path of brinkmanship. It amassed the bulk of its troops on the Sutlej-Ravi corridor, started to shell Indian positions with increasing intensity, went in for a military exercise of its army, navy and airforce, talked about withdrawing its troops from Sierra Leone and deploy its 750 km range Shaheen missiles.[51] Rumours of a pending Indian strike were floated by the ISI and a war psychosis was built up in Pakistan throughout 2002[52]. Acknowledging that the threat of war between India and Pakistan existed, the High Commissioner of Pakistan to India, Ashraf Jehangir Qazi tried to pin the blame for the increasing tensions on India as it was "planting the idea in the minds of Pakistanis that it might go to war with Pakistan; that this way, it wants Pakistan to comply with India's conditions."[53]

In spite of giving assurances to the US and other countries that he would put a stop to the infiltration of jehadis into Kashmir, General Musharraf either failed in fulfilling this commitment or deliberately chose to ignore the rising international concerns in order to safeguard his strategy on Kashmir.[54] General Musharraf tried to wriggle out of his commitments to stop cross border terrorism by stating in a BBC interview on 29 August, 2002, that he had not given any timeframe to the international community to stop infiltration across the line of control in Jammu and Kashmir and hinted that in view of sympathy within Pakistan for Kashmiris, there could be no end to violence until there is forward movement towards resolution of the Kashmir issue.[55]

President Musharraf's lie of curtailing the ISI activities, specially its Kashmir cell, also stand exposed following denial of the same by the former Director General of ISI, Javed Ashraf Qazi, who has said that the ISI personnel were required to keep a watch on India's troop movement. He also said that the ISI was a dynamic organization and adjustments would be made according to the changing conditions but no large-scale reorganization will take place.[56] There has also been no shift in the Kashmir policy of the Pakistan Army or the ISI. Hints towards projected strikes in J&K had started appearing in July 2002, following official Pakistani briefings to their Western allies that they would not be able to keep Kashmiri militants inactive beyond summer if status quo on the ground was to continue.[57] Officially, Pakistan does not associate with these terrorist groups and, therefore, maintains the aspect of deniability. Furthermore, by maintaining the issue of unsolved 'Kashmir dispute' it attempts to de-legitimize the Line of

Control (LoC). Interestingly, the JKLF (Amanullah faction) maintains a similar approach to the question saying that crossing of the LoC for an armed struggle does not come under the definition of cross-border infiltration.[58] In June 2002, President Musharraf had stated that "there is nothing happening across the Line of Control."[59]

Pakistan has always opposed an electoral process in Kashmir. It does not want any legitimisation which this process may bring about in favour of India. That is why they manoeuvred the Pak-based jehadis to intensify their activities in Kashmir in the run-up to the assembly elections in the State in September-October, 2002. A wave of terrorist attacks swept across Jammu and Kashmir in July, August, September and October 2002, targeting candidates and workers of the local political parties. Over 800 civilians were killed during the two months the election process was conducted. The Pakistani protege, the All Party Hurriyat Conference (APHC), also chipped in by giving a call for boycott of the elections. However, the Pakistani attempts to terrorise the people of Kashmir failed when the State witnessed an average of over 44 percent voting despite the immediate threat to the lives of the voters.

The failure of APHC and other indigenous groups involved in insurgency (with Pakistan's support) has prompted the policy makers in Pakistan to dump them. They have become increasingly critical of the Hurriyat. In July 2002, the United Jehad Council, an amalgamation of 23 militant organisations based in Muzaffarabad, PoK, had asked the Hurriyat Conference to either initiate a poll boycott campaign or step down. It had warned that those who participated in the electoral process would be dealt with severely.[60] Through this warning, the United Jehad Council also wanted to deter the former militants who were showing interest to participate in the elections. Similarly, the Jamaat-e-Islami of Kashmir was criticized for the statement by its chief, Ghulam Ahmad Bhat, that the Jamaat was not fighting for the State's accession to Pakistan.[61] Following the elections in Jammu and Kashmir, Pakistan is lying low for the moment perhaps analysing the impact of the elections in Kashmir. However, this deceptive calm will not last long as the professional jehadis will be straining on the leash. The increased presence of the fundamentalist parties in Pakistani politics will definitely create an impact on any future course of action on Kashmir.

Political Trends

Following 11 September, 2001, General Musharraf made an all-out effort to improve the image of Pakistan by promising to carry out reforms aimed at curtailing the activities of the madarsas and the jehadis. In a 62-minute televised speech on 12 January, 2002, he promised to regulate the madarsas and stop external funding. "If any madarsa is found indulging in extremism, subversion or militant activity, it will be closed". He promised to shut down the activities of militant organizations, enforce the rule of law and seemed determined to cast Pakistan in the vision of its founding fathers – Mohammad Ali Jinnah and Mohammad Iqbal. His banning of seven major militant parties, condemnations of the Taliban's repressive policies, introduction of reforms to regulate politico-religious groups were all geared to present Musharraf as the new *avtaar* of Mustapha Kemal Attaturk. According to Lt. General Talat Masood, former staff officer to

General Zia-ul-Haq, Musharraf wanted, ideologically and politically, "to cleanse Pakistan of extremism and foster the positive and liberating tenets of Islam in its body politic."[62]

The General, however, had more on his mind than the welfare of his country. The post 9/11 scenario in Pakistan, with the US breathing down his neck, gave him the god-sent opportunity to acquire legitimacy. His usurping of power by ousting the democratic government of Nawaz Sharif in October 1999, had not been received well both within and outside Pakistan. To achieve legitimacy he had to increase his powers, bring all actors in domestic politics under his control and appear to be a ruler pursuing the democratic and correct path leading towards his acceptance by the international community.

In his quest for absolute power, General Musharraf set the ball rolling by seeking a referendum so that he may remain President for another five years. The referendum, held on 30 April, 2002, in the face of fierce opposition from the majority of political parties including the hardliners and the Alliance for the Restoration of Democracy (ARD), saw him emerging victorious with 97 percent votes going in his favour. The referendum was, however, criticized as a farce amidst allegations of rigging, intimidation and low turnout of 6-7 percent.[63] After having 'democratically' secured his position as President of Pakistan, Musharraf, on 22 August, 2002, announced wide-sweeping constitutional amendments, as a consequence of which he acquired absolute powers and practically erased any opportunity for political opposition to his position in the foreseeable future. The Legal Framework Order (LFO) gave him powers to unilaterally dismiss the government and the national and provincial parliaments.

He also created a super-cabinet in the form of the National Security Council. The body, dominated by military officers, retains greater power than any elected civilian cabinet and shall serve as a consultative and advisory body on "democracy, governance and inter-provincial harmony". The LFO also disqualified from political participation all defaulters, criminals, convicts, defaulters on loan and utility bills, absconders from court proceedings as well as those individuals convicted under the National Accountability Ordinance (NAO). Finally, all laws promulgated by General Musharraf and actions taken thereon could " not be called into question in any court on any ground whatsoever."[64] In Musharraf's view these amendments were necessary in the larger interest of the country, more so for ushering in a sustainable democracy in Pakistan.[65]

In a very smooth operation, General Musharraf had practically removed every semblance of political opposition to his rule. Nawaz Sharif had been exiled to Saudi Arabia, Benazir Bhutto was in a self-imposed exile – shuttling between the UK and Dubai, and the Alliance for Restoration of Democracy (ARD) was being openly coerced. That left only the militant and religious political groups to cut a deal with Musharraf. Even Imran Khan, the cricketer-turned-politician leading Tehrik-E-Insaf, alleged and Musharraf had personally threatened him after he questioned the referendum. Their choice was limited. Either they toe Musharraf's line or suffer the same fate as the rest of civilian political parties like the PPP or the PML (NS).

With the ARD declaring that it would not be part of any coalition to form a government, the MMA is sure to call the shots in any future government. Musharraf has also exploited the current environment to establish his control over tribal areas in Pakistan which had earlier successfully opposed attempts by the Pakistani authorities to come under their direct administrative control. Again, Musharraf achieved this through convincing the tribesmen that they could escape the threat of immediate US intervention only by agreeing to come under Islamabad's protection.

Indications on the ground were clearly pointing towards an army-hardline group combine emerging as the new power brokers in Pakistan. This was a repeat of the Zia era politics, with the army playing a dominant role. In spite of oft-repeated statements by Pakistani officials that the army has no intention of ruling Pakistan,[66] the General himself has made no bones about an institutionalised role for the army in Pakistan's governance. Speaking to German newspaper *Die Welt*, he stated that "In Pakistan's politics, the Army has always played an important role ... so why should we be so shy and not institutionalise this reconciling role? We are considering constitutional role for the Army, and we are not ashamed of it."[67]

Musharraf's attitude has been best analysed by former Indian High Commissioner to Pakistan G. Parthasarthy who stated that the General "has come to realise that, apart from wielding power and acquiring wealth without responsibility, many of his army colleagues genuinely believe they have a divine right to wield political power in Pakistan."[68] Over the years, the Pakistani military establishment has maintained a lifestyle courtesy, its power and commissions skimmed off from defence purchases. Recently, a report published in the *South Asia Tribune* by Shaheed Sehbai carried a list of more than 100 Pakistani officers who have "grabbed land at throwaway prices". Large tracts of land located in areas having 400 acres or more have been bought by General Pervez Musharraf, General Moinuddin Haider, General Zubair Chak, General Aziz, etc. This list is practically the 'who's who' of Pakistan.[69] Musharraf realised that in order to continue in power he had to keep his generals in good humour. Therefore, even while talking of ushering in democracy and reforms, he has ensured that the generals have a permanent role in the civil governance of Pakistan through the NSC. In addition, several military officers have been appointed in various capacities in Pakistan's civil and economic administration. They also occupy senior positions in the Diplomatic Corps and public sector corporations. Criticizing this military encroachment in civil governance, a Pakistani journalist Irfan Husain writes that "these worthies who seldom have any professional qualifications to match their assignments are generally beyond the reach of mere politicians. This is specially true of those appointed to a vast array of civilian jobs over the last three years."[70]

For those who had assumed that the growing political opposition to Musharraf will result in major victories for the Pakistan Peoples Party (PPP) and the Pakistan Muslim League (PML–Nawaz), the outcome of the October 2002 election must have come as a rude shock.[71] Irrespective of the allegations of massive rigging and intimidation, the victory of the Pakistan Muslim League (Qaid-e-Azam) and the Muttahida Majlis-e-Amal (MMA) gives an indication of the underplay which went on between the government and these parties. The overt support given by Musharraf's Government to PML (QA), 'ensured that it secured the highest number of seats (77) from a total of 272 seats. According to Ayaz Amir, the credit of PML (QA) victory is to be credited to the ISI and Pakistan military intelligence efforts over the past one year.[72] What is interesting, however, is the stunning 45-seat victory of the MMA making it a strong player in any future government that comes to power.

Nearly all Pakistan observers and analysts are of the opinion that the anti-Americar and anti-establishment sentiments brought about by socio-economic hardships and the government's decision to allow the US troops to operate from Pakistan translated in electoral success for the MMA. For once, the Islamic right-wingers had sunk their differences originating from the Deobandi, Barelvi and Shia schools of thought. The coming together of Jamaat-e-Islami, Jamaat Ulema-e-Pakistan and Jamiat Ulema-e-Islam, and their political strategy owe a lot to the efforts and patronage of the Islamists in the ISI and the Pakistani military establishment.[73] According to several articles/editorials appearing in *Ausaf* in October 2002, the success of the MMA indicates that the jehadi noose is tightening around Pakistan. There are also hints of the MMA trying to widen its base by attempting to induct other militant groups like the Sipah-e-Sahaba.[74] The MMA agenda for Pakistan is clear cut. They want a reversal of 'un-Islamic' financial policies being followed by the Pakistani government. They promise equal rights to women, including equal job opportunities and promise to ban honour killings in Pakistan.[75] The Jamaat-e-Islami Chief Qazi Hussain Ahmad has said that there will be no restriction on women, including on wearing of *burqa* (veil) but at the same time they would have to live according to the teachings of Islam. They plan to establish separate universities for women and abolish co-education.[76] It appears that the MMA has plans to strictly monitor the information and entertainment industry to reduce western influence especially 'indecent' shows on Pakistan television. This is bound to cause concern amongst both the cable operators as well as western channels as they are bound to incur a sudden loss of revenue.[77]

While taking a moderate approach towards women and promising Islamic fiscal and poverty alleviation programmes, the MMA has made it clear that it supports the Taliban and would not like any outside interference in Pakistan's domestic or 'neighbouring' affairs in Afghanistan. Syed Munawaar Hasan has announced that "the Taliban and al-Qaida fighters are our brothers and the witch hunt against them should stop."[78] The Jamaat-e-Islami leader Qazi Hussain Ahmad is assuring the international community that they are not terrorists and will not use Pakistan for terrorism. However, he has also made it clear that they do not approve of foreign interference and do not require American help or their bases in Pakistan.[79] Some sections in the MMA are toning down their anti-US rhetoric and are ready to 'negotiate' to promote an atmosphere of mutual trust. This, however, is being seen as influenced by the need to present a softer and acceptable front of MMA to enable it to achieve a power sharing arrangement with the PML (QA).[80] The need to reach a compromise with the US-Musharraf agenda also stems from MMA fears that Musharraf might try to sideline the alliance by cobbling together a coalition of the PML(Q), PPP, the National Alliance and the MQM.[81] This viewpoint gathers more credence in view of recent efforts of Maulana Fazlur Rehman, Chief of the MMA, to assure the British High Commissioner in Pakistan that the alliance would let the US and UK complete their agenda against international terrorism on Pakistani soil.[82]

Maulana Fazlur Rehman has also stated that the religious parties have for the first time given an opportunity to the jehadi forces to tread the political path. If the aspirations of these people are not respected, and if MMA is not given a part in governance then these forces will be disillusioned and might go back to their old ways. Rehman has called the election results a mandate for change–in the context of the prevailing situation in the region since the last 18 months.[83] Knowing the background of these religious parties and the complexion of their support base, MMA's participation as part of a coalition government can only help promote the jehadi agenda.

It may be noted that since 1947, the Jamaat-e-Islami has laid a strong foundation of the Wahabi doctrine in Pakistan by penetrating key institutions. Though its activities got a boost during Zia's regime, the Jamaat could not translate it into political power. Today, for the first time, the hardline religious organizations have the numerical strength on the basis of which they can play a critical role both inside and outside the government. The perception of the leadership of these parties is that by and large the election results confirm the people's support for their views on the kind of change to be brought about in Pakistan. MMA is, therefore, not likely to play second fiddle to any party. By declaring Maulana

Fazlur Rehman as its candidate for premiership, it has thrown the gauntlet in the political arena of Pakistan along with not so subtle hints that any political party will find it difficult to form a government without the MMA.[84]

Tragically, there are few chances of a positive change in the offing. Any government in Pakistan comprising MMA representatives shall lack stability. It will be wrought with factionalism and dissent within its constituent members. Even till the end of October 2002, political parties like the MMA and the PML (Q) which in popular opinion were to come together to form a government, had failed to reach any agreement on the basic issues of the country's foreign policy, economic policy and the kind of 'Islamisation' which the MMA wants to impose upon Pakistan. It has been observed that in secular political systems, parties which are in no position to singly achieve a popular mandate go in for alliances with other parties, sometimes even with those professing radical religious ideas. The opportunity to share in governance provides these parties to fulfil their own agendas – examples of which can be seen in Turkey, Egypt and Israel. In fact, the situation developing in Pakistan will add the country to this list of countries which have been witness to tremendous violence and misery. It would place the country in an even worse situation than it was in the eighties. One will see an increased official dose on obscurantist values which shall discourage and demoralise the moderate and progressive elements in Pakistan, and shall encourage those whose sole alternative to a life of poverty and misery is to achieve a respectful identity of a jehadi. The internal turbulence expected in Pakistan would have serious repercussions both within and outside the country, which will result in its isolation within the international community including Muslim countries. In all probability one will see Pakistan slowly and steadily sliding towards self-destruction.

Conclusion

It would be wishful thinking to presume that things would change for the better in the near future for Pakistan. The recently held elections in the country have not only thrown up a fractured mandate, but also strengthened the hands of the fundamentalist forces like the MMA. The elections also prove that there is a sizeable population within Pakistan which pins its hope on the Islamic option for governance as compared to the democratic and martial law fiascos in the past. They still perceive themselves as leading players in the worldwide Islamic movements, and would like to see the jehadi forces, including the Taliban re-assert themselves–though in a 'moderate' role under the present circumstances.

The fractured mandate also suits the interests of the Pakistan military establishment and the ISI. It ensures that in the absence of a strong civil government, they will be able to continue to be the destiny-makers of Pakistan. Musharraf's desire to consolidate his power dictated his twin strategy of his overt support for war against terror and covert support to the terrorists. The first keeps Pakistan from being obliterated and secures the country from an economic collapse. The second serves to use the jehadi elements as (a) symbol of support for the wider Islamic cause, (b) an effective tool against India, (c) a ruse to milk the Americans for more material gains. Reuel Marc Gerecht, a Resident Fellow at the American Enterprise Institute for Public Policy Research, has cautioned that the US Government should see beyond the façade of cooperation extended by Pakistan. He has mentioned that the slow process of 'Talibanisation' of Pakistan will continue and the Americans should not place too much trust on Pakistan in the war against terror. "If we allow ourselves to be blackmailed because of our fear of chaos in a nuclear-armed Muslim country, then we will surely get blackmailed repeatedly. Even our Pakistani friends would be hard pressed not to take us to the cleaners again and again."[85]

By 'detaining and surrendering' small groups of inconsequential foot-soldiers and sympathisers of the al-Qaida and Taliban, in a staggered fashion, Musharraf has so far been successful in keeping alive the US interest in himself and in Pakistan. This strategy has also helped in ensuring the safety and anonymity of the larger groups of hard-core jehadis and their leadership. These groups have conveniently melted away in different parts of the country and are now regrouping in Karachi, Waziristan and at various locations in POK. There has been no change in Pakistan's Kashmir policy, only the approach has changed for the time being. Pakistan's continued interest in the affairs of Afghanistan and India, along with the increasing role of the MMA in domestic politics do not signal a peaceful future for either Pakistan or the region. Of utmost concern is the emerging political scenario in Pakistan, where the growing political power of militant religious parties is taking them closer to the command and control systems of the Pakistani nuclear arsenal.

Notes:

1. Rory McCarthy and Hasan Zaidi, "Can Pakistan Change," *India Today,* 28 January, 2002, pp. 31-32; "Pak grooming ultras for Bosnia too," *Hindustan Times,* 20 January, 1996.
2. Anat Lapidot, "Islamic Activism in Turkey since the 1980 Military Takeover", in Bruce Maddy-Weitzman and Ifraim Inbar (ed.) *Religious Radicalism in the Greater Middle East.* London: Frank Cass, 1997, p.68.
3. Syyed Vali Reza Nasr, *The Vanguard of Islamic Revolution: The Jamaat-e-Islami of Pakistan.* London: I.B.Tauris Publishers, 1994, pp.63-64; Zohair Hussain, "Islam in Pakistan under Bhutto and Zia-ul-Haq," in Hussien Mutalib and Taj-ul-Hashmi (ed.) *Islam, Muslims and the Modern State: Case Studies of Muslims in Thirteen Countries.* New York: St. Martins Press, 1994, pp. 59-63.
4. Sreedhar, "Pak hand in Boudiaf assasination?" Sunday Mail, New Delhi July 26, 932.
5. Kapil Kaul, "US Capabilities and Intentions in the Gulf," *Strategic Analyses,* August 1987, Institute for Defence Studies and Analyses, Delhi.
6. Ken Silverstien, "When Osama Met The Taliban," 9 October, 2001, slate.msn.com/?id=116991
7. Ahmad Rashid, "Pakistan, Taliban and the US", *The Nation,* Lahore, 8 October, 2002.
8. ibid.
9. "Pakistan: Taliban is not terrorist", 16 October, 2001. arabicnews.com/ansub/daily/day/011016
10. Mahir Ali, "loves US, loves US not," *India Today,* 16 September, 2002, p.61.
11. Dexter Filkins and Carlotta Gall, "Pakistan Evacuates Taliban Supporters," The *New York Times,* 24 November, 2001; Kirk Spitzer, "Report: Pakistan rescued Taliban," usatoday.com/usatonline/20011127

12. Ken Silverstien, n.6.
13. Syed Saleem Shahzad, "Pakistan and the Taliban revisited," *Asia Times* Online, 22 December, 2001; atimes.com
14. Raja Asghar, "Pakistan bars foreign aid for Islamic seminaries", 19 June, 2002. In.news.yahoo.com
15. Majid Khadduri, *War and Peace in the Law of Islam.* Baltimore: The John Hopkins Press: 1955, p.78,{Koran IV, 62}.
16. "Pak HRC pulls up Musharraf", *The Statesman*, 28 March, 2002.
17. "Musharraf shouldn't play games about terrorism : US", *Hindustan Times*, 10 March, 2002; Rory McCarthy, "Consulate bomb kills 11 in Karachi", *The Guardian*, 15 June, 2002.
18. "Pak crackdown on jehadis", *Hindustan Times*, 10 May, 2002; "Musharraf shows terror an iron fist", *The Times of India*, 12 May, 2002; "27 held in crackdown on ultras in Pak", *The Tribune*, 15 August, 2002.
19. "Pak Militants plan strike at US targets", *Hindustan Times*, 23 July, 2002.
20. "Bombing brings back Al Qaida into focus", *The Times of India*, 5 May, 2002.
21. Hussain Haqqani, "Uniform Mistrust", *The Indian Express*, 24 July, 2002.
22. Jason Burke, "Where is Osama?", *India Today*, 16 September 2002, pp. 50-52 ; "Bin Laden is dead: Al Jazeera", *The Statesman* (World Focus) 10 September, 2002.
23. David Rohde, "Karachi is Al Qaida's new base," *The Times of India*, 2 November, 2002.
24. M.Ilyas Khan, "Al Qaida in Pakistan : The 'guests' who stayed on", *The Indian Express*, 14 June, 2002.
25. Ibid.
26. Jason Burke, "Desperate Jehadi", *India Today*, 24 June, 2002, p.47.

27. Ibid.

28. B.M. Bhatia, "Pakistan's Burden-I", *The Statesman*, 5 September, 2002.

29. ibid.

30. Najam Aziz Sethi, "Musharraf's hands full, pockets half-empty," *The Indian Express*, 21 May, 2002.

31. IANS release, *The Times of India*, 11 September, 2002.

32. Najam Aziz Sethi, n.30.

33. Radhica Sachdev, "The Cost of Conflict," *Hindustan Times*, 3 July, 2002.

34. G. Parthasarthy, "Powell pats the all-American Pervez," *The Pioneer*, 1 August, 2002.

35. Speech delivered by Assistant Secretary of State, Christina Rocca at the American Enterprise Institute in Washington on 10 October, 2002.

36. B. Muralidhar Reddy, "Pak plans to build four frigates with Chinese help," *The Hindu*, 25 August, 2002.

37. "UK alarm over Pak nuke purchases," *The Statesman*, 26 August, 2002.

38. "Lethal arms flood Pak tribal areas", *The Tribune*, 22 August, 2002.

39. G. Parthasarthy, "General and his labyrinth", *The Statesman*, 23 May, 2002.

40. Chidanand Rajghatta, "Pak hand in N. Korea bomb," *The Times of India*, 20 October, 2002.

41. Prakash Nanda, "The Gulf Widens for Pakistan", *The Asian Age*, 26 June, 2002.

42. Sumit Mitra, "Supping with the enemy", *India Today*, 12 August, 2002.

43. Arun Joshi, "Six attacks in six days: Army camps are sitting ducks", *Hindustan Times*, 21 May, 2002.

44. Talat Masood, "Give Time For Reform", *India Today*, 28 January, 2002; p.35.

45. "Pervez ups the ante, India calls it interference", *The Statesman*, 6 February, 2002.

46. Jason Burke, n.26.

47. Rory McCarthy and Hasan Zaidi, n.1, p.34.

48. Siddarth Vardarajan, "Slowly, Pakistan's new Kashmir Policy takes shape", *The Time of India*, 23 March, 2002.

49. "Pervez asks all nations to mediate in S. Asia", *The Asian Age*, 14 March, 2002.

50. Arun Joshi and Jay Raina, "India puts Pak on 2-month notice", *Hindustan Times*, 24 May, 2002.

51. Kulwinder Sandhu, "Pak army's 10-day exercise from today", *The Tribune*, 16 July 2002; B. Muralidhar Reddy, "Pak to pull out troops from Sierra Leone", *The Statesman*, 21 May 2002; "Prakram peaks, Shaheen deployed", *The Statesman*, 21 May, 2002.

52. "ISI warns Pak of high-risk conflict with India in weeks", *The Asian Age*, 8 May, 2002.

53. Sonia Trikha, "If India has reservations about Pak, let us resume, sustain a dialogue", interview with Ashraf Jehangir, *The Indian Express*, 22 May, 2002.

54. Ravindra Kumar, "Musharraf must crack down on Kashmir Terror" *The Statesman*, 3 May, 2002.

55. "No time limits on LoC insurgents", *The Asian Age*, 30 August, 2002.

56. K.J.M Verma, "ISI's Afghan, Kashmir Cells to Continue", *The Statesman*, 20 March, 2002.

57. Mubashir Zaidi, "Track 2 for terror : jehadi unity under Kashmir Liberation Army", *The Indian Express*, 23 July, 2002.

58. "LOC crossing not infiltration : JKLF(A)", *The Statesman*, 18 June, 2002.

59. Hasan Suroor, 'Kashmir may become another Palestine warns Musharraf', *The Hindu*, 25 June, 2002.

60. Muzamil Jaleel, "Come clean or clear out: Jehadis tell Hurriyat", *The Indian Express*, 3 July, 2002.

61. Shabir Choudhary in the *Dawn*. Reported in *The Times of India*, 23 July, 2002.

62. Talat Masood, n.44, p.35.

63. "Thousands march against Pakistan referendum", *ABC News Online*, 28 April 2002, at www.abc.net.au/news/newsitems and Akhtar Soomro, "Musharraf wins Pakistan Referendum, but doubts remain about its fairness", 3 May, 2002, www.europaworld.org.week80/musharrafwins

64. "Pakistan : Entire Election Process Deeply Flawed", Human Rights Watch Background Briefing, 9 October, 2002, HRW Documents on Pakistan @ hrw.org/press/2002/10/Pakistan-bck1009

65. "Pakistani President extends his powers", *The Guardian*, 22 August, 2002.

66. Statement by Pakistan's Ambassador to the US, Ashraf Jehangir Qazi, at the John Hopkins University. Ashish Kumar Sen, "Army has no intention to rule Pakistan, says Qazi", *The Statesman*, 18 October, 2002.

67. "Musharraf sees bigger role for army, 'why be so shy?", *The Indian Express*, 8 May, 2002.

68. G.Parthasarthy, n.34.

69. "Pervez in scam of the generals", *The Asian Age*, 20 August, 2002.

70. Irfan Husain, "The Politics of Jobs", *The Asian Age*, 16 October, 2002.

71. Hussain Haqqani, "Free? Fair? Farce? Don't ask the General about elections", *The Indian Express*, 17 August, 2002.

72. Ayaz Amir, "Thank you Busharraf for mullahs", *The Asian Age*, 19 October, 2002.

73. Syed Nooruzzaman, "Pointers from Pak elections", *The Tribune,* 15 October, 2002; G. Parthasarthy, "Politics in Musharraf's Pakistan", *The Tribune,* 9 September 2002; Adnan Adil, "Religious Parties settle for poll adjustments", *The Tribune,* 20 August, 2002.

74. "Rise of hardliners", Strategic Foresight Group, *The Times of India,* 21 October, 2002.

75. "MMA promises women equal rights", *Hindustan Times,* 21 October, 2002.

76. B.Muralidhar Reddy, "MMA seeks to ban co-education in Pak", *The Hindu,* 22 October, 2002.

77. Umar Farooq, "Indecent TV may have to go", *The Asian Age,* 21 October, 2002.

78. Hasan Zaidi, "Enter the Mullahs", *India Today,* 28 October, 2002, p.45.

79. "No using Pak in the name of terror : Hardliners", *The Indian Express,* 15 October, 2002.

80. Hasan Zaidi, n.78, p.45.

81. Gen. Mirza Aslam Beg, "Pakistan's anti-US verdict", *Hindustan Times,* 20 October, 2002.

82. "MMA to go soft on US crackdown", 21 October, 2002.

83. Interview with Talat Husain, News Night, PTV World, 28 October, 2002.

84. Qazi Hussain Ahmad interview with Talat Husain, News Night, PTV World, 1 November, 2002.

85. Reuel Marc Gerecht, "Pakistan's Taliban Problem", *Weekly Standard,* 5 November, 2001.

2

Army's Quest for Power and Legitimacy

Dr Smruti S Pattanaik

The Pakistan Army's motivation to interfere in politics has much to do with the protection of institutional interests than to govern. The first military takeover experimented with constitution making to implement the Army's vision of democracy and to perpetuate the military's dominance in politics. General Zia and General Musharraf introduced far-reaching changes that consolidated the army's dominance in a civilian democratic system. Though in form Pakistan reverted to civilian rule in 1985, it remained military to the core with the Chief of the Army Staff (COAS) being the President. After 1988, the army had dominated through a system of troika. Though General Zia informally inducted the army into the sphere of decision-making through the infamous Eighth Amendment, General Musharraf has introduced amendments to the 1973 Constitution to formalize the role of the army in governance. Frequent army interference in Pakistan has led to institutional decay. In spite of the well-demarcated separation of power between the three organs of the government, the army has played a role of arbitrator and acted as extra-constitutional authority. Given this context, the formalisation of the army's role in national politics theoretically would not make much difference to the functioning of government as has happened in the past, but practically the armed forces are going to scrutinize the functioning of the civilian government. Instead of selected interference at the insistence of political leaders to accomplish the dirty job of making the system function, the army by Constitution would have legitimate authority to interfere in the political domain that the civilian leadership considers as its own.

In the post-11 September political scenario, General Musharraf's support to the US war on terror not only gave him international legitimacy, but the military used the situation to strengthen itself in politics. The referendum and amendments to the Constitution are cases in point. Far-reaching institutional changes which the military regime introduced to the Constitution were subjected to less international scrutiny. To gain approval of the international community, the military government projected itself as the best bet in Pakistan in terms of stability against the threat of growing fundamentalism. As the International Crisis Group report emphatically puts it, "Far from being besieged by Islamic extremists, Pakistan's military government has carefully used that phenomena as an essential tool to justify its hold on power, improve its standing with the West, and resist restoring secular democracy and as a tactical means to advance its goal in both Afghanistan and Kashmir"[1]. In this context it is important to analyse the Pakistan Army's position in politics, public perception of its role in governance and future of the polity under an army-dominated system given the socio-political dynamics of the country.

Army Consolidating Power

The problem in Pakistani politics is fragmented political opposition. The naked struggle for power and lack of commitment to democracy has made the military manipulate political leaders to its advantage. The military always has a ready and willing partner among the political circles to co-opt and thereby reduce the effectiveness of the political parties to challenge their rule. After taking over, General Musharraf tried his best to divide the political parties, to weaken the opposition there by to reduce their ability to challenge the military government. In the name of accountability many of the political leaders were brought into the purview of Ehtesab Bureau, which was mandated to look into the corruption charges. Politically motivated corruption proceedings were initiated to coerce leaders into political submission. Of course the functioning and neutrality of the Ehtesab Bureau was questioned during the regime of Nawaz Sharif who had initiated action against his political rival Benazir Bhutto. The military placed its own men in the accountability bureau thereby making the anti-corruption drive questionable.

The only political party that was amenable to the temptation of power formed a new party, the Pakistan Muslim League (Qaid-e-Azam). This party aligned with the military government and became the front-runner in the October 2002 elections. Moreover, personality clashes between the senior PML (N) leaders and Nawaz Sharif were simmering when General Musharraf took over. The military was not only able to win over the anti-Nawaz Sharif leaders, but corruption charges against many of them willing to align with the military were dropped. There were reports that top PML (Q) leaders like Chaudhury Pervez Elahi, the Chief Minister of Punjab, and Iftekhar Gillani had their loans written off[2] for the cooperation they extended to the military. Though the military government had promised its anti-corruption drives with much fanfare, political expediency gave way to their moralistic rhetoric. Interestingly many of the political parties dissatisfied with the functioning of the Nawaz Sharif government had welcomed the military takeover. It is the politicians whose faith in the political system and democratic change of regimes is so lacking that they want the military to resolve political problems and effect change and then withdraw to the barracks. Nowhere has such political naivety and immaturity been this apparent as in Pakistani politics. After welcoming the army intervention the same politicians are being critical of the military government. Interestingly, the PML came into being as a political party with direct help from the military in 1988. It won the first general election as a part of *Islamic Jamoohri Ittehad* with active help from the ISI and with the blessings of the establishment. Though the differences between the establishment and the party surfaced in 1993, the ultimate blow to the relationship came with the sacking of General Pervez Musharraf as army chief.

To deal with institutional challenges after coopting the politicians, the judges of the Supreme Court and the High Courts were given oath under the Provisional

Constitutional Order (PCO). The independence and impartiality of the judiciary can be gauged from the content of the PCO No. 1 of 2000 which reads that:"A person holding office immediately before the commencement of this order as a judge of the superior court shall not continue to hold that office if he is not given, or does not take, oath in the form set out in the schedule, before the expiration of such time from such commencement as the Chief Executive may determine or within such further time as may be *allowed* by the Chief Executive".[3] The parameter of functioning of the judges was defined by the General. They drew their authority to deliver justice from the PCO and as 'allowed' by the Chief Executive. The Supreme Court quite expectedly gave breathing space to General Musharraf and granted him extraordinary power to amend the Constitution. The PCO no. 1 of 2000 reads, "Whereas Pakistan is to be governed, as nearly as may be, in accordance with the Constitution, the Chief Executive has and shall be deemed always to have had, the power to amend the Constitution".[4]

Army Formalising its Role

The army has defined a role for itself not only in internal politics but also in foreign and defence policy matters. Though the army always had a role informally, their formal induction to a structured decision-making sphere has been opposed by the successive civilian governments. The idea of a National Security Council (NSC) has been debated by each regime, both military and civilian. The idea of NSC is always seen as an answer of the military to the civilian inefficiency and to protect its interests in matters of decision-making that would have direct bearing on the military. The military always perceived that the civilian government would compromise with the 'national interest' for political power. The civilian government has always looked with contempt at the military's attempt to intrude itself into the civilian sphere. Both Ayub Khan and Yahya Khan constituted the National Security Advisory Council to run the affairs of the state. But there was no controversy regarding its functioning because political power was concentrated in the hands of these military rulers without effective political opposition. General Zia had set up a National Security Council through Presidential Order 14 of 1985, to recommend on issues pertaining to the proclamation of emergency, security of Pakistan and any matters of national importance. Later, this was abolished as a result of intense political bargaining where the elected members of the National Assembly agreed to concede power to the President by voting for the incorporation of the 8th amendment to the Constitution. Apart from this, establishment of the Council for Defence and National Security (CDNS) was mooted again in 1996 during the regime of Malik Miraj Khalid, the caretaker government after Benazir's dismissal "to aid and advise the government in the determination of national strategy and fixation of priorities in terms of overall national security".[5] The CDNS had only advisory capacity. However, given the dynamics of Pakistan politics this advisory capability became actually binding with implicit repercussion to the stability of the regime. When Nawaz Sharif came to power in 1997, he allowed the ordinance on CDNS to lapse. Later, when Jehangir Karamat mooted the idea of the establishment of a NSC in his lecture to the cadets in the Navy War College, he had no option but to resign after it created an unprecedented political furore. It was reported that he apprised Nawaz Sharif about the reason why he floated the idea. He reportedly admitted that he was pressurized by his service to float the idea[6]. The civilian government's contempt to such an idea is understandable due to the fact that the army had been playing an important role in political intrigues since 1985.

It is important to mention here that it was the Nawaz Sharif government which had amended article 58 2(b) or the eighth amendment in 1997 which was welcomed by the entire political spectrum. However, surprisingly, many political analysts and retired army generals believed that the reason why Nawaz Sharif behaved arbitrarily was the amendment of this article, which served as a check on his absolute authority. This reduced the all-powerful President, who had earlier dismissed three elected governments, to a mere figurehead. This also ended the army's leverage in the political system because in all the three cases where the civilian governments were dismissed, the army in collaboration with the President had played a significant role. According to Sharifuddin Pirzada, the renowned lawyer associated with 1973 constitution making, had the 58 2(b) not been repealed, the army would have taken its supreme commander into confidence and, as a consequence, a constitutional change would have taken place and democracy continued to flourish.[7] Similarly, Jehangir Karamat, former chief of the army staff, commenting on Sharif's dismissal said that had Nawaz Sharif pondered over his suggestion to create a National Security Council, the military intervention would not have happened because its basic purpose is to keep the democratic dispensation intact.[8] This reflects the kind of thinking Pakistan elites have regarding military's role and their indispensbility to political stability.

Interestingly the eighth amendment was passed by the National Assembly in 1985 with 188 members present out of a total 217 members and the house passed the bill unanimously as a compromise formula to restore power to the civilian government. However, the army's centrality in the political power structure is admitted by the former Prime Minister Benazir Bhutto. Speaking after the 1988 elections she said, "Anyone thinking that after the elections the power of the army will automatically wane is being unrealistic".[9] This assessment holds true in the context of the 1999 military coup. Shortly after taking over General Musharraf said, "few at the helm of affairs in the past were intriguing to destroy the last institution of stability left in Pakistan by creating dissension in the ranks of armed forces".[10]

Over a period of time, the army's interests have been extended from protecting its institutional interests to include internal security issues ranging from political stability to economic sustenance. It is true that in Pakistan the army does not want to be a mute spectator to political and economic degeneration, which in the long run would affect the army's institutional interests. Army's role as perceived by the first martial ruler Ayub Khan is pertinent to mention in this context. According to him, though it is distasteful for the army to assume political function but "the army alone can act as a corrective force and restore normalcy".[11]

The confidence of the army and its ability to govern emanates from the lack of faith they have in the institution of democracy and the political leaders. According to General Tanvir Naqvi, Chairman of the National Reconstruction Board who finalized the Legal Framework

Order, "The army has a role, which is a de facto role. That role should disappear"[12] with the NSC coming into being. Though it is only now that the army has formalized a role for itself with the establishment of the National Security Council.

A cursory glance at the Constitution of the present NSC brings out clearly what would be the army's role in politics. The NSC consists of the President, Prime Minister, leader of Opposition, four Chief Ministers, Chairman of Joint Chiefs of Staff Committee (JCSC) and the three service Chiefs. The role of the NSC would be to deal with matters pertaining to Islamic ideology, national security, sovereignty, integrity and solidarity of Pakistan. The agenda of the NSC is extremely vast and the President has discretionary power to take decisions. The role of the NSC would be advisory and not binding. However this clause would have little relevance in practice with army's overarching role. One of the rationales behind the Constitution of the NSC is that the council would provide a forum to the President to influence the "federal and provincial governments to consolidate and continue the reform process". In addition to this, the NSC would serve "as a forum for consultation on strategic matters pertaining to the sovereignty, integrity and security of the state, and the matters relating to democracy, governance and inter provincial harmony". These broad functions take away the legitimate power of the Prime Minister. Thus in the new political dispensation with President; also being a Chief of Army Staff, the army would emerge as a dominant centre of power. The President (i.e. Gen. Musharraf) would have the power to dismiss at his discretion the Chairman of the Joint Chiefs of Staff Committee, all the service Chiefs and the provincial governors. Thus their functioning and survival would depend on the pleasure of the President and this in turn would strengthen the President's power.

The Supreme Court of Pakistan had entrusted the military government to initiate changes but it had also made it clear that such amendments must not alter the federal and parliamentary character of the Constitution. However, the changes suggested by the military government would substantially alter the basic structure of the parliamentary democracy. Though by name it would be parliamentary, but in practice the President would have far-reaching powers to initiate changes without the concurrence of the Prime Minister. The Supreme Court's formulation of the army's intervention as 'doctrine of necessity' in practice is going to be a legitimization of the perceived 'necessity' by granting a constitutional role to the army. The introduction of checks and balances is to curtail the power of the Prime Minister because the argument put forward by the military government is that a powerful Prime Minister would behave arbitrarily. Notwithstanding the criticism about the formation of NSC, the military government is determined not to allow any political parties to introduce amendments to the system introduced by them. One of the reasons attributed by General Musharraf to his decision to become the President of Pakistan was to implement reforms introduced by his regime and see to it that the civilian government does not change the amendments brought in by the military government to the 1973 Constitution. Interestingly, Part XII Chapter 7 of the Legal Framework Order clearly envisages that notwithstanding any judgment of the court or anything contained in the Constitution the legal framework order (LFO) shall not be called into question in any court on any ground. Political parties like the religious parties represented by the MMA, and PPP are opposed to the amendments and want that the amendments cannot be part of the Constitution unless adopted by the elected representatives of the people in the National Assembly. However, with present divided mandate the political parties do not have the required political strength to challenge the LFO. The present amendment has overriding power over anything contained in the Constitution.

Interestingly, the 1973 Constitution describes military takeover as treason punishable by death. Though the civilian government tried to protect democracy from the army's predatory impulses but they used the army to further their political interests. Whether it was using the army in 1973 in Baluchistan to settle a political problem or seeking the army's active intervention to deal with the political impasse in 1977, the army was attributed a role, which it had not formally looked for.

Army and its Legitimacy to Govern

Does this imply that the Pakistan Army has a legitimate role in politics or does the state, the ideological orientation and its security predicaments involve the army's indulgence in politics? The role of the Pakistan Army in politics has followed a well-defined parameter and is based on public assumptions which superficially seem to be a correct assessment. If one takes into consideration the first military takeover in 1958, it followed an era of unabashed struggle for power where the process of Constitution making suffered due to the conflict regarding placing the center of authority, whether it should be the Prime Minister or the President who would be the real center of power. The struggle between the Prime Minister and the President regarding their power and function saw the fall of governments and of course, its effect on governance was blatantly evident. In this struggle the army was the only organized force; and the army articulated perceived security imperatives of Pakistan, and the army suddenly assumed greater importance than it deserved. The frequent use of military in law and order enforcement duty, which is a primary function of the civilian government, also proved the army's ability to deliver and the inefficiency of the civilian government. While faith in the civilian government was on the decline, the army's legitimacy as ultimate saviour of Pakistan grew proportionately. These general perceptions ultimately widened the army's mandate from security of the borders to governance. The army's role in the anti-Ahmediya riots in 1953 and its efficiency in restoring normalcy certainly boosted its image as an institution in the eyes of the people. Moreover, Ayub Khan, the first military ruler, also watched from close quarters the political intrigues taking place around that time. Thus he also developed his own views and perceptions about the politicians. His close interaction with various politicians also convinced him about their incapacity to govern. Iskander Mirza openly invited Ayub Khan to take over the political reins because he could not take the constitutional onslaught where the post of the President was becoming more ornamental under the 1956 Constitution. The contempt with which the armed forces viewed the politicians is evident from Ayub's writing in his book *Friends not Masters*. Stephen Cohen, who has studied the Pakistan Army, wrote that the military's description of themselves as an organization has always regarded the armed forces as the special expression of the idea of Pakistan due to their role in defence. According to him few officers in the Pakistan Army have "advocated an activist role in reforming or correcting the society where it has fallen below the standard of excellence".[13]

Political parties in Pakistan have also helped in accentuating the army's image by their own inefficiency in governance. Whether it is during the 1970 elections where Bhutto played an important role or his uncompromising attitude to respect the democratic mandate given to the Awami League which resulted in the country getting divided. Though the army was discredited for its role in 1971, the role played by Bhutto was not above board. Bhutto however had political charisma and his political credibility increased after he was able to give the country its first consensus Constitution. Later, his handling of domestic political developments discredited his democratic credentials. Moreover, Bhutto constitutionally ensured civilian supremacy and increased the defence budget and tried to rebuild the morale of the army. However, the shattered image of the army got a boost after Bhutto employed the army in Baluchistan for internal security duty. Bhutto charged the provincial leaders of treason and arrested them. This strengthened Bhutto's position politically. At the same time these actions consolidated and convinced army's opinion about politicians. To quote a political analyst, the army "sees itself as a national force, which must intervene to cement and preserve a nation threatened by treacherous politicians. Bhutto by operating within this matrix, provided further evidence to the army that these dangers existed".[14]

Credentials of the military as an uncorrupted organization dedicated to national security is acknowledged by the politicians themselves. For instance, during the 1977 rigged election, the opposition parties under the Pakistan National Movement were so distrustful of Bhutto and his commitment to hold fresh election that many of the political leaders openly expressed their willingness to participate in the elections under martial law.[15] The image of the military as the only viable organization is not propounded by the military alone, but the politicians themselves have credited the military in its self-propagated image. Moreover, not only by words but also by actions, the politicians have discredited themselves, the government and the institution of democracy. This is evident from the fact that during the talks between the Pakistan National Alliance (PNA) and the government, Bhutto apprised General Zia of political developments almost on daily basis. Bhutto himself at one point asked the army to take over after he failed to reach an agreement with the PNA regarding fresh elections. He reportedly told Zia, "Do not worry, I will give you justification", for imposing martial law. "My brain is your power" and "we would run the country together".[16]

Moreover, the army's commitment to democracy was demonstrated when after Zia's death, the military did not take over the governance of the country but played an important role in restoration of democracy. Of course the army had certain reasons for not taking over the reins of power. One of the important reasons was that dissatisfaction against army's rule in general and General Zia's regime in particular had been widely manifest. The army would have discredited itself as an institution conscious of the well-being of the state, had it taken over. The institutional credibility it retained by holding elections certainly boosted the image of the army.

Declining faith of the people in the political system is evident from the way the civilian governments conducted themselves after the restoration of democracy. The lack of cooperation between the two major political parties frequently created political instability. The smaller political parties with limited regional agendas have lacked national political perspective. However, this is not to say that the regional parties should not have protected their constituency but at the same time they remained vulnerable to political manipulation by the establishment, which was a part of the troika after the restoration of democracy. The army played an important role in the formation of the governments and their downfall. The military by acting behind the scenes, effectively discredited the politicians again. During the years 1988-96, due to the eighth amendment the army retained its political control over the civilian government. Thus it is not surprising that the army emerged as the final arbitrator in the squabbling among various institutions of the government. The extra constitutional role of the army portrayed an image of its commitment to the civilian government but at the same time the politicians took blame for malfunctioning of the government; whether it was intervening in the conflict between Prime Minister Nawaz Sharif and President Ghulam Ishaq Khan in 1993 where both of them were asked to resign or whether it was the conflict between the Prime Minister and the Judiciary in 1997 which saw the exit of the Chief Justice. All these incidents raised severe doubts among the general public regarding the ability of politicians to govern or settle institutional differences without the army's intervention. At the same time this conveyed army's indispensability to the political system. According to General Jehangir Karamat, "ours has been an assertive military. It has been an interventionist military" because of circumstances, but the military should not be dragged into resolving problems between various institutions of the state[17]. In Pakistan, the military has always intervened in politics after the politicians and the system of governance are completely discredited. Thus legitimacy to its intervention is acquired through the degeneration of the political system itself. Therefore, military interventions are welcomed with a sigh of relief[18]. Apart from the image of the army, the faith and trust of the people in the institution itself is immense. Through the portrayal of an image of India as an immediate threat, the army is seen as the sole rescuer of the state, both in the time of war and peace. The defence budget and the army's various economic interests have hardly been questioned in Pakistan. The function of the army and depiction of a larger than life role have all contributed to the indispensability of the army in the political system itself. Lack of effective political opposition has contributed to the deterioration of the democratic system where political leaders at the helm of power have behaved arbitrarily whenever they are in a numerically comfortable position in the National Assembly. This enabled the military in Pakistan to fragment the political parties and muster political support for its actions. In fact, some of the political parties have cooperated with the military regime to further their political interests. Thus, there is no dearth of political support to Pakistan's military establishment in their effort to rule. The establishment has not only furthered its interests by dividing political parties, but at the same time some of them have boasted about creating alliances and played a role in the formation of government[19]. As a well-known Pakistani commentator writes, "The October coup was different from previous military interventions.... Moreover, because Sharif had concentrated all power in himself in the process disposing of all democratic checks and balances, undermining state institutions, abusing and amending the Constitution repeatedly, and destabilizing the economy the public had widely demanded that the army act"[20]. During Nawaz Sharif's regime he had used the army in accomplishing the tasks of the elected government. Whether it was to conduct the census, the collection of electricity bills, fixing the sewerage — the army had a role to play. This not only attested to the inefficiency of the civilian government, but also reinforced the credibility of the armed forces' ability to deliver and enforce the rule of law. In the recently unveiled report in August 2002 on the achievements of the military government entitled *"Three Years of Reforms"*, it is described that "military rule was a *fait accompli* and was attributed to a crisis provoked by the rulers' inept handling of sensitive affairs that would have shattered national unity and landed Pakistan in an invidious position. There was no alternative but for the army to step in".

After the October 1999 coup, the army has been engaged in defining a role for itself. When General Musharraf took over, in his first address to the nation, he said that the army took over reluctantly to protect the national interest of Pakistan. Like his predecessors, Gen. Ayub Khan and Gen. Zia-ul-Haq, he maligned politicians branding them as corrupt and inefficient. In the first two years after taking over political power, the army was engaged in a systematic campaign to generate an opinion which was supportive of a role for the army.

What has helped the military as an institution at the cost of democracy is the marginalisation of civil society from the sphere of decision-making. Years of martial rule have stunted the growth of civil society in Pakistan. Due to various draconian measures, the elites have remained mute spectators. The press which could have helped the growth of a culture of debate and discussion itself was under the Press and Public Ordinance till 1988. In addition, the emergence of radical elements with their narrow view of religion emerged as a new menace further silencing the civil society. The protection given by the establishment and the intelligence agencies to these radical religious groups strengthened their power to enforce compliance to their view by everyone including the press. It became difficult to openly criticize the social evolvement of the Pakistani state.

General's Referendum

General Musharraf entrenched his position by holding a referendum to get himself elected as the President of Pakistan. Citing the reason for choosing direct election as President he said, "it will give a boost to my self-confidence and I will have the moral strength that the entire Pakistani nation is with me". In his address to the nation on 5 April, 2002, General Musharaff stressing the need for the referendum said, "...the essence of democracy has to be introduced in Pakistan" otherwise "all the reforms and restructuring that we have done in various sectors will go waste if we do not cap it with true democracy". Defining his role in the future political structure he said, "I want to have power to the extent that he dares not undo what I have done. He dare not violate national interests. He dare not reverse the reform agenda. I want to assure that I will support the Prime Minister if he practices governance rightly and in the interest of Pakistan, I will back him up. I will strengthen him fully. That is how democracy in Pakistan will function". Talking about the future of democracy, General Musharaff said, "I am involving myself in politics in the interest of democracy, maturing democracy and consolidating democracy"[21].

General Musharaf's political campaign had two objectives. First, to garner support from the people for his continuance in the office of President for another five years to implement his already outlined seven point agenda. The seven point agenda includes (i) rebuild national confidence and morale, (ii) strengthen federation, remove inter-provincial disharmony and restore national cohesion, (iii) revive economy and restore investors' confidence, (iv) ensure law and order and dispense speedy justice, (v) de-politicise state institutions, (vi) devolution of power to the grassroots level, and (vii) accountability. Secondly, he used this public campaign not only to malign the politicians but also the democracy that existed earlier in Pakistan.

Referendum in Pakistan politics was invented by the army to gain political legitimacy for their rule. Cleverly, the military rulers have always put certain issues to vote to garner public support and have conferred on themselves the right to implement these measures by remaining in power. For example: The question General Zia put to the voters was, "Do you endorse the process initiated by the President of Pakistan, General Muhammad Zia-ul Haq, for bringing the laws of Pakistan in conformity with the injunctions of Islam as laid down in the Holy Quran and Sunnah of the Holy Prophet and for the preservation of the ideology of Pakistan; and are you in favour of the continuation and further consolidation of that process and for the smooth and orderly transfer of power to the elected representatives of the people?" Voters were required to answer 'yes' or 'no'. Similarly, General Musharaf's question to the electorate was whether they supported the continuation of the seven-point reforms outlined by the President. Chief Executive's Order No 12 of 2002 pertaining to referendum reads, "Notwithstanding anything contained in the Constitution or any law for the time being in force. If the majority of votes cast in the referendum are affirmative, the people of Pakistan shall be deemed to have given the democratic mandate to General Pervez Musharraf to serve the nation as President of Pakistan for a period of five years to enable him to consolidate the reforms..." Ayub Khan was more direct regarding the question he put in his referendum to the basic democrats unlike General Zia and General Musharraf. The question that was put to the electoral college by Gen. Ayub Khan was, "Do you have confidence in the President Field Marshal Ayub Khan, Hilal-I-Pakistan, Hilal-I-Jamat?"

The large-scale rigging in the 30 April 2002 referendum discredited General Musharraf. At the same time it consolidated him politically for the next five years as the President of Pakistan. Some of the challenges to his consolidation of power and his seven-point agenda of governance are outlined below which would have strong bearing on the future of Pakistan.

Internal Challenges

The war on terrorism and General Musharraf's unstinted support to the USA brought cleavages in the domestic political context to the fore. The religious parties, forerunner of Pakistan's Afghan policy, were bitterly opposed to General Musharraf's decision as the Taliban regime was their brainchild. War on terror and endorsing the US attack on Afghanistan was largely perceived by the religious parties as an attack on their political constituencies. For example, leader of the Tehrik Nafaz Shariat-e-Muhammadi (TNSM) chief Maulana Sofi Muhammad declared that the US strikes on Afghanistan were an attack on Islam and the support to these strikes is only by the non-believers. It was reported that the TNSM registered around 40,000 volunteers who were ready to fight in support of the Taliban[22]. Apart from the Pakistan Army's institutional interests, one of the reasons why General Musharraf made last minute efforts to save the Taliban regime was to contain domestic dissatisfaction which led to terming him as a 'stooge of the US'. Moreover, the Pakistan military played an important role in the creation of the Taliban and they were apprehensive of a Northern Alliance dominance in Afghanistan.

Various political parties gave broad support to the US led operation in Afghanistan. However, most of the parties were critical about supporting the US without adequate proof of Osama's involvement in the WTC and Pentagon attack. This is one of the reasons why General Musharraf intially urged the US government to show the proof. The government later announced that the proof given by the US was conclusive and satisfactory. The government was able to deal with demonstrations by the radical groups and religious parties by resorting to pre-emptive arrests and detention. However, the discontentment regarding Pakistan siding with the US remained. Pakistan's approach to some of the jehadis who had crossed over to Afghanistan to fight for the Taliban and were arrested by the Northern Alliance, angered the people in the (NWFP)[23]. Pakistan did little to rescue them from getting deported to the Guantonamo Bay. It was reported that some of the Pakistani Army officials were airlifted from Afghanistan just before the bombing began in October 2001. Since the public was largely unaware of the kind of proof the US provided to the government, they were vocal in their criticism. The civil society was critical of the government policy and some also felt that the government was in a hurry to join the coalition. They felt the benefits which Pakistan got by joining the coalition were superficial.

Opposition to General Musharraf's policy is evident from the victory of Muttahida Majlis Amal in the October, 2002 general election which encashed on this dissatisfaction. In the foreign policy sphere, General Musharraf is going to face more political opposition in his Afghan policy. Though after the election, the military regime announced that there would not be any change in Pakistan-US relations, there were many embarrassing moments for the government.

Rising Religious Fundamentalism

Religious fundamentalism has emerged as a major challenge to Pakistan's internal stability. However, most of the steps to curb radicalism adopted by the Musharraf government are cosmetic in nature. The army has not yet abandoned the idea of using these jehadis for its political and strategic purposes. The jehadis have been able to provide motivated cadres to carry out the army's objective in Kashmir. The 13 December 2001 attack on the Indian Parliament put pressure on Musharraf to take decisive action against these groups. But the ban imposed on many of the jehadi and sectarian groups in reality has been ineffective and superficial. Though the accounts were frozen, the militant groups were given enough time to transfer their money to safe accounts. Moreover, the strong linkages between the army and the jehadi groups ensured that before effective steps were taken, the jehadi groups were well prepared for the official onslaught on them. Sincerity and commitment of the government to take action against the radical elements can be questioned on various grounds.

What would challenge the internal socio-political stability is the return of battle-hardened radicals from Afghanistan. These highly motivated and hardened jehadis are likely to create problems inside Pakistan. Due to the changed international situation Pakistan would not be able to export them to Kashmir to reduce internal pressure. However, these groups are unlikely to stay dormant for a long time. These radical groups with pan-Islamic identity are a threat to the western capital investment. According to Pakistani columnist, Ayaz Amir, "It was the army and the intelligence services which brooked no assault on the 'obscurantist elements' because they were seen as serving the 'national interest' - a bogey in whose name every act of lunacy can be justified".[24] In his 12 January 2002 speech, President Musharraf said that the campaign against extremism is in the national interest of Pakistan. "The extremist minority must realize that Pakistan is not responsible of waging armed jehad in the world".[25] However, there are reports that elements in the ISI continue to maintain linkages with these militant groups. In this context, a special branch policeman and a sympathizer of Jaish e-Mohammad were arrested in connection with the Daniel Pearl kidnapping case. It is difficult to break the two-decade long ties. By the time action against the militant groups was announced they have entrenched themselves financially and politically with active patronage of the establishment.[26] Moreover, some sections in the Pakistan military are reluctant to disown them as they form the backbone of Pakistan's Kashmir policy. For instance, the Al-Rasheed charity organization, which was banned, was functioning under the ISI patronage which sanctioned their 'charity activities' and arranged meetings with Mullah Omar.[27] As a source one of the provincial home departments remarked, "The country today bristles with armed units, which have the temerity to call themselves Sipah, Lashkar, Jaish (soldiers and armies), consequently undermining the notion that state is sole repository of all coercive powers".[28]

The problem in effectively banning these groups or curtailing their activities after 9/11 is that the jehadis are fighting the battle of the army. The International Crisis Group in its report on linkages between the army and madrasas concluded, "The militant clergy and the Pakistani military share a common hostility towards India and a perception that Pakistan should be ruled not as a democracy but as an authoritarian state...madrasa reforms, political reforms, economic reforms are all dependent on whether the military can reform itself and submit to the people's will expressed through the ballot".[29] The Pakistan Army's linkage with the conservative elements is deep-rooted. Tanzeem-al-Ikhwan, a militant religious outfit having a madrasa in Chakwal in Punjab, has close contact with the Pakistan Army.[30] What is worrisome is that well organised groups of zealots belonging to various radical religious groups have penetrated the army. Unlike the traditional religious parties, these groups want power.[31] The linkages between these groups and the army has provided immunity to them from persecution. To deal with the sympathizers of the Taliban elements in the army, General Musharraf reshuffled some of the senior army officers, and tried to deal with the discontent to pre-empt any effort to remove him. General Musharraf went for a major revamp in the army hierarchy; he appointed a new Vice Chief of Army Staff and removed the ISI chief General Mehmood Ahmed who had close links with the Taliban. Mohammad Aziz, Corp Commander Lahore and a known sympathiser of religious parties, was removed and made the Chairman of JCSC.

The government arrested and detained many of the leaders of religious and sectarian parties and their followers. But no effective measures were intiated to deal with the problem at the institutional level. Government limitation can be gauged from the fact that action was taken against non-Pakistani madrasa students and jehadis. This was publicized as the government's resolve to fight fundamentalism and extremism at home.[32] But their domestic cadres have been left untouched. The jehadis are opposed to the government's announced policy to reform madrasa, introduce a new curriculum or in any way controlling their activities. The government is yet to implement measures like the madrasa reforms which include revealing sources of funding and auditing the funds. It is important to mention here that foreign funding to the madrasa started in Z.A. Bhutto's time when Arabic was introduced as a compulsory subject and this brought into the picture Saudi Arabian funding to madrasa. According to a report, over 2,600 *deeni madrasa* in Punjab with more than 200,000 students are actively involved in sectarian and terrorist activities.[33]

The 19 June, 2002, Madrasa Registration Ordinance is a much diluted one compared to government pronouncements on madrasa reforms. It is now required that foreign students and teachers have to obtain no-objection certificate from the Interior Ministry to enrol themselves in a madrasa. The government announced that any madrasa not complying with the government directives would not receive any *zakat* money. However, the foreign donations that the madrasa receive are huge compared to the government donations. Especially the ones that get donations from Saudi Arabia would be much better off by following the lines of radical Wahabi belief rather than complying with the government directives. Quoting interior ministry sources, the *Newsline* reported that around 70 percent of the madrasa are self-sufficient and do not rely on the government for funding. Only the Punjab government has banned the foreign funding to all the schools in the province.[34]

In the past two decades, the civilian governments have also adopted a half-hearted approach to madrasa reforms, as, the radical groups and their part and parcel of the government. Whether it is the coalition of Islamic Pasand Party (Islamic Jamoohri Ittehad) or support given by the JUI to the Benazir government, the religious parties have always resisted the government's interference in the madrasa which they consider as their domain. With the MMA emerging as the third largest party in October 2002 the future of madrasa reforms is doomed. The government cannot legislate now through ordinances. It would require the approval of the National Assembly. Thus, it is likely to face tough opposition from the MMA. The MMA after spectacular electoral success would not like to lose its conservative constituency which has voted it to power.

Though the government has unveiled budgetary plans for madrasa reform it would be difficult for the government to achieve success given the larger socio-political context. Without improving the formal educational system and making secular education accessible to the poor sections of society, the government's effort is bound to fail. According to a report, despite state intervention madrasa still follow curriculum based on traditional literature and teaching methods. "Its rationale of existence is virtually unchanged and as emotive as ever: to defend the faith of Islam – if need be through jehad".[35]

Proliferation of Small Arms

The de-weaponisation campaign which General Musharraf launched to deal with growing violence was taken in a haphazard spirit. According to statistics given by the Ministry of Interior, from 21 June, 2001, to 12 March, 2002, as many as 141,180 weapons and 848,407 pieces of ammunitions were recovered from four provinces.[36] The commitment to the de-weaponisation campaign is doubtful given the politico-military strategies of the Pakistani establishment vis-à-vis the jehadi groups. The growth of these jehadi groups and proliferation of small arms are inextricably linked. In a national seminar, the Interior Minister Moinuddin Haider was skeptical whether the move to de-weaponise would be successful given the unresolved Kashmir problem.[37] The monthly *Herald* quoting senior government officials wrote that the de-weaponisation campaign was sabotaged by the ISI. It feared that this campaign would affect jehadi organisations in Pakistan fighting in Kashmir.[38] According to one estimate, there are 20 different parties with their independent military type establishments in Pakistan. [39] Thus the demand for weapons is overwhelming given the kind of agenda these parties have which ranges from sectarian violence to jehad, to criminal activities and elimination of political rivals and opposition. The commitment of the government to this campaign is evident from the fact that the government agencies are themselves not serious about the implications of weaponisation. The Interior Ministry has no record for license holders of non-prohibited bore weapons that are issued as a political bribe by the elected governments. It was reported that Benazir Bhutto during her second stint as the Prime Minister had issued 20,000-25,000 licenses for AK-47s.[40] Recently, the Pakistan police during the de-weaponisation drive arrested a group of people belonging to Jaish-e-Mohammad in Bahawalpur and captured a cache of AK-47s, grenades etc., which the ISI in contravention to government law had authorised the group to carry. Later, the group held 17 government officials as hostage and demanded that the government should free their members. After the intervention of the ISI these members were freed and the situation was diffused.[41] Until the linkages between the military establishment, jehadis, their relevance to the military strategy of Pakistan vis-à-vis India is not broken, these measures would remain on the list of wishful thinking that the government of Pakistan wants to accomplish.

Economic Revival

After taking over, General Musharraf declared that economic reconstruction, restoring investors' confidence, and reducing debt burden would be the priorities of the government. Due to various sanctions on Pakistan, it was difficult to achieve economic goals since the economy was dependent on external aid. The debt burden rose to $38 billion during Nawaz Sharif's time due to corruption, mismanagement and lack of transparency. However, the war on terror and Pakistan being a frontline ally of the US brought in certain economic benefits. The balance of payment situation improved and its foreign reserves indicated positive signs. Through the Acquisition and Cross Servicing Agreement (ACSA) between Pakistan and the US, Pakistan provided the US forces the use of facilities, training services, repairs and maintenance. The government also charged for facilities like air bases and storage to the US forces and provided food, water, transportation, oil, communications and medical services. Quoting the official sources, the *Newsline* wrote that $60-70 million would be charged per month from the US in this regard.[42] The charges for the services provided by the government are shown in the Central Bank data, though it does not contain the details. Under the category of 'other goods and services and income' an amount of $431 million has been shown against a negative $43 million of the corresponding previous year 2001.[43] After the war on terror was launched, the FBI initiated investigations in the US against the *hawala* system to deal with the money flow to finance terrorist activities.

As a result of this, the money that was remitted through the hawala channel was diverted to the legal channel. This is one of the factors why the forex reserves have gone up in 2002.

Pakistan's economy suffered because of the US strikes in Afghanistan due to increased freight rates and imposition of war risk insurance which made both imports and exports expensive. However, due to external economic aid Pakistan was able to post a current account surplus of $331 million and the rupee-dollar parity depreciated by 18.6 percent, which was the largest adjustment since 1982.[44] The US government also promised that it would help Pakistan in its balance of payment problem by allocating funds for Pakistan Oil limited, and edible oil and fertilizer imports. Moreover, the European Union under a new arrangement agreed to scrap seven per cent duty on import of textiles from Pakistan.

Debt rescheduling also gave breathing space to the Pakistani economy. The immediate tasks would be reduction of government spending in unproductive sectors in the next five years. At the same time Pakistan needs to improve the investment climate to attract foreign direct investment. That would largely depend on how Pakistan tackles political instability, fundamentalism and violence in the society.

Rise of the Religious Right

The October 2002 election saw the spectacular rise to power of Muttahida Majlis Amal, a group of religious parties. The question that arises here is how the religious parties, which hardly had any strength in the previous elections were able to muster such large-scale support. The poll statistics make it evident that the MMA percentage-wise have polled only 11 per cent vote and the average turnout of voters in the NWFP, Baluchistan and FATA was 29.5 percent compared to Punjab and Sindh which accounted for an average 42.3 per cent turnout. Percentage of votes polled attest to the fact that the support base of the MMA has remained narrow. In the North West Frontier Province, the MMA had fielded 82 candidates for the 99 provincial assembly seats whereas major political parties like PPP had put up 53 candidates, PML (N) 52 candidates and the PML (Q) 63 candidates. Regional parties like the Awami National Party had fielded 57 candidates. However, having the highest number of candidates contesting the provincial seats did not ensure their victory. The MMA's strategy of some important seat adjustments with other parties like the PPP (Sherpao) paid dividends. The lowering of the voting age also helped the MMA because many of its cadres are young. Apart from this the religious parties exploited the anti-American and anti-Musharraf sentiments. The military government's approach to the Taliban regime had angered many. The US bombing and civilian casualties in Afghanistan made the Pushtuns who have strong socio-cultural linkages with their ethnic compatriots in the areas bordering Pakistan-Afghanistan feel betrayed. The dominance of the Tajik and the Uzbek ethnic minorities in the new regime in Afghanistan and sidelining of Pushtuns made the situation still worse. The US is generally perceived as anti-Muslim and its policies towards Israel and Iraq are largely seen as deliberate anti-Muslim stances. Moreover, the continuance of bombing during the Ramadan month in 2001 had deeply hurt the religious sentiments of the conservative elements. It is important to mention here that many of the jehadis who fought along with the Taliban in various military adventures inside Afghanistan belong to this region. It seems that in many constituencies the MMA candidates captured the PML (N) seat, which has an ideological affinity with the religious right. Whereas the PML(N) vote was split due to the PML (Q), the MMA vote got consolidated.[45] In addition, the military did not allow leaders like Nawaz Sharif and Benazir to come back to their constituencies and did everything to weaken their parties. This enabled the religious parties gain to strength. Initially the government also introduced a clause to Election Order 2002 barring people convicted for corruption to contest elections. Later it added another clause to place a bar on individuals who have been declared absconders as is the case with Benazir Bhutto. Absence of mainstream political leaders affected political mobilization. Introduction of graduation qualification kept out many veteran political leaders from the election fray. Moreover, a degree from the madrasa being equated with a formal university degree helped the religious leaders. The military introduced amendments to bar any person to be Prime Minister more than twice, irrespective of the fact whether they had completed their term in office or not.

For the first time major religious parties belonging to disparate ideological orientations have come together under a single platform. Interestingly, this conglomeration has both Shia and Sunni parties. The longevity of this alliance would depend on their coherent political programme and how effectively they overcome ideological orientation while charting various policy programmes. Though the alliance fought the election as a unified front, the internal divergences are too apparent to be concealed. In the past, the fierce fighting between the two major Shia and Sunni parties has led to bloody violence challenging the social fabric of Pakistan. To what extent the religious parties can overcome the differences would remain to be seen. Already differences have surfaced between Qazi Hussain of the JI and Noorani who wants to adopt a flexible approach to the PML (Q) with Fazlur Rehman opposing it. Rehman has expressed his displeasure over Qazi's nomination as the MMA Parliamentary party leader. Similarly JI was not happy with Fazlur's nomination as the Chief Minister of NWFP. But MMA has managed to overcome these contradictions quickly. Jamali government US-Pak relations—arms supply etc. How the army has used the US to consolidate power.

The rise of MMA is going to have far-reaching implications on the social fabric of the frontier region. Already NGOs are feeling threatened since many of them are funded by Western sources. The religious parties have expressed their intention to implement Sharia and have publicly articulated their views against co-educational institutions. Conservatism and radicalism are certainly going to get a boost with the electoral victory of the religious parties. Maulana Fazlur Rehman has condoned the disenfranchisement of women in the tribal areas.

Future of Pakistan

The current political development is going to have severe implications not only on the internal stability of Pakistan, but on its foreign policy as well. The already fractured polity is going to be fragmented along the lines of various policies that are going to be adopted by the government of Pakistan. After coming to power General Musharaf had initiated various reforms to deal with madrasa. The problem all along has been that most of the madrasa have resisted reforms. The amendments brought in by the military government in July 2002, have clearly envisaged that "no political party shall promote sectarian, ethnic, regional hatred or animosity, or be titled or constituted as a militant group or section".[46] It is really not evident how the government by making such pronouncements without effective implementation is going to deal with the ground reality. While the credibility of mainstream political parties has declined, the influence of religious parties has increased. Organisations like the Hizbul-Taheer are rising to prominence due to their orthodox views about Islam. Both Hizbul-Taheer and al-Mujaheerin have their linkages to British radical Islamic groups. Both these groups have challenged General Musharraf's rule and have openly called for his removal. These groups consisting of radical youth have been vocal in their articulation and are committed to the belief of Salafi Islam and its mission is to establish Khilafat in Pakistan. The administration has not been able to deal with these groups and has arrested many of its activists. According to the Interior Ministry, approximately 4,200 suspected activists were in jail and they were released after the Lahore High Court rejected the government plea that Hizbul-Taheer is anti State.[47] This group would seriously challenge the government in future. Though these organizations are in its infancy in Pakistan but its linkages to various radical international organisation in countries like Egypt, the UK, Uzbekistan, Tajikistan and Israel speaks volumes about its potential as organizations able to create problems for General Musharaf.

Though the government has promised to take action against the radical Islamic groups, its failure to deal with extremism is going to create more problems for the government. The organizations have changed their names and transferred their account to other names just before the ban was imposed. Their cadres have remained intact. In fact, it is possible that they are waiting for an opportune moment. Many of these jehadis see General Musharraf as a stooge of the United States, which is perceived as anti-Muslim in its policy orientation. They are disheartened to see the plight of the Taliban - their ideological compatriots and role model. With their pursuit to establish a truly Islamic state being shattered after the US bombing many jehadis' perception of the valour of the Taliban fighter is also being questioned. However, the Taliban cadres' sympathizers and supporters are still intact. Their capability to strike back is temporarily disabled but the motivation and determination to fight the so-called infidel still dominates their thinking. Some of these groups have been accused of killing Western civilians in various suicide strikes inside Pakistan. Along with this the message is sent to General Musharraf of the dangers of close collaboration with the US. Such strikes have adversely affected Pakistan's credibility to provide protection to various Western interests. In addition they have sent wrong signals to foreign investors regarding the investment climate in the country. In the long run, Pakistan's economic potential will be severely undermined with mindless violence.

Pakistan has become a hub of international terrorism with many of the al-Qaida elements taking refuge in various urban centers. Though the government has been denying the existence of any al-Qaida group in Pakistan, in October 2002, people like Bin al-Shib were extradited to the US amidst tight security. The existence of strong supporters and sympathisers of the Taliban regime explains why Pakistan has become a safe haven for the fleeing al-Qaida elements.

The General needs to deal with the extremist elements to stabilize the internal security of Pakistan. If the government does not introduce serious reforms to the madrasa system and at the same time improve the primary education system it is likely that the challenge to Pakistan's security would most likely emerge from within. Though the present regime attributes religious radicalism to General Zia's period there is no let up to their relevance to the military in Pakistan. The army does not perceive radical Islam of Jehadis as a substitute to professionalism and service discipline but a component of it.[48] Given the support including funding, weapons, transport, intelligence and immunity from persecution that was provided to these jehadi groups and leaders by the establishment with the direct connivance of elected political leaders to serve their strategic interest has led to a situation where Pakistan itself is threatened by the gun culture. According to a report, "While the military government's control over more radical religious parties is clearly not absolute, these groups would exist even farther on the margins of Pakistani society if it were not for the frequent sustenance they have received from the military government and security services".[49]

The international community, especially the US, want democracy to be restored in Pakistan, but have adopted a mild approach to political developments inside Pakistan terming them as 'internal problems'. The Afghan crisis provided the military government with much needed international legitimacy. This new-found international acceptability made it easy for the General to deal with his political detractors at home. The approach of the US has demoralized mainstream parties in their effort to restore the 1973 Constitution. "The prevailing but unexpressed view in Washington seemed to be that a military government was better able to deal with the difficult demands the US was placing on it than a political one would have been".[50] The army has created for itself an image of a secular army that is committed to liberal values. General Musharraf has been posing as the liberal administrator heading a country, which is threatened by the onslaught of growing fundamentalism. Many of the American policy makers have thus argued that General Musharraf is the best bet for the Americans; and if he is not supported there is a chance that the fundamentalists would control power in Pakistan.

The rise of MMA to power is going to pose problems for General Musharraf in dealing with fundamentalism. Of course the MMA was vocal in its criticism of the Pakistan-US relations but after the election it has been careful in airing its views regarding the US. The MMA couched its words with deliberate moderation and ambiguity. For example, in an interview given after the October election, Jamiat-e-Ulema-e-Pakistan chief Maulana Shah Ahmed Noorani said that the "MMA would not do anything that harms Pakistan's national interests but any policies that aimed at harming the very spirit of Pakistan and the Ummah will be resisted".[51] It remains to be seen how the MMA defines national interests that include both Pakistan's foreign policies vis-à-vis India and the US and imposing clamps on militant activities. An analysis of their past behaviour shows that they would not support the anti-fundamentalist policies in the interest of their party and they would not allow the government to wipe out their cadres.

The constituent parties of the MMA are Jamiat Ulema-I-Islam (Fazlur), Jamiat Ulema-I-Islam (Samiul), both followers of Deoband school having a strong base in the Pushtun areas of NWFP and Baluchistan, Jamiat Islami (Qazi Hussain) which has been strong supporter of jehad in both Afghanistan and Kashmir, Jamiat Ulema-I-Pakistan of Maulana Shah Ahmad Noorani, a follower of Barelvi school which have ideological differences with the Deoband group, Jamiat Ahle Hadith of Sajjad Mir that follows Hadees school, and Tehrik-I-Jafria Pakistan, a Shia party headed by Maulana Syed Sajid Naqvi which follows Jafaria fiqh and does not play any important role in jehad. Both JI and JUI have a strong support base in NWFP and Baluchistan, and JUP (Noorani) has a strong following in Punjab and Sindh. This alliance helped in giving the MMA electoral success in all the four provinces and helped the religious parties to keep their support base intact. Though the Shia party does not have a strong base in any part of the country but it served the purpose of presenting a united front to the people. Significantly the MMA election symbol is a book, which the MMA claimed was a vote for the Holy book and their commitment towards the Islamic system.

The divided mandate can also be attributed to the fact that in many segments the candidates of the major parties were contesting against each other. At the same time absence of clear-cut electoral understanding or seat adjustments between the parties cut into each other's votes. The PML (N) concluded as the fourth largest party in the election due to the fact that the party faced a split and in many of the National and Provincial Assembly constituencies were facing their rival PML (Q). Since political activities were banned in the country earlier and was lifted only three weeks before the election, these political parties could not reach to the people with their political agenda. With the State controlled electronics media have faster impact in the mind of the people the military regime did not leave any stone unturned to malign the politicians by accusing them of corruption and inefficiency. The politicians did not get enough opportunity to clarify their position. At the same time both Nawaz Sharif and Benazir could not return to Pakistan and neither could file their nomination papers or lead the election campaign due to the various electoral reforms introduced by military regime to keep both of them out of power. Thus the leadership vacuum helped the 'Kings party' who were given official patronage to campaign. In this context the comments of the European Union Election Observer remains valid.

Pakistan entered the era of coalition politics with no political parties having cleared two third majorities. Though this phenomenon is not new in Pakistani politics, but the bitter experiences in the past has seen how the establishment has manipulated such weak governments in consonance with the President powered by the notorious eighth amendment in the past. The military to help the King's party to form the government restored the Constitution on 15th of November. However 75 articles that include 63 (a) were suspended. The LFO delineates that the Constitution to be restored in phases. Article 63 (a) which pertains to members disqualification that stipulates that any member of a political party if he violates Constitution, code of conduct or declared policies of his party or he votes contrary to the direction of his parliamentary party in relation to any legislation that is to be adopted by the Parliament will be disqualified from the government by encouraging floor crossing in the National Assembly. Finally the military managed to divide the PPPP and some of its members voted for Mir Zafarullah Khan Jamali to win the vote of confidence by one cote and later with the help of Muttahida Quami Movement, Jamali won the trust vote on 30th December.

Internally, the newly emerged political dispensation would remian too weak to challenge the military establishment's decision. They would be proxies of the military regime with a democratic face to give legitimacy to General Musharraf's democracy. Pakistan's democracy would be sustainable as long as the military wants. Secondly, since most of the time the politicians would be concentrating on their political survival, their ability to govern would be substantially as long as the military wants. Secondly, since most of the time the politicians would be concentrating on their political survival, their ability to govern would be substantially reduced. This would give credence to the General Musharaf's floated theory that politicians are inefficient. Finally, with weak political parties, the religious parties would gain more political prominence. The future of madrasa reforms, introduction of new curriculum and all the seemingly sensible steps promised by General Musharaf in his January 12 speech are more likely to be in a limbo.

The army is going to be dominant in Pakistani politics for many years to come. This became more so after 9/11

Its assertion in politics to a large extent would depend on how the political parties are conducting themselves in the National Assembly. If the political parties are fragmented and remain organizationally weak it will be difficult for them to challenge the military from asserting political power. As is evident in the past the army's ability to fragment political parties and keep them divided is enormous.

Notes:

1. International Crisis Group, "Pakistan: The Dangers of Conventional Wisdom", p.2. see www.intl-crisis-group.org/projects/
2. Imran Khan in his letter to General Pervez Musharraf quoting from the Muslim Commercial Bank Annual report wrote that the 22.792 million rupee loan outstanding against Chaudhury Manzoor Elahi, Chaudhury Shujaat Hussain and Chaudhury Pervez Ilahi were written off during the calendar year ending 31 December, 2000. As cited in Mubashir Zaidi, "Winning Ways", *Herald*, October 2002.
3. Italics mine. See *Herald*, February 2000, p.24.
4. *Herald*, February 2000, p.24.
5. Amir Mir, "Unholy Resurrection?", *Newsline*, p.47.
6. As per some reports the crisis originated at the corps commanders conference on 19 September, 1998, where concerns were expressed about the situation in the country by a number of officers and General Karamat was urged to do something about it. *The Khaleej Times*, 24 August, 1998.
7. Amir Mir, "Unholy Resurrection?", *Newsline*, February 2000, p.47.
8. *The Nation*, 2 April, 2002.

9. Christina Lamb, *Waiting for Allah*, London: Hamish Hamilton, 1991, p.41.
10. Text of General Musharraf's speech, *Dawn*, 18 October, 1999.
11. Ayub Khan, *Friends not Masters*, London: Oxford University Press, 1967, p.58.
12. See the interview by Syed Ali Dayan Hasan with General Tanvir Naqvi, "We only had three years of democracy – from 1985-88", *The Herald*, July 2002, p.29.
13. Stephen Cohen, *The Pakistan Army*, Karachi: Oxford University Press, 1998, p.105.
14. Omar Norman, *Pakistan: Political and Economic History Since 1947*, London: KeganPaul, 1990, p.68.
15. Such a view was expressed by Nasim Wali Khan of the National Awami Party and Air Marshal Asghar Khan who was heading Tehrik-I-Istiqal. After General Zia took over, the Central Committee of the PNA favoured postponement of election by General Zia. PPP of Bhutto was divided on this issue but did not reject it.
16. K.M. Arif, *Working with Zia,* Karachi: Oxford University Press, 1995, p.81 and p.113.
17. Refer to Karamat's interview in *The Herald*, March 2001, p.77 and p. 83.
18. See the statements given by various politicians after General Zia took over in 1977. K.M. Arif, *Working with Zia: Pakistan's Power Politics, 1977-88*, Karachi: Oxford University Press, 1985, pp.135-147.
19. Lt General Assad Durrani had revealed through an affidavit that money was passed by former Army Chief General Mirza Aslam Beg to the tune of Rs 60 million to ensure the defeat of the Benazir Bhutto government. General Hamid Gul also openly brags about his role in creating the Islamic Jamhoori Ittehad. See Zafar Abbas, "True Confessions?" *The Herald*, July 1996, p.15.
20. Ahmed Rashid, "Pakistan's Coup: Planting the Seeds of Democracy", *Current History*, December 1999, p.410.

21. Interestingly, Pakistan Peoples' Party, Pakistan Muslim League (PML-Nawaz), the Jamaat-I-Islami, the Jamiat Ulema-I-Pakistan, the Jamiat Ulema Islam (Fazlur), the JUI (Sami-ul), the Jamhoori Watan Party, the Awami National Party were opposed to the referendum. The PML (QA) led by Mian Muhammad Azhar, the Millat Party, the Pakistani Awami Tehrik, the Tehrik-I-Insaf, the Mottahida Quami Movement, the PML (Functional), the National Awami Party Pakistan (NAPP), the Grand Democratic Alliance headed by Hamid Nasir Chatha, the Quami Jamhoori Party of Ashghar Khan were supportive of the referendum which they defined as "in the interest of democracy". For the speech see www.pak.gov.pk/public/Address-5 April.htm.

22. *Dawn*, "TNSM Shoora to decide sending Jehadis to Afghanistan", 16 October, 2001. Rahimullah Yusufzai, "Recruitment has begun in Tribal Areas", *The News International*, 16 October, 2001.

23. The Musharraf government sought the repatriation of pro-Taliban Pakistani fighters in Afghanistan but the US brushed aside the demand and wanted to cross question them to find out about the al-Qaida. *Washington Post*, Ed., "Pakistan's Choice", 27 November, 2001.

24. www.dawn.com/ayaz.htm

25. For Gen Musharraf's 12 January speech see www.pak.gov.pk/public/President_address.htm

26. Zahid Hussain, "Holding the Country Hostage", *Newsline*, February 2002, newsline.com.pk

27. *The Washington Post*, 30 January, 2002.

28. As cited in Masood Ansari, "The Crackdown Begins", *Newsline*, February 2002, newsline.com.pk

29. ICG Asia report, pp.30-31.

30. Khalid Ahmed, "Fundamental Flaws" in *On The Abyss: Pakistan After the Coup*, n.21, ibid, p.97.

31. Tariq Ali, "In the Doghouse", *On the Abyss: Pakistan After the Coup*, n.11, p.30.

32. See ICG Asia report no 36, 29 July 2002, "Pakistan: Madrasa, Extremism and the Military', p.23.

33. Amir Mir "Sects and Violence", *Newsline*, October 1999, p.70.

34. Massaoud Ansari, "The Crackdown Begins", *Newsline*, January 2002.

35. ICG report on Pakistan: *Madrasa, Extremism and the Military*, 29 July 2002, p.3.

36. The weapons included 02 missiles, 03AA guns, 446 hand grenades, 120 dynamics, 43 rocket launchers, 123 repeaters, 100 pashposas, 89 mines, 7 bren guns, 124 LMG, 1 ganger machine, 111 daggers/knives, 03 mines, 229 RPG shells, 369 mortar shells, 565 AA Ammo, 11 shotgun shells, 05 anti-personnel mines, 18 anti-tank mines, 99 explosive fuses, 22 rockets, fuses 107 mm, 384 anti-aircraft gun rounds, 407 rocket launcher shells and 18 mines shells. See Mohmmad Asghar, "People to Get Back Licensed Weapons", *The Dawn,* 16 March, 2002.

37. Ayesha Siddiqa Agha, "The Demand and Supply Dynamics of Small Arms and Light Weapons in Pakistan", unpublished paper, (Islamabad), p.25.

38. Aamer Ahmad Khan, *The End of Jehad,* December 2001, p.21.

39. These are Sipah-e-Sahaba, Harkat-ul-Ansar, Dawat-ul-Arshad, Alkhalid Force,Lashkar Jangvi, Lashkar-e-Toyaba, Sipah-e-Ali, Tehrik-I-Nifaz-e-Fiqah-I-Jafriya, Sipah-e-Mohmmad, Sipah-e-Abbas, Almukhtar Force, Imamia Student organization, Salafi Students Organisation, Sunni Tehrik, Khaddam-e-Ahmadia Students Union, Ahl Hadith Youth Force, Mustafavi Students Federation, Hizb-ul-Mujaheedin, Jaish-e-Mohmmad, Jammat-I-Islami, as cited in Ayesha Siddiqu Agha, "The Demand and Supply Dynamics of Small Arms and Light Weapons in Pakistan", unpublished paper, (Islamabad), p.9.

40. Ayesha Siddiqua, ibid, p.15.

41. Ayesha, p.18.

42. Nadeem Malik, "The Maths of Mayhem", *Newsline,* June 2002. See www.newsline.com.pk
43. Nadeem Malik, "The Maths of Mayhem", *Newsline,* June 2002. See www.newsline.com.pk
44. See the State Bank of Pakistan Annual Report, July 2000-June 2001, www.sbp.gov.pk
45. Ijaz Haider, "Why and Whither MMA", *Friday Times,* 18-24 October, 2002, Vol.XIV, no.34.
46. See the *Legal Framework Order, The Gazette of Pakistan Extraordinary,* 21 August 2002, Part-I, pp.1033-34.
47. Khaleed Ahmad, "The Rise of Hizb al-Taheer", *Friday Times,* 18-24 October, 2002, vol XIV, no.34, thefridaytimes.com
48. Hasan Askari Rizvi, *Military State and Society in Pakistan,* St Martin Press, 2000, p.245.
49. ICG Report *Pakistan: The Dangers of Conventional Wisdom,* p.3, ICG Asia Briefing paper, 12 March, 2002.
50. Ambassador Teresita C. Schaffer and Mandavi Mehta, *Political Institutions and the Army,* A Report from the CSIS Project Pakistan's Future and US Policy Options, 17 April, 2002.
51. "We Will Move Carefully on the Issue of US Presence...", interview with Maulana Shah Ahmed Noorani, Chief of Jamiat-e-Ulema-e-Pakistan, in *Friday Times,* 18-24 October, 2002, vol.XIV, no.34.

3

Quick Fix Foreign Policy

Pinaki Bhattacharya

Prologue

Foreign policy is a medium by which a state - and by extension a nation—seeks to express itself in the world arena. By choosing various instrumentalities of policy, modern countries seek to maximise national interests; gain influence in international fora; and try to minimise physical conflict in pursuit of political gains.[1] Pakistan is also not different from this praxis. Keeping this in mind a historical reconnoitring of Pakistan's role in international politics is thus needed to contextualise what can be said about its emerging worldview post-9/11.

The country had a rather ambivalent birth, tinged with the blood of millions who were killed during "exchange of population" between India and Pakistan. Based as its nationhood on principles of religious nationalism, Pakistan began this search for attaining such foreign policy goals early in the 1950s, just a few years after it gained independence on 14th August, 1947. Eager to establish its Islamic credentials, Pakistan sought to orient its foreign policy to fit with the priorities of other Islamic nations as they began emerging in the wake of World War II. Early on, in February 1952, when a meeting of Muslim clerics from the world over was held in Karachi, Khwaja Nazimuddin, the then Prime Minister of Pakistan, had declared: "(Pakistan's) existence has brought the unification of the Muslim world and the cohesion of the *Millat* (Faith) within the pale of possibility."[2]

In fact, earlier, on August 18, 1951, the country's first Foreign Minister, Sir Muhammad Zafarullah Khan, considered brilliant by any standards, had made an inexplicable statement. He had stated: "It (Pakistan) has served brilliantly in the cause of the independence of Indonesia, Libya, Eritrea and Somalila."[3] Yet, history shows Pakistan has sought to align itself with the British, other colonialist Western nations and the USA. Of course, on all such occasions it has been under the rubric of "anti-Communism" that Pakistan had joined the South East Asia Treaty Organisation (SEATO) in 1954, and the Central Treaty Organisation (CENTO) in 1959. Thus, even as early as late fifties, the USA had emerged as the first major pivot of Pakistan's foreign policy.

Pakistan's neighbour India, on the other hand, had moved quickly on the world stage professing the cause of the newly liberated, former colonised nations and even seeking to maintain distance from the two contending Cold War blocks. India's first Prime Minister, Jawaharlal Nehru, even inked an agreement to create a block of its own, the Non-aligned block, at Bandung, Indonesia, in April 1955. Even though Sir Zafarullah Khan had earlier claimed to have helped Indonesia in gaining its independence, Pakistan broke ranks with the country-having a majority Muslim population-as Karachi abrogated its non-aligned status in 1954 by accepting the US military aid.

A crucial reason for this flip-flop was the policy manifestation of Pakistan's questionable birth. The leaders of Pakistan like Mohammad Ali Jinnah had propagated the theory in 1940s that undivided India was really two nations with two peoples, thus a ripe case for a division. That argument had won the day with the British who were then on a spree of redrawing national boundaries. But even at the hour of its birth, Jinnah and his followers had felt cheated because Kashmir was not accorded to them, following their logic.

So the first act of the new government at Karachi was to launch an attack against India in 1947-48 to get Kashmir. The Indian attempt to expose Pakistan's aggression by taking the case of Kashmir to the newly formed United Nations proved a bonanza for Pakistan. Skilled oretong accompanied by misrepresentation of facts by Pakistani representative at the UN gave a boost to their objective of seeking international intervention to legitimise their claim over Kashmir. And that remained the defining moment of Pakistan's diplomatic history, an event that continues to wield enormous, if not almost total, influence on Pakistan's foreign policy till present. Unlike a self-confident nation, Pakistan needed the active support of the major powers like the British and then one of the two superpowers, the USA, to keep the Kashmir pot boiling. This, in turn, had reflected on its postulations in the international fora.

On the other hand, Pakistan's forays to carve out another plank of its diplomacy on the basis of its effervescent Islamic identity, too, faced serious hurdles. The Islamic world, dominated by Iran and Egypt in the 1950s and 1960s, sought to look down upon the sub-continental Muslims as at best pretenders, and at worst usurpers of the Islamic holy grail. Still, the closest friend of Pakistan in the Arab block those days was Iran, which historically was the main source of Arab Islamic civilisational influences in the sub-continent.[4]

The Shah of Iran, Reza Pahlavi, had even offered to broker for peace between Afghanistan and Pakistan when the two had threatened to begin a shooting war in late-1950s and early-1960s on the issue of Pakhtunistan.[5] We shall revisit this detail of Pakistan's history later, at an appropriate place. But meanwhile, the two protagonists could not agree on accepting the Shah's offer. Yet, that did not stop Gen Ayub Khan, the then military ruler, to consider aloud that Pakistan, Iran and Afghanistan could fuse into a greater political entity.[6] That proposal, unsurprisingly, found no takers. And Pakistan's intention of emerging as a leader of the Islamic world remained unrequited.

Foreign Policymakers' Domestic High Jinks

Be that as it may, before one continues ahead to discuss these foreign policy developments, it is important to take stock of the framers of these policies at the helm of political power in Pakistan. Thus, notwithstanding these machinations at expanding Pakistan's influence on the world stage, it is noteworthy to observe that the power-elite who handled the levers of the state were going through a series of convulsions. The reasons for these were many. Not in the least was the fact that the country's identity was under severe strain. The leaders who led the movement for the formation of Pakistan in British India were the English-educated privileged class who were on the other side of the gulf that separated them from the Muslim mass that formed the body of the nation. In fact, readers would do well to recall that Jaamat-e-Islami, a hardline Muslim communal organisation, had opposed the partition of India on the ground that it would fragment the Muslim community of the sub-continent and thus weaken them. But for Muhammad Ali Jinnah and his followers, the idea of sharing political power with the Congress was an anathema.

So Pakistan was born like a Siamese twin, attached at the bodypolitik but with two heads. The west of the country was 2,500 miles away from its eastern part separated by the Indian landmass and two seas, the Arabian Sea and the Bay of Bengal. That this was a recipe for disaster was evident when the Constituent Assembly of Pakistan, also acting as its federal assembly, mandated to write a Constitution for the new country, was dissolved in 1954 after producing just the Objective Principles of the proposed document. A new Constituent Assembly formed at the behest of Pakistan Federal Court produced a Constitution in 1956 that was abrogated two years later in 1958. In this little over a decade since independence, till the time the formality of a civilian prime minister was discontinued in 1958, the country had seen seven premiers.

So in October 1958, Pakistan had for the first time slipped into the control of the army, as general and later

Field Marshal, Ayub Khan took over the reins of power, and Martial Law was imposed. But earlier, in 1954 itself, the rulers of the western part of the country had merged all the separate provinces of the west into one composite province called West Pakistan to bring it at par with the numerical majority of East Pakistan. Ayub Khan added to this miasma of political confusion by inducting his own ideas of nation-building laced with his concepts about how a democratic polity should function. The military rulers, principles were quaintly named 'Basic Democracy.'

This was a pyramidal structured power that devolved on various governmental bodies composed of a curious amalgam of democratically elected peoples' representatives and nominated members of the bureaucracy. At the apex of this pyramid were the two provincial development advisory councils headed by governors, which functioned as the government. The governors were under federal ministries and were appointed by the President, which in this case was Ayub Khan himself from 1960 till 1969. Thus Pakistan's first tryst with democratic general elections was in 1959 under the 'Basic Democracy' system, 12 years after it gained its independence. Till then the country was ruled by a group of bureaucrats and politicians who had exhausted their popular mandate, having been elected before 1947.

Political parties, meanwhile, had fared worse than the legislative and government institutions. The two main contenders of power, the Muslim League of Pakistan's founding father, Jinnah, and its first prime minister, Liaquat Ali Khan, and Awami Muslim League of Dr HS Suhrawardy, were at each other throats soon after independence. Liaquat Ali proffered the argument that partisan political fights could be a bane for a new nation like Pakistan faced with so many hurdles on its path. The sub-text of that statement was a demand of political monopoly for the Muslim League. Naturally, the Awami League, more popular in East Pakistan, could not countenance that especially since they did not even consider the Muslim League homegrown.

Till 1954 when the first Constituent Assembly was dissolved, the Awami Muslim League parties could do little to stake a claim on the federal level cake. Only that year, after the first dissolution, a coalition central ministry was formed where the non-Muslim League parties were accommodated. But the governmental prowess of all the political parties was evident in the provinces where they were in power till 1954. That was a story of factional feuds, incompetence and even wanton political violence.[7] So when Field-Marshal Ayub Khan proscribed political parties in 1958, little tear was shed in their memory.

Two critical events had shaped Pakistan's worldview in the decade it was ruled by Ayub. In 1962, China went to war against India following border disputes. As is now known the Indian armed forces were found so abysmally unprepared that the Chinese could make deep inroads into Indian territory. After these initial advances in November that year, the Chinese unilaterally declared that they would withdraw from their advanced positions. This they did in the east but not in the west, the area abutting Pakistan-controlled Kashmir.

In reality, this area of the state of Jammu and Kashmir held the key that unlocked for Pakistan the hearts of the Beijing leadership. And that led to a Sino-Pak relationship that has acted as the second major pivot on which Pakistan's foreign policy is based. Pakistan, as it was planned in 1947, by the British did not share a boundary with China. But after it fought the war with India over Kashmir in 1947-48, it retained control of some parts of the state, which shared a border with China. Now at the height of the war of words between India and China in the late-1950s over the border disputes, Pakistan's then Foreign Minister, Mr Zulfiqar Ali Bhutto, saw a window of opportunity.

He returned to Pakistan from a visit to the United Nations in 1959, convinced because of his interactions with the Burmese, that his country could do business with Beijing[8]. The issue he chose for an intense engagement with China was the settlement of the Pakistan controlled Kashmir's border. But the Chinese did not bite the bait initially. They had reasons for not doing that. The status of Kashmir, Beijing knew, was a sore point with India: a Chinese acceptance for negotiations with Pakistan about its borders shared with the part of the contentious territory would be tantamount to tacit acceptance of Pakistan's suzerainty over the disputed land.

But this Chinese reticence vanished in 1961 when the negotiations began. They were concluded by the end of the year and an announcement was made on 26th December, 1962, that an agreement on principles had been reached. This, incidentally, was also the day when an Indian delegation was in Rawalpindi to begin negotiations with Pakistan on Kashmir. Formidable Bhutto apparently had urged the Chinese to make the announcement on that day so, as he thought, the USA could pressurise India to follow on the footsteps of the

Chinese and strike a solution to the Kashmir problem.[9] The matrix for future being laid out, some would say!

The boundary that was agreed upon between Pakistan and China gave the former a trans-Karakoram boundary in one sector, while for the Chinese it involved gaining territory adjoining the Xinjiang province. In some people's opinion, what Pakistan ceded were map claims.[10]

For the sake of the record it must be mentioned that the Chinese were less well-disposed towards Pakistan than they were towards India. They had felt that Pakistan, at the instance of the USA, had voted in the UN against discussions on China's representation at the body. They had even noted Pakistan's unofficial contacts with the Chiang Kai-shek regime of Formosa, now Taiwan. And on top of that China knew that Pakistan was a member of such avowedly anti-communist blocks like the SEATO and CENTO.[11]

Besides these memberships and Pakistan's flowering relationship with China, Ayub and his armed forces had been emboldened by the induction of American arms which had begun in 1954 under the USA's military assistance programme. The Ayub regime had already been conducting a low intensity conflict in Kashmir for more than a year when on September 1, 1965, the country launched "Operation Gibraltar," a full scale war against India. Under Prime Minister, Lal Bahadur Shastri, India's riposte was a quick expansion of the war-front to include areas in the west like the Punjab province of Pakistan and the desert terrain of Sind.

This time, as is known the then USSR got into the act, and effected a truce between the countries, and invited Shastri and Ayub to meet at Tashkent for talking peace. The Tashkent talks remained inconclusive as Shastri tragically died while being there, but the troops of both countries returned to the pre-war lines which was named the ceasefire line. Russia, really, had been involved in the Kashmir issue since earlier. Even in 1962 when the UN Security Council wanted to vote–at the urging of the USA and Britain-on a motion directing India and Pakistan to begin dialogue on the Kashmir issue, the Russians had vetoed it. They had thus earned the opprobrium of Pakistan for that act.

But for Ayub, who was convinced that Pakistan's armed forces "could lick them (Indians) in the field" and "win back Kashmir"[12] the result of the 1965 war was a hard lesson. He had to witness the USA's withdrawal of support at the crucial time when they suspended arms supplies to Pakistan during the war and which continued till 1968. Thus, by 1969, he was at the end of his tether and laid down office of the President but not in favour of a democratically elected people's representative. Instead he transferred power to another army general, Agha Mohammad Yahya Khan.

The new general, presiding over Pakistan, had one dubious distinction. He held Pakistan's first free and fair general election in 1970, under the 1962 Constitution. And that led to the dismemberment of the country. Even if one need not go into the details of this poll and the events that led to the Bangladesh's (East Pakistan) liberation war, the happenings during the battles, one needs to keep in mind the international environment of the time. And therein lay two very important developments, which favoured Pakistan immensely and had long lasting impact on its foreign policy, the effects of which can be felt even now.

The first of that is now a part of the international diplomatic folk lore. This is about how the then US National Security Adviser, Mr Henry Kissinger, had a "stomach upset" on a visit to Islamabad, and ended up in Beijing shaking hands with Chinese premier, Zhou En-lai. In realpolitik terms, this was a classic case of *quid pro quo* between nations that transcended the boundaries of political morality, a rare commodity as it is.

What Romania couldn't do in right earnest, Pakistan did with panache. It traded in its friendship with China for an opening to Washington, the residents of which were eager to create another layer in their containment circle around the then Soviet Union. China's relationship with the USSR, a fraternal communist country, had by then reached the nadir. The result of this transaction was the continuous flow of American arms to Pakistan even when it was using them against Indian armed forces in the 1971 war. Also critically evident was the presence of the *USS Enterprise,* the aircraft carrier-led task force, in the Indian Ocean waters. But then India too had struck a 20-year treaty of friendship and cooperation with the then USSR.

The other important development was less noticed by the world but had equally important effect on the sub-continental politics. Pakistan's former prime minister, Khwaja Nazimuddin Zhou En-lai had once said: "Islam is a body, and the Muslim states represent the limbs of this body. Pain inflicted on any one part of the body gives pain and anguish to the whole body."[13] Almost on cue, the 1962 Constitution of Pakistan had elements clearly Islamic and it was to no one's surprise that Jordanian King Hussain visited the country in January-February 1968, when the words about mutual friendship and peace were expressed. But more importantly, during the Indo-Pak war of 1971, Jordan worked as the channel for supply of US warplanes to Pakistan.[14] This Arab acceptance of Pakistan's Islamic credentials would go a long way into establishing a more profitable relationship with the kingdom of Saudi Arabia and the like, at a later date.

The Islamic Bomb

The turbulent beginning of the '70s decade for Pakistan saw the rise of ZA Bhutto to the apex of the political hierarchy of the nation. Mr Bhutto, who had gained his political legitimacy from the 1970 polls in Pakistan, saw in the nuclear bomb, a way of emancipating a nation, licking its wounds after a comprehensive military defeat in 1971. So he declared: "We know that Israel and South Africa have full nuclear capability. The Christian, Jewish and Hindu civilizations have this capability. The Communist powers also possess it. Only the Islamic civilisation was without it, but that position was about to change."[15] This statement had followed the disastrous developments for Pakistan's nationhood: the embarrassing Shimla agreement in 1972 with India, and the 1974 nuclear test by India. Worse, the formation of a Muslim Bangladesh, on the basis of ethnic and linguistic identity, had knocked the stuffing out of the "two-nation" theory, which stood on the argument that Muslims of the subcontinent were one nation by themselves. The argument of religious homogeneity leading to political unity had taken a severe beating.

So the concept of an "Islamic Bomb" was Pakistan's way of escaping the subcontinental rut and integrating instead with the broader West Asian Islamic nations in search of nutrients for its roots, thus, in turn, discovering a *sine qua non* for existence. The decision to build a nuclear bomb by Pakistan was taken formally at a meeting in Multan, in January, 1972, presided over by Bhutto. One of his associates, Khalid Hassan, has testified that soon after the Multan decision, Bhutto traveled extensively in several Arab countries to mobilise needed resources for his ambitious plan and found an enthusiastic partner in Libya.[16]

The Libyan connection paved the way for more mainstream Arab support to the Pakistan programme. Libya, a north African offshoot, was viewed suspiciously by the Arab leaders like the Saudi Arabian royal family[17], for Libyan leader, Mr Muammar Qadaffi's pan-Arab ambitions. But by then, Bhutto had been handed over to the hands of the hangman by one of his chosen cohorts, the army chief, Gen. Zia-ul Haq. Still, Saudi Arabia's role as the country which funded Pakistan's nuclear programme cannot be ignored,[18] making it the third pivot of Pakistan's foreign policy.

Yet, the most important connection in this emerging whodunnit of nuclearisation of South Asia was China. The tel-tale signs of China's support to Pakistan had materialized in the words of one of the people who helped strike the Chinese deal. Bhutto, writing in 1978 from his solitary confinement in a death cell in Pakistan, where he was incarcerated by the latest military ruler of the country, Gen Zia-ul Haq, wrote in his final testament: "If out of the whole mosaic of the past, I had to select one piece from my most crucial and momentous achievements, I would not refer to my contributions in the 1965 (Indo-Pak) war, nor the creative bilateral foreign policy I embarked upon for the glory of my nation........ In the light of the recent developments which have taken place my single most important achievement, which I believe will dominate the portrait of my public life is an agreement which I arrived at after an assiduous endeavour spanning over eleven years of negotiations. In the present context, the agreement, concluded in June 1976, will perhaps be my greatest achievement and contribution to the survival of our people and our nation."[19]

A closer examination of this dying declaration reveals certain clues. In 1976, the month of May to be precise, prime minister Bhutto had led a high level military-scientific delegation to Beijing. Two overt agreements were signed; no secret protocol has come to light till date. But it was considered significant then that Bhutto could meet the dying chairman of the Chinese Communist Party, Mao Zhe Dong. Bhutto was, in fact, the last foreign dignitary to meet Mao before he died four months later.[20] Now, dying men don't tell lies, so the saying goes. And Bhutto could not have been referring to any other agreement he signed in 1976 which could have been so "momentous" for the survival of Pakistan's people.

For China, the politics then prevailing in the subcontinent must have been disconcerting. This was because of the ascendance of India in the developments that were taking place since the birth of Bangladesh. India had exploded its first nuclear device in1974, clearly a reply to China's nuclear status attained in 1964. And Green Revolution in the country was providing signs of attaining a level of food security, which was making India independent of handouts from external sources. So, if China viewed that India needed to be contained, one could not have found much fault with Beijing's logic. A nuclear Pakistan was thus the Chinese gambit in South Asia.

But before he was hanged to death in 1979, and still was the prime minister of Pakistan, Bhutto had made major strides in establishing Pakistan's credentials in the Arab Muslim world. Though he was hamstrung with a defeated army, he still risked becoming the sword arm of the Organisation of Islamic Countries.[21] This was also the time of the first "Oil shock." The Organisation of Petroleum Exporting Countries (OPEC), mostly having West Asian members, had become a source of unfathomable wealth. The cash-rich kingdoms like that of Saudi Arabia were eager to buy security. They found in Pakistan a well trained, professional Islamic army ready to provide security at a price. And the political synergy was established.

Cold Warriors

Bhutto's successor, Gen Zia-ul Haq, was quick to grasp this reality. Still more importantly, within three years of his ascendance to power, Zia was provided an opportunity to play a far more important role, a role that changed Pakistan's political idiom and had a lasting impact on its contemporary society. It began with the Cold War directly knocking at the doors of South Asia for the first time. In December 1979, the then USSR unleashed its military might on Afghanistan. Zia, like an eager child, found in this confounding mess an opportunity to redeem his nation, himself and Pakistan's armed forces. He offered the services of his country as the frontline for Afghan resistance, mounted by the Western powers led by the USA, bankrolled by the West Asian countries like Saudi Arabia, and peopled by the Afghan tribesmen.

In the next eight years, billions of dollars worth war matériel was pumped into Pakistan *en route* to Afghanistan. The Afghan *mujahids* had in Pakistan army and its intelligence service, the Inter-Services Intelligence (ISI) their fairy godfathers. And the provinces of North West Frontier Province (NWFP) and Baluchistan became their playgrounds. Zia projected this military endeavour to his countrymen as an effort at rescuing Islam from the hands of the Communist non-believers. The fervour thus created was reflected in the mushrooming of schools specialising in Islamic studies or *Madrasas*. The Islamisation of Pakistan polity, sporadically attempted by both political leaders and military rulers, was completed during Zia's regime.

Foreign aid flow increased to such levels that Pakistan became a country of spenders. The short-term attitude of the political leadership and the people alike was reflected in one of the lowest savings rate among developing countries.[22] In this country of more than135 million people, 800,000 large farmers held 26 per cent of the total cultivable land. One per cent of the total national budget is normally accorded to development of education; even less for other social sector areas.

This was also the time when Zia took the crucial decision of launching another offensive against India. This time he decided prudently not to launch conventional, full scale war against the neighbour. Instead, he decided to bleed the country through low intensity conflicts fought by trained irregulars. He chose to foment internal political tension in Indian provinces like Punjab and Jammu & Kashmir. It was easy for him to do this as he could financially support this effort through the Afghan war chest. He ringed the Indo-Pak international border in Punjab and the LoC in Kashmir with training camps for cash and carry 'freedom fighters' seeking to free Indian states of Punjab and Jammu & Kashmir.

But to the eternal regret of Zia, the Afghan war eventually wound down. The USSR disintegrated the Cold War ended with Communism ceasing to be the number one enemy of the West. Yet, Pakistan was saddled with the vast terror infrastructure that was built in that turbulent decade of '80s. The country's strategists decided to turn the resultant threats, emerging out of lesser interest of traditional allies like the post-Cold War USA, into an opportunity. In the subcontinental context, they decided to prop up a government in Afghanistan, that was not just friendly to them, but was indeed their creation. Afghanistan's importance, in the minds of Pakistan's strategic planners, lay in its ability to provide 'strategic depth' in case of a military threat to mainland Pakistan. The Taliban was born.

On the other hand, the Islamic band of marauders symbolised by the Taliban forces or other Islamist *mujaheedins* gave Pakistan its much coveted status of primacy among the Islamic nations. These mujahideens also needed to be gainfully employed fighting 'holy wars' *(jihad)* around the globe, wherever the cry arose that

'Islam was in danger.' This was to be the new currency for power of a post-Cold War Pakistan. These strategists even convinced the West Asian allies that they too would gain from the stratagem. So we see that though - after the death of Gen Zia in an aircrash in 1988 - domestic political convulsions have wracked Pakistan, the army-ISI establishment has continued to flourish irrespective. Whether it was Ms Benazir Bhutto or Mian Nawaz Sharif who had nominally been in the saddle of power as prime ministers, they had rarely been able to do much to change this dispensation, even if they wanted to.

Rudderless In the Brave New World

But the world around Pakistan had been changing. India had launched major economic reform programme in the country, as initial steps towards globally integrating its economy. The huge consumer market in India, now accessible to the world, was a major attraction to the capitalist West. Also, at the end of the Cold War, in an environment extolling the virtues of a new world order based on the liberal democratic principles, India with its 50-year old democracy was proving to be an example of a political success in an underdeveloped country. Its economic potential was considered enormous, what with the country enjoying the third largest gross domestic product (GDP) in terms of purchasing power parity.

In this world where trade, commerce and economic development were becoming a byword for diplomatic exchanges, and market access was becoming more important than political powerplay, Pakistan was fast becoming an anachronism. In contrast to India's burgeoning balance of trade, Pakistan's economy was being seen to be fuelled by the ill-gotten wealth of the *jihadis* –in other words, the world was waking up to the fact that a major part of Pakistan's unofficial GDP was actually raked in from trade in narcotics. And the only notable export of the country was the *jihadi mujaheedins.*

This was happening at a time when Western scholars were speculating that the next frontier of the post-Cold War battleground will be at the faultlines of civilisations. The possibility of a final confrontation between Islam and other religionists was being spoken about. In this environment, it had become fashionable to refer to Pakistan as a failed or a failing state. Even Pakistan's main foreign policy pivot, the USA, was being urged to overlook any thoughts of ensuring the country's security. To quote one scholar who wrote, "First, I believe that the United States should be highly reluctant to provide military sales to Pakistan under current circumstances. The greatest threat to Pakistani security today is internal, not external. It stems from the corruption and thorough-going cynicism of Pakistan's ruling elite and its unwillingness to reform the basic institutions and policies governing the political economy."[23]

In the midst of this, India under the hardline BJP government exploded six nuclear devices in 1998 and declared itself a nuclear weapon state. While there was an eruption of global consternation and condemnation of the Indian act, Pakistan too followed suit with its own series of explosions. The USA, other western nations and Japan slapped trade and economic sanctions against both countries. But what the USA did next with India was symptomatic of the future. It invited the country to engage in a series of intensive strategic dialogues. This was a signal to the world that India's nuclear tests were being viewed at least in some sections as a claim of assertion of an emerging great power. Pakistan's nuclear weapons, on the other hand, gave rise to speculation of destabilisation of the world order as they could fall in the hands of a runaway, roguish military ruler or worse, could end up in the hands of terrorists.

What followed next seemed to substantiate this picture of doom? Pakistan, in the concluding year of the millennium, launched an offensive of nuclear brinkmanship across the Line of Control in Kashmir. Even as Pakistan's forces were being pulverized by Indian artillery barrage, the then Prime Minister, Nawaz Sharif, was summoned to the White House by then US President, Bill Clinton, and told to vacate the incursion and not to try and change the character of the LoC by force, in future. This was a rather stark counterpoint of history turning a full circle from the 1970s when the Nixon administration's National Security Adviser, Henry Kissinger, had claimed in an internal memo 'that the President wanted the US policy to tilt towards Pakistan.'

Nawaz Sharif, on his part, even made it seem that he was not aware what his armed forces had been planning. This gave an impression that Pakistan's security establishment was like a hydra-headed monster, sponsoring a well-organised foreign army of Taliban fighters on the one hand, and leading a motley gang of murderous Islamic fanatics on the other, much beyond the reasonable control of any civilian institution. Even more a cause for consternation was that these were the people who had control of fully operational nuclear bombs.

For the sake of Pakistan, worse news was the reaction of its closest allies like the Saudi Arabia, or the attitude of the former allies and current Arabian stalwart nations like Iran and Egypt. They seemed to believe the worst case scenario about Pakistan. While Saudi Arabia felt that the terror attacks on its territory were the handiwork of the Afghanistan-based Pakistan sponsored militants and were thus weary of indulging Pakistan too much, Egypt, under the rampage of Islamic Jihad movement too felt the same. For Iran, Pakistan's complete support of the Taliban regime in Afghanistan bode ill because of the latter's visceral enmity towards the Shia sect of Islam. Iran was also angry at the wanton killing of Shia minorities in northern Afghanistan, after Mazar-e-Sharif fell to the Taliban forces, reportedly bolstered by even regular Pakistan armed forces personnel.[24] The diplomatic isolation of Islamabad seemed complete when even these Islamic countries rejected pleas from Pakistan to condemn India and support the Kargil adventure.

Saudi Arabia, earlier mentioned as the third key pivot of Pakistan's foreign policy, has been the most important member of the Organisation of Islamic Countries, the umbrella body of 54 Muslim nations. They have brought the chestnuts out of the fire for many of Pakistan's leaders at their moments of reckoning. The latest was when Nawaz Sharif-who could not be prosecuted in Pakistan for his crimes in defrauding the nation on account of mounting international pressure–was provided sanctuary in Saudi Arabia, saving face for the Gen Parvez Musharaf regime after it ousted Sharif from power in the wake of the Kargil adventure.

Even Saudi Arabia, made it clear to Gen Musharaf that with dwindling petroleum prices it would not be able to fund Pakistan's economic profligacy anymore. They had indicated they would be cutting back their subsidy to the religious educational institutions, which proliferated in Pakistan in the wake of the Soviet-Afghan war. This was the message they delivered to Musharaf when he visited them barely ten days after he had taken over power on October 12, 1999.

China, which the General visited in January 2000, for the first time as the Chief Executive of Pakistan, was warmer in its reception. For Pakistan the strategic relationship with Beijing was one of the most prized, next only to its relationship with the USA. Thus it had been reassuring to Pakistan that Chinese did not lecture Musharaf on the necessity of democratic governance or even fiscal prudence. In fact, they promised to reschedule loan repayments and were generally strong in their statements about traditional closeness of the Sino-Pak relations, much to the relief of the Pakistani delegates.[25] Whether the Chinese leadership talked to Pakistan leadership about its fledgling relationship with the Taliban or even its concerns about the support of Islamic *jihad* Diaspora to the Uighur Muslims in provinces like Xinjiang, is not known.

In Teheran, Musharaf faced rougher weather for the same set of reasons he was feted in Beijing. Visiting Iran, three months after he took over power, the General was under pressure about issues of peace in Afghanistan and killing of Shias in Pakistan and Afghanistan. In fact, former Iranian president, Hashemi Rafsanjani, was quoted in the vibrant Teheran media saying: (Pakistan's) overly militaristic policies....which were responsible for much killing, would not serve the purpose."[26] An ominous portent for Pakistan's military ruler and a particularly harsh message from a country that had been its only "land route to the West"[27] for a long time.

The General was thus desperate. That was why he virtually beseeched India for reopening dialogue so he could break out of his "diplomatic isolation."[28]The Agra summit between India's Prime Minister, Atal Behari Vajpayee and him followed, concluding on an inconclusive note as was expected. At the end of the summit though Gen Musharaf claimed that a joint declaration had been agreed upon between him and the Indian prime minister, only to be torpedoed by the hardliners in the ruling BJP government of India, like its Home Minister, Lal Krishna Advani.[29]But during the summit it almost seemed that the swaggering General was conducting the summit for the sake of the media than for finding solutions to the intractable problems besetting the relations between the two countries. To the media, he seemed too keen to collect every possible debating point against the ponderous Indian prime minister.

9/11 And After

The posturing apart, the ground realities in Pakistan were not conducive for engaging the world's attention in any charitable way. But September 11, 2001, changed all of that. When in its aftermath, the US stitched its alliance against terror and pointed at Pakistan as the frontline state in this first war of the new millennium, many international observers had a sense of *déjà vu.* Like the

1980s, this time too a largely discredited Pakistan, under a military ruler, suddenly emerged as a key player in an international coalition created to take on forces in Afghanistan that threatened the global *status quo ante bellum*. Will Musharaf, like Zia of two decades ago, be able to steer this development into strengthening his own position and the country's, almost fortuitously?

An objective analysis of the facts at hand indicates to the contrary. The most important aspect of this Afghanistan operation is the commitment of the USA, its own armed forces, besides resources. This time around Pakistan cannot take on the mantle of an arbiter of Afghanistan's politics because of influence garnered as a clearinghouse of American military aid. In fact, Pakistan in 2001, is a country who was having to rollback its own policy of propping up a fundamentalist Islamic regime like that of the Taliban. Inaction on its part would have attracted international opprobrium and indeed possible armed action. Within the American policy establishment, there were two key realisations. One, the roots of Islamic terror, which they were seeking to remove, was deeply embedded in Pakistan. Secondly, the Pakistan armed forces could not be trusted to deliver the deadly force required to overcome the hydraheaded monster it has helped to create. This notion actually stemmed from the understanding that the USA and its allies had committed a major folly by withdrawing from Afghanistan so soon after the departure of the Soviet forces, thus seeking to run US interests piggybacked on Pakistan's agencies.[30]

Thus the world witnessed that the United Nations Security Council (UNSC) resolution 1373, which condemned terrorism and redefined it in terms of accounting for the direct perpetrators and indirect state and non-state sponsors, refused to accept a separate classification for those people, whom countries like Pakistan call 'freedom fighters.' So it may not be too farfetched to say that unlike Gen Zia, Musharaf will not be able to get a Kashmir dividend for his support to the international cause. Indeed, when on December 13, a militant attack was conducted on Indian Parliament House and India mobilised its armed forces for launching possible operations against terrorist infrastructure across the LoC, Musharaf had to appear on the state television to clarify and articulate his views on militancy and terrorism.[31]

The international reaction to this speech was reflective of the politics of the day. China, the strategic ally of Pakistan, had expressed cautious optimism at the promise of a new direction for the nation that Gen Musharaf had held out on that day. Still, the Chinese spokesperson had not failed in pointing that, "this (the speech) will help relieve tension in the region, and it conforms to the consensus of the international community on anti-terrorism. It is also in the long term interest of Pakistan." In other words, Beijing was concluding that Pakistan's new resolve to confront terrorism was as much for its own benefit as it was for others.

Still, there were some who were skeptical about Islamabad's intent to back the words of its chief executive. At the first Conference on Interaction and Confidence-Building Measures in Asia (CICA) at Kazakhstan's Almaty, five months after Musharaf's January 12th, 2002, speech, most members were still insisting that Pakistan should fulfill its promises, thus backing with action its words.[32]

The newly formed CICA had amongst its members, besides the Central Asian countries, Iran and Egypt.

This was a summit shadowed by the world's fear of a conflagration between two nations armed with nuclear weapons. The Almaty Declaration that was CICA's signal contribution resolved that, "Separatism is one of the main threats and challenges to the security and stability, sovereignty, unity and territorial integrity of states. The Member States shall not support on the territory of another Member State any separatist movements and entities, and, if such emerge, not to establish political, economic and other kinds of relations with them, not to allow the territories and communications of the Member States to be used by the above-mentioned movements and entities, and not to render them any kind of economic, financial and other assistance. We reaffirm the right of people living under foreign occupation for self-determination in accordance with the UN Charter and international law."[33]

The day the Almaty Declaration was being signed by its founding members, the US Secretary of State, Gen Colin Powell, was in Barbados and he told the media, "I spoke to President Musharaf over the weekend, once again encouraging him to do everything to restrain all activity, to end all activity across the Line of Control (in Kashmir). And when that takes place in a way that is obvious and demonstrable to all, then we would call upon India to take de-escalatory steps so we can start moving in the other direction."[34]

Earlier, at the 11th SAARC summit in January 2002, the member-countries had agreed to a resolution that had recognized "terrorism in all its forms and manifestations is a challenge to all states and to all of humanity, and cannot be justified on ideological, political, religious or any other ground. The leaders agreed that terrorism violates the fundamental values of the United Nations and the SAARC charter and constitutes one of the most serious threats to international peace and security in the twenty-first century." This categorical assertion by Pakistan's closest neighbours could not have been lost on Musharaf, who had otherwise seemed more enthusiastic about stagecraft.[35]

So it was apparent that the world was waiting for Pakistan to take concrete steps in thwarting terrorist elements operating from its soil. Gen Musharaf, knowing he had few options otherwise, seemed bent on taking action. Sporadic reports began appearing in the media about how Pakistan's armed forces were encountering alleged al-Qaida/Taliban cadres, on the run from the US and allied forces. The two bomb blasts at Karachi in mid-2002 expressed the disapproval of the Islamic *jihadi* forces at the Pakistan establishment's *volte face,* by which yesterday's friends had turned into foes.

Still, Gen Musharaf knew that even if Pakistan's *jihadi* elements understood his predicaments that led to his siding with the US and its allies, they would not countenance a move on his part to de-escalate on Kashmir. Yet, the world community could not have maintained double standards on terrorism, which would have called for opposing it in every corner of the world excepting in Kashmir. Instead, it allowed Musharaf to walk on the tight rope. While the General maintained his rhetoric about Kashmir, on the ground he took measures to reduce the activities of terrorists targeting it.

In the process of legitimising his regime in the eyes of the international community, General Musharaf has almost ended up delegitimising himself in the eyes of his people. Here was a man who had to give up the traditional Islamic fundamentalist constituency of most military rulers of Pakistan. Yet, he also failed to gain a countervailing domestic political force by rallying the moderates. The first group sees in his US alliance seeds of betrayal to the *jihadi* cause, while the second rue the loss of sovereignty and liberty as the US and allied security agencies get a free run of the country.[36]

The inherent instability of this arrangement was evident even more after the showcase general elections of Pakistan. The fact that the six-party Islamist fundamentalist alliance, the Muttahida Majlis-e-Amal (MMA) has not only secured 53 seats in the national Parliament, but a controlling majority of 48 seats out of 99 in the North West Frontier Province (NWFP) Assembly, and the largest single party status in Baluchistan, with 14 of 51 seats,[37] reflects on this reality. Even in Sindh and Punjab the MMA has made deep inroads.

The enormity of this achievement can be measured against the fact that no combination of religious parties has ever secured more than 11 seats (1988) in any previous National Assembly, and the religious parties were down to just two seats in the last elections in 1997.[38] Maulana Sami-ul-Haq, the Vice President of the MMA, and the head of the Madrassah Dar-ul-Uloom Haqqania at Akora Khattak that spawned virtually the entire leadership of the Taliban, interprets the mandate as proof that "the masses have rejected the 55-year old tyrannical system of governance and want a just system based on Islamic values."[39]

These results may not have surprised most Pakistan observers. The progressive deligitimisation of political parties, and indeed the political class, by the only surviving institution of the country, the Pakistan army, has been the story of the country for the last five-and-a-half decades. The exercise has only been completed by Gen Musharaf when he blocked the path of most possible political rivals like Benazir Bhutto and Nawaz Sharif to make an electoral comeback. On the other hand, the faith of the people in the army itself has been severely shaken after the fate that befell the Taliban government in Afghanistan. They have witnessed their country's 20-year old Afghan policy lie in shambles. Kashmir policy that has a history of even longer duration seems stuck in the court of international public opinion with a threat of a statute of limitation being served upon it. Not for long can Pakistan ignore what the UN Secretary General, Kofi Annan, had said on a trip to Islamabad in 2001. He was categorical about the UNSC resolutions on Kashmir being under chapter VI of the UN charter, thus making the concurrence of both parties mandatory for them to take effect[40]

Hence a question arises: will this mandate for the fundamentalist parties cause the expiry of Musharaf's authority to rule? Doubtful is the best answer possible at the moment. For Musharaf has the ability to turn this adversity into an advantage as he can emerge as the man whom the West recognises as the 'known devil.' Those in the Pakistan army who harbour ambitions of replacing him will be deterred by the significant presence of the US security agencies on the nation's soil. And going by the present indications, few Pakistan army officers would be willing to preside over an ignominious decline of Pakistan army's influence over the country's politics and society. Recent reports about assassination attempts on Musharaf point at this complex correlation of causes.

Notwithstanding these factors, the key to Musharaf's survival strategy may lie in how he manages his relations with the third pivot of Pakistan's foreign policy, Saudi Arabia. Since October 1999, when Musharaf usurped power from the elected government of Mian Nawaz Sharif, Saudi Arabia has been his constant beacon for finding the political path. He had visited Riyadh barely a fortnight after taking over power because as he described it "to express my respect and appreciation to the Custodian of the two holy mosques, King Fahd Ibn Abdul Aziz."[41] The other reason was to brief the Saudi leadership about his political and economic plans.[42]

The next crucial exchange between the two countries took place in October 2001, a little over a month after 9/11. This time the Saudi Foreign Minister promised to do whatever his country could do to alleviate the adverse economic condition of Pakistan.[43]He also recognised Pakistan was a bastion of Islamic *ummah* and that solidarity with Pakistan was the responsibility of all Muslims.[44]During his next visit to Saudi Arabia in June 2002, Musharaf disclosed closer collaboration between Saudi and Pakistan's intelligence officials to "purify the Pakistani atmosphere of this dirt (terrorists)."[45]And Musharaf showed that he had not forgotten to remember that whenever Pakistan faced a problem, Saudi Arabia was its "first resort."[46]

This is the same Saudi Arabia which had financed Afghan Mujahideen, approved and supported Pakistan's creation of the Taliban, and yet had finally fallen foul of the rabid Islamists like Osama bin Laden, because of the ruling family's close proximity to the USA on issues relevant to West Asia. This is the time when Riyadh began to feel the heat and the pinch of cheque-book politics, souring its relations with Pakistan a bit as most of the Saudi-baiters operated out of Taliban-controlled Afghanistan or even Pakistan.

Despite that, the status of Saudi Arabia being the religious leader of the Sunni school of Islam is unchallenged. And they can bring to bear some of that moral might to work for Musharaf should he require it for being rescued from the hands of his countrymen. On top of that, the Saudi Arabian regime of King Fahd has enormous influence with the Americans, as it remains the only bulwark of the US in a region where not many would like to advertise their relationship with the USA. This US-Saudi Arabian strategic relationship could be an important parallel channel for Musharaf to tap into at moments of crisis.

But the present dynamics of the world favour change, not *status quo*. Even if one applies a set of first-cut theories of international relations–classical realism and defensive realism-to the situation that Pakistan finds itself in, the dynamics favour those who can buck the trend. But first, an explanation about the two set of principles. These two theories of foreign policy try to explain the external behaviour of a nation–its reasons for trying to expand its influence or interests beyond its borders. The adherents of classical realism think that nations turn expansionist when they consider their power (material resources) to be more than others. Those in the opposing camp of defensive realism feel that nations seek security rather than influence and thus say that nations throw their weight around when they themselves feel threatened.

Like most theories, there is a group of dissidents for this set too. This group of realists call their theory state-centred realism. It says that nations do not frame or conduct foreign policy, states representing them do. And the state expands when it feels strong, irrespective of the nation. The more famous adherents of this are scholars like Fareed Zakaria. Samuel Huntington, the Harvard University professor who gained popular notoriety with his theory of 'Clash of Civilisations,' has explored the influence of character of the state on national policy but has not really ventured into the relationship of these variables on foreign policy.

Applying these theories to the position of Pakistan foreign policy manoeuvres, one sees they are limited in their ability to explain the country's national behaviour. These theories are really fit to explain great power behaviour. Pakistan's two lode stones for foreign policy or even its nationhood are the issues of its nuclear option and Kashmir. Islam in Pakistan's international politics has always been a guiding principle but never an overriding one. And all these determinants of foreign policy of the country are in the hands of the state. That state may be elected or may not be elected.

So when Musharaf talks of the "full might" (read nuclear) of Pakistan to bear upon an adversary who refuses to hand over Muslim Kashmir, he may be talking about a situation where the state of Pakistan decides on a course that the people may not countenance. Or when a Pakistan seeks to create strategic space for itself in the heart of Afghanistan, which really may be a machination of its army irrespective of the consequences to its own territory or its people. And all these are manifestations of survival strategies of a defensive, weak state feeling insecure about its own existence. Even though this wary state contaminates the people with its sense of insecurity, it does so without the existence of a credible threat to the nation.

Let's examine Pakistan's relations with Afghanistan as a test case. At the formation of Pakistan in 1947, the Pushtu speaking people of the new country belonging to North West Frontier Province and Baluchistan felt no sense of ethnic connection with the mainland Punjab or Sindh. Afghan leadership too fomented such sentiments and caused serious problems for the fledgling Pakistan leadership. When Pakistan's first Prime Minister, Liaquat Ali Khan, was assassinated in 1951, many feared that the killer, a Pathan, had done it for the cause of Pakhtunistan.[47] But that proved to be incorrect as the killer was later identified as one belonging to an Islamic fundamentalist party.

Yet, when General Zia-ul Haq sought to expand Pakistan's influence in Afghanistan domestic affairs in 1980s, he did it because he was seeking to consolidate his shaky hold on the domestic polity of Pakistan. Also, as a way to bolster his position he chose to side with one of the superpowers in this Cold War great game. In no circumstances was Pakistan then strong enough to seek expansionist mileage in Afghanistan. And the Pakhtunistan demand had remained dormant for so long, that it could not even have been *casus belli* for Pakistan's action.

Then let us look at the time when Pakistan chose to begin its quest for a nuclear bomb. This again was at a time when the country had just been vanquished in a battle with India in 1971, even dismembered and the administrative hold of the ZA Bhutto government was at best tenuous. The frail and an enfeebled state sought to redeem itself by choosing the nuclear option purely as a defensive strategy. The identification of Pakistan's people with the nuclear issue came much later.

On Kashmir too Pakistan has been most belligerent when it has been weak. In 1947-48, just after its creation the country sought to settle this issue in its favour by a stratagem which smacked of diffidence. If the Pakistani state would have been strong and self-confident politically, it would have approached the United Nations and the international public opinion for a just settlement. Instead, it chose the use of indirect force by sending marauders who were to create the ground for a popular insurrection in Kashmir. In 1965, a politically embattled Ayub Khan sought to externalise his problems by fighting a war with India, which he thought was weak too. A gross miscalculation, as he later discovered. Then in the 1980s, when Zia launched his low intensity warfare on India, more than Pakistan, it had been his goal to weaken India from within, incurring the least cost for Pakistan-a sign of a defeatist tactic and a lack of confidence.

So it can be argued that a stable and self-confident Pakistan will be least expansionist in terms of its neighbourhood, thus fostering stability in the subcontinent. The question is whether Musharaf can lead the country to that goal. The situation seems ripe for a change in direction for the country. And this arises from another crisis, the one that has engulfed the whole of the Islamic diaspora. The bellicose proselytisers of the religion have given the politics of its people a label of being illegitimate. But that should hardly be the case.

Whether it is West Asia or the Indian subcontinent, the common Muslims' popular aspirations are not different from those of the other communities. Yet, it is noteworthy that the USA treats countries like Saudi Arabia, Bahrain, Oman, Kuwait or the United Arab Emirates as lands where the normal rule of law should not apply, ostensibly for maintenance of "traditional" systems. The US supports regimes in these countries that have no mandate from their people. The result is ferment as newer generations, more globalised, tend to gauge that their existence in the political Middle Ages is a result of a Western strategy to keep them contained so. They seem to conclude that their interests are not commensurate with the interests of the developed West as the latter seeks monopoly in sourcing its raw materials from these regions. So the political anger of the Muslim youth finds expression in religious terms as they have few avenues to express it otherwise.

This is where a self-contained and a self-confident Pakistan can provide leadership lessons. Because politics in Pakistan may have been murky but its idiom has been that of democratic compromise, much different from the nakedly confrontationist attitudes of the likes of Osama bin Laden. It is important in this light to allow the electoral majority that the MMA has gained in the recent elections, to further the political process. It will be an important experiment to see whether these religio-political entities can learn the systems of mainstream politics and shed their ideological rigidities. For the Maulanas of MMA are not cut from the same cloth as that of Ayatollah Khomeini.

If Musharaf too can learn to live in the political centre, as a progressive moderniser and develop a way of actualising Pakistan's self-worth without needing to brandish its nuclear arsenal, the country then can truly go a long way in fulfilling the dreams of its founding fathers, which is to be the leader of the community of Islamic nations. And that will break the mould of a defensive realist state about whom has been this write-up.

Notes

1. Robert Gilpin, *War and Change in World Politics* (Cambridge: Cambridge University Press), P.23
2. W Norman Brown, *The United States and India, Pakistan, Bangladesh,* (Cambridge, Mass.: Harvard University Press), P. 368
3. Ibid. P. 380
4. Ibid. P. 380-381
5. Ibid. P. 351
6. Ibid. P. 351
7. Ibid. P. 275
8. Neville Maxwell, *India's China War,* (Jonathan Cape Ltd, London) P. 215

9. Ibid. P. 217n.
10. Ibid. P 217
11. Ibid. P.274
12. Stanley Wolpert, *Roots of Confrontation in South Asia* (Oxford University Press) P.118
13. W.Norman Brown, *The United States and India, Pakistan, Bangladesh* (Cambridge, Mass.: Harvard University Press), P.380
14. Ibid
15. Sreedhar ed. *Pakistan's Bomb: A Documentary Study* (ABC Publishing House), Preface P.xiii
16. Ibid
17. Ibid P. xiv
18. Ibid
19. Ibid P. xvi
20. Ibid P. xvii
21. Ibid. Introduction to Second Edition by K Subramanyam, P. xxiii
22. Sreedhar & Neelesh Bhagat, *Pakistan: A Withering State* (Wordsmith) P. 126
23. Richard N Haas and Gideon Rose ed. *A New US Policy toward India and Pakistan*, (Council on Foreign Relations) Additional Views by George Perkovich. P. 50
24. Qamar Agha, "Pakistan's Isolation," *Hindu,* Dec 23, 1999
25. "Friendship with China," Unsigned Edit, *Dawn,* Jan 20, 2000
26. Mahdi Masud, "Mending Fences with Iran," *Dawn,* Dec 23, 1999
27. Ibid
28. Qamar Agha, "Pakistan's Isolation," *Hindu,* Dec 23, 1999

29. kkkk

30. This was mentioned by Prof Frank Katz of George Mason University at a video conference organised by USIS, Kolkata, on September 9, 2002, which the writer attended.

31. *Dawn,* January 13, 2002

32. M P Bhandara, "Falling into the Yahya syndrome?" *Dawn,* June 9, 2002

33. Almaty Act, Clause 18, *http://www.mfa.kz/english/cica_decl02.htm*

34. M P Bhandara, "Falling into the Yahya syndrome?" *Dawn,* June 9, 2002

35. The famous handshake, a swaggering example of showmanship, with Indian Prime Minister, Mr AB Vajpayee on stage, at the 11th SAARC summit, Kathmandu, in January, 2002

36. Ayaz Amir, "Creative Anarchy Pakistan Style," *Dawn,* August 10, 2002

37. Ajai Sahni, "Dictator's Democracy," *South Asia Intelligence Review, South Asia Terrorism Portal,* www.satp.org

38. Ibid

39. Ibid

40. "Pakistan's Lies and Propaganda on Kashmir," *www.armyinkashmir.org*

41. King Fahd Ibn Abdul Aziz Discussed Saudi-Pakistan Relations and the Developments in Pakistan with General Musharaf. Gen Musharaf: Respect and Appreciation are behind choosing Saudi Arabia to be the first country to Visit after the coup," *http://www.ain-al-yaqeen.com/issues/19991029/feat3en.htm*

42. Ibid

43. "Saudi Arabia expresses Solidarity," *http://www.contactpakistan.com/PakEmbassy/latestnews/archives/news091.htm*

44. Ibid

45. Ibid

46. Ibid

47. Stanley, Wolpert, *Roots of Confrontation in South Asia,* (Oxford University Press), P.121

4

Future of the Jehadi Groups

KALIM BAHADUR

The emergence of Pakistan's Jehadi groups and the so-called Jehadi culture was not an unexpected and sudden development. For a variety of political and social reasons the Muslims of the Indian sub-continent have always been conscious of their community's international fraternity. Every important development affecting the Muslims anywhere in the world has aroused them. It was at the end of the nineteenth century that an Afghan intellectual called Jamaluddin Afghani came to India to mobilise the Indian Muslims in their struggle against the British war against the Turkish empire. He influenced the Indian Muslim elite profoundly. Muslims in India were greatly exercised during the Turkish war in the Balkans during the first quarter of the twentieth century. A Muslim medical mission, led by the famous Congress leader, Dr Mukhtar Ahmed Ansari, had gone to Turkey to attend to the Turkish soldiers injured during the fighting there, although it was the war of independence of the people of the Balkans against oppression by the Turkish autocracy. The Indian Muslims were moved by the overthrow of the Turkish Caliphate by the Turks themselves, and by the problems of the people of Palestine, etc. The concept of one monolithic Islamic community called the Ummah and the widespread belief that conspiracies were being hatched against Islam and that there was need for the Muslims to unite and defend the faith germinates and strengthens the idea of jehad. In this chapter it is attempted to analyse the evolution, the meaning and implications of jehad in the context of Pakistan and the Indian sub-continent. Further, an attempt has been made to study the ideology of the jehadi groups in Pakistan and their future in the context of the 9/11 attack on the Twin Towers in the United States and later the decimation of the al-Qaida and the Taliban. The jehadi groups are also studied in the context of the India-Pakistan conflict over Kashmir. The *raison d'être* of the jehadi groups in Pakistan has been the Kashmir issue, which is portrayed not as a territorial dispute with India but as an ideological and religious conflict. Pakistan has never denied providing "diplomatic, political, and moral" support to the "freedom fighters" in Kashmir. It is well known, though, that the Pakistan military's links with the militants in Kashmir run much deeper. General Musharraf has claimed that jehad (the freedom struggle) in Kashmir and terrorism must be differentiated. Almost all fighting groups, especially the orthodox Sunni factions, drew inspiration from Osama bin Laden and the Taliban. Most of them owe their origins to the Afghan Jehad. Pakistan's Kashmir policy depends on their support. In fact, jehadi groups are considered of great importance for Pakistan's strategic objectives, i.e. a favourable settlement of the Kashmir dispute. The military standoff with India in 1999, when Mujahideen and Pakistani soldiers occupied the strategic hills of Kargil, only to retreat later, graphically illustrates this relationship between the religious militant groups and the Pakistan military. One writer has argued that since jehad is a part of the Islamic lore and it is being interpreted as one of the duties of Muslim jehadi groups, are likely to survive in Pakistan and elsewhere. The end of the Taliban is only a setback, but the strong showing of the hardline Islamic religious parties in the recent election in Pakistan reveals that the ideologies of jehad have deep roots in that country.

Some scholars have claimed that Muslims had forgotten about jehad, but it was Washington which re-invented jehad to mobilize Muslims to confront the Soviet intervention in Afghanistan in the early eighties. This is only partially correct, but the concept of jehad was not totally dead when the United States picked up the standard of jehad in Afghanistan. Washington only resurrected it and gave it a new life. However, the concept of jehad had already been given a new lease of life by the Pakistanis during the early months after the inception of Pakistan. Jehad was the central theme during the first Kashmir War in 1947, though subsequent India-Pakistan wars were not called jehad. During the long history of Muslim invasions of India, of the so many wars that were fought between the Muslim invaders and local Hindu Rajas, some of them were fought in the well-known battlefield of Panipat but none of them was called a jehad. The first time that a campaign was called jehad in the Indian sub-continent was the one led by Syed Ahmed Barelvi in the late twenties and the early thirties of the nineteenth century. Interestingly, this was provoked by declarations by several Indian Muslim theologians of the time that India had been turned into a *Darul-Harb* (a land of war); the exigencies of the political situation pushed the Mujahideen in a frontal clash with the rising power of Maharaja Ranjit Singh, and the jehad movement was decimated in the battle of Balakot in 1831. The Mujahideen who followed Syed Ahmed Barelvi through the length and breadth of the Indian sub-continent were moved by the ideal of purifying Islam of all unIslamic accretions and building an Islamic state in India. Syed Ahmed Barelvi had visited Arabia in 1821 for Haj and had reportedly met Abdul Wahab, the Arab theologian, and later the British had given the name of Wahabis to the Mujahideen movement. Some of the Mujahideen survivors of Balakot had participated in the 1857 uprising in North India and two Ulema under the influence of the Mujahideen ideology had founded the famous seminary at Deoband in 1867. The Ulema of Deoband were committed Sunnis and called themselves *ahle al-Sunnah wal Jama'at* (people of the practice of the Prophet and the community) who accepted the authority of the four orthodox schools as opposed to the Barelvi school, with their acceptance of the intercession of saints and worship at tombs, etc. The Barelvi school should not be confused with followers of Syed Ahmed Barelvi.

Jehad has been a hazy concept and a part of Muslim psyche throughout the centuries and therefore, it has come to mean any war which Muslims chose to call it as such. Jehad has also been a controversial issue. First of all, what is the objective of jehad? Who can declare a jehad? Does jehad mean only war with weapons or there are other kinds of jehad? All these issues have been debated throughout the history of Islam. Jehad is not among the five pillars of Islam at par with prayers, fasting, etc. There is much more confusion and difference among the Islamic scholars about these questions. Some of the modern scholars have given different answers to these questions. This dilemma was highlighted in the twentieth century by the response of the Head and the founder of the Jama'at-i-Islami in the Indian sub-continent, Maulana Abul Ala Maududi, to the Pakistan government's request to him in early 1948 to ask the members of his party to join the Pakistan Army and also the jehad in Kashmir. The Maulana's response was that he could not instruct his members to join the so-called jehad as he did not consider the war in Kashmir as jehad as the Government of Pakistan had not openly declared it a jehad. According to him it was not Islamic morality that you secretly engage in fighting a war while publicly you deny that you are fighting a war and further that Pakistan was not an Islamic state. Pakistan until that time had not been declared an Islamic state. It was only later in 1949 that the Pakistan Constituent Assembly passed the Objective Resolution which provided that the country would be an Islamic State. Moreover, there could not be jehad on one part of the border with the other country and peace in another part. To the request for Jama'at members joining the Pakistan Army his answer was that since Pakistan was not an Islamic state he could not ask the members of his party to join the army of a non-Islamic state. It was clear that according to Maulana Maududi jehad could only be declared by an Islamic state. This also means that no individual or a group of individuals could declare a jehad. Other Islamic intellectuals have also spoken about various aspects of jehad. Maududi's views were challenged by the prominent theologian Maulana Shabbir Ahmed Usmani who was the leader of the Jamiat al Ulema-i-Islam who gave an entirely opposite *fatwa*. He argued that since India had flouted an agreement by occupying Junagadh, Pakistan was also not obliged to abide by the agreement. Maududi answered by raising the issue of the continued maintenance of diplomatic relations with India which were also evident by the import of coal, sugar, and cloth from India. Maulana Usmani countered by saying that India had waged war with Pakistan and it was left with no option but to retaliate against the aggression. He went on to claim that Pakistan had admitted before the Kashmir Commission that her forces were at war with India. Maududi had to agree later that after Foreign Minister Zafar Ullah Khan's admission that the Pakistan Army was present in Kashmir the war in Kashmir was jehad. In the opinion of some scholars in the language of the Shariah the word jehad is used in the sense of war (*Jehad-bis Saif*). However, this war is aimed at bringing an end to oppression and aggression against Islam. The idea is not to use war as a means of propagating Islam but to remove those tyrannical forces which are inimical to Islam. Jehad has been defined in two ways; one greater, which is the one Imam Ghazali has used that is the *Jehad al Nafs*. According to Ghazali *Nafs* has two meanings, one, power of anger and sexual appetite in human beings; two, soul i.e., human beings in reality, his self and his person. However, the common understanding of Muslims is that jehad means struggle against oneself to overcome evil and also in the cause of Islam. Islamic scholars have defined jehad in two ways one is *al-Jehad-ul-Akbar*, the greater jehad, and *al-Jehad -ul-Asghar* or the lesser jehad. Jehad could be defined both as defending against and\or attacking an enemy. However, as commonly understood by Muslims and others jehad is taken to mean war with all its connotations of murder and bloodshed.

The concept of jehad has been at the core of Islamic strategic thinking throughout the history of the Islamic world. This in spite of the fact that there have ' een many different interpretations of the Quranic teachings on the subject. Some of the contemporary Islamic thinkers like Maulana Abul Ala Maududi, founder of the Jama'at-i-Islami movement in the Indian subcontinent, Hasan al Banna and Syed Qutub of the Muslim Brothers of Egypt and the Ayatullah Khomeini of Iran. The earliest to write on the subject was Maududi whose work on jehad was among his first major publications as far back as 1930. This work has been a major influence on the thinking of the militant Islamists through most of the Muslim world. In fact Maududi shares with most other fundamentalists his jehad paradigm as the core of his ideology on the achievement of an Islamic state. According to one scholar some common themes in the Islamic revivalist discourse are the failure of the western models of political, social and economic domination which foster secularism, materialism, and spiritual bankruptcy; the need to return to Islam in order to restore lost identity, moral purpose and character; an emphasis on the unity and totality of Islam to politics and society and the introduction of Shariah law.

The central theme of all the three Islamic ideologies is on the violent overthrow of the existing state and forcible seizure of the levers of power to establish an Islamic state. They emphasized that political power was essential for the setting up of an Islamic society. Peaceful means cannot bring about reforms of the society, which Islam wants to put in effect; state power was essential to bring them about. In spite of Maududi, Qutub and Khomeini differing with each other on sectarian and theological issues they were agreed that Muslims of the world constituted one community and they were not divided by racial, ethnic or territorial nationalism. They all had common belief in jehad. The most radical among the three was Syed Qutub who had given a call for the violent removal of all those who stood in the way of the achievement of Islamic society.

Khomeini had targeted imperialism even before the revolution as he thought its objective was to oppose Islamic militancy and separated religion from politics. He gave a call to the world Muslim community to wage jehad against imperialism. With the approach of the revolution, he became increasingly strident about revolution and republic. He believed that revolution would transform itself into an Islamic state. That was the only way to rid society of despotism, poverty, cultural alienation, and alcoholism. Khomeini did not envisage the revolution as peaceful, step by step or as a gradual process. To him a revolution was abrupt, political and violent. Maulana Maududi, who founded the Jama'at-i-Islami in India and later migrated to Pakistan and headed the Party in that country till his death in 1979, has been the most influential ideolog of Islamic fundamentalism. His writings have been translated and republished in most of the Muslim countries and they influenced the militant groups in several countries and he has been considered the ideological mentor of several militant parties in several countries in West Asia. He is one of the first theoreticians who has presented Islam as a logical, well argued, cogent system of ideas, of course if one accepted his basic premise. He was a relentless opponent of western civilization, western secular democracy, and socialist doctrines. He believed that the Quran provided a complete guide to every sphere of life. Though as opposed to other fundamentalist thinkers he recognized the possibility of advancement and evolution in it to meet the needs of the changing world. Maududi's views on jehad have influenced the militants and radical Islamists and his claim that the most significant type of jehad was the use of violence as an element of general strategy. In his early years, he appeared to oppose violence as a means to achieve political objectives. However, once Pakistan came into existence and the Jama'at came to play an important role in the politics of that country Maududi appeared to be not averse to the use of violence to gain its political objectives. During the anti-Ahmediya agitation in Pakistan in 1953, he justified violence against the community and later during the 1971 civil war in Pakistan in which the Jama'at supported Pakistan's military regime against the freedom fighters and confirmed it as a party that would not hesitate to utilize force when it could be handy for political purposes. These parties and the ideology propounded by them were progenitors of the militant Islam which spawned the radical and terrorist groups which planned and executed the 9/11 attack on the Trade Towers in New York.

When the civil war broke out in Afghanistan in the wake of the revolution in April 1978, General Zia-ul-Haq was in power in neighbouring Pakistan. He had no legitimacy and was insecure in power; he saw an opportunity to sponsor resistance to the "Godless" communist rule in an Islamic country which might have given him a fig leaf of legitimacy. The US had seen the communist takeover in Afghanistan as the Soviet move into a vitally strategic area near the mouth of the Gulf of Hormuz which was too close to the oil sources of the

Persian Gulf, Kuwait, Iraq and Saudi Arabia. The April Revolution had been naturally not welcomed by all the Afghans and the adventurism of the Khalq regime had also amply contributed to this by its extremist left policies. The Soviet intervention in the civil war had only complicated the situation in the region. Added to this was intense factionalism within the ruling party in Afghanistan. In the early period of Soviet intervention Washington wanted only to strengthen the resistance to keep the struggle going on, but in 1984 the CIA's goal became explicitly to defeat the Soviets. The CIA provided weapons to the Mujahideen, turning a blind eye to the heroin production being used to add to the US funds. The US provided Stinger anti-aircraft missiles to the Afghan resistance. Washington also encouraged the Mujahideen to conduct raids into the Soviet Central Asian Republics. The CIA played a very important role in mobilizing the Muslims from all over the world to fight in the Afghan civil war. Between 1982 and 1992, 30,000 Islamist radicals from 40 different countries joined the jehad. General Zia-ul-Haq thought it was a golden opportunity to make Pakistan once again the frontline state in the struggle against communism. That would ensure the economic and military support of the United States and Arab countries to Pakistan while the General would also get legitimacy at home. It is also claimed by some that had the co-incidence of several events not happened General Zia could not have survived the rising opposition to his rule in his country. The interests of United States and those of Pakistan coincided in Afghanistan. Thus was the Afghanistan jehad born. It was in the common interest of both the countries to use the Islamic slogan of jehad. General Zia-ul-Haq who was almost a pariah in the world community suddenly became the spokesman of the Islamic countries. The jehad in Afghanistan came as a morale booster for the Islamic parties in Pakistan. These parties were used by the Intelligence agencies of Pakistan to mobilize Pakistanis and Muslim militant groups from other countries for fighting in Afghanistan in the name of jehad. In fact, they did not need any prompting as they had already become active in this respect.

The religious parties in Pakistan were the offshoots of the Ulema parties in India. The Ulema throughout the history of the Muslim world have rarely led a revolution unless their privileged position in matters of religion was challenged by the ruling regime. The Ulema in India had opposed the concept and the demand for Pakistan. The leading Ulema organization, the Jamiat al Ulema-i-Hind, had been a consistent opponent of the Muslim League and its demand for Pakistan. At the time when an overwhelming majority of Indian Muslims had walked over to the Muslim League's demand for Pakistan, the Ulema remained firmly opposed to it. The religious opposition included the Jama'at-i-Islami which was not exactly an Ulema organisation. It opposed Pakistan though it also opposed the composite nationalism of the Indian National Congress. The Ulema's opposition basically stemmed from their belief that the Muslim League leadership was Western educated and therefore, they would not build an Islamic state in Pakistan. They claimed that Pakistan would be a Muslim national state which they believed was against Islam. The Ulema remained united and all attempts by the supporters of the Muslim League to win them over to the idea of Pakistan were not successful till the end. However, it was only in 1945 that a separate Ulema Party was set up called the Jamiat al Ulema-i-Islam led by Maulana Shabbir Ahmed Usmani. Once Pakistan came into existence these Ulema arrived in Pakistan and reorganised their parties in the new country but most of them faced difficulties as they had to live down their own opposition, sometimes bitter opposition to Pakistan. To some extent they were able to retrieve the ground and re-establish their legitimacy by catching on to the demand for Islamising the country. Their argument was that since Pakistan was demanded in the name of Islam and now that it had been achieved it should be declared an Islamic state.

Almost all religious parties have developed around the individuals rather than around an ideology. The Ulema are notoriously prone to factionalism. All the major religious parties like the Jamiat al Ulema-i-Islam led by Maulana Fazalur Rahman, earlier by his father Maulana Mufti Mahmood, and the Jamiat al Ulema-i-Pakistan led by Shah Ahmed Noorani have several splinter groups. The Jama'at-i-Islami because of its tight discipline and rigid ideology and selected membership has escaped splinters, but there are known factions in the party and many prominent leaders including some of the founders have left it during the last two decades. The religious parties had come close to the establishment during the regime of General Zia-ul-Haq. This process started first because General Zia began to talk of setting up an Islamic system in Pakistan and used this Islamic card to secure the support of the religious lobby in Pakistan. After the war in Afghanistan broke out and refugees from Afghanistan began to pour into the country, the military regime set up refugee camps in Baluchistan and the North Western Frontier Province (NWFP). Only two religious parties were allowed access into these camps i.e. the

Jamiat al Ulema-i-Islam led by Maulana Fazlur Rahman and the Jama'at-i-Islami. These two parties and some other religious groups were already being used to mobilize Muslims for the jehad in Afghanistan. These two parties were also allowed to set up madrasas in the camps for Afghan refugee children. Some Afghans had already joined the major seminaries. These seminaries were the Binnori seminary in Karachi and the one that is headed by Maulana Sami-ul Haq in Akora Khatak in the NWFP. These religious parties had been running hundreds of madrasas in various parts of Pakistan. Very little notice had been taken of those madrasas till the emergence of the Taliban in Afghanistan in the early nineties.

Madrasa is an Urdu/Arabic word for school. There are no exact figures for the number of madrasas in Pakistan. Their number could be tens of thousands throughout the Muslim world, including the United States. Most of the schools promote moderate, traditional and liberal interpretations of Islam. Some are actually secular schools and have nothing do with religion and they are simply schools attended by Muslims. But there are thousands of Madrasas in Pakistan that preach a highly fundamentalist interpretation of Islam. They are the breeding and training grounds for terrorists. A number of the most radical Madrasas, including one where many of today's Taliban leaders were educated, are on Pakistan's border with Afghanistan. These jehadi schools are free and provide board and lodging for boys from the ages of 8 to their early 20s. They hold attraction in a country where many suffer from severe poverty, even starvation. In most cases parents who cannot afford to feed their kids send them away to Madrasas to escape that poverty. The schools say they want to improve the plight of

Muslims worldwide. They teach students that America, Israel, India and western countries in general are the enemies of Islam; and it is the duty of the Muslims to remove Americans, Israelis and other perceived enemies from Muslim lands. Pakistan's most militant Madrasas teach fundamentalist Islam and little else. It is not uncommon for students to spend entire school days simply memorizing and reciting portions of the Koran, the Muslim sacred scripture. In such Madrasas there is no provision for teaching subjects such as mathematics, science, geography and history. Generally, questions and critical discussions are not allowed so students develop a closed mind. Teachers teach, students listen and repeat. These are the Madrasas that preach jehad, or holy war, against the West and produce suicide or *fidayeen* volunteers. Students are taught that the United States is the enemy of Islamic values and culture, it wants to destroy Islam, and seize their natural wealth. And they are encouraged to join Muslim armies fighting in territories such as Kashmir and Afghanistan. Though they are outside the mainstream of Pakistani culture, fundamentalist Madrasas have substantial resources. Jamia Darul Uloom Haqqania, one of the most radical Madrasas in northwest Pakistan, sent nearly all 3,000 of its students to fight in Afghanistan in 1997. Many of al-Qaeda cadres and those of the Taliban and other jehadis are believed to have graduated from Madrasas in Pakistan as well.

One result of the spread of the jehadi movement in Pakistan was the growth of religious sectarianism in the country. Eleven years of General Zia-ul-Haq's Islamisation had spawned sectarian groups and sectarian Madrasas which were in most cases funded by the state. As one writer has pointed out that in seeking legitimization and a social base for his rule, General Zia's policies encouraged fundamentalism, strengthened its institutional base and provided a fertile base for sectarianism to grow and prosper. For bringing this about, the Zia regime worked with great enthusiasm while it created a divided polity. In Sindh, General Zia-ul-Haq had been held responsible for the creation of the MQM which was supported as the urban counterweight to the Pakistan Peoples Party, which had a popular base in Sindh province. Similarly, the deepening of sectarian divisions, an outcome of General Zia's policy of a bias for the interpretation of one religion as understood by one sect; one result of which was of dividing the opposition which was less likely to challenge the seizure of the state by those who had captured power by a military coup and not by a popular election. The major sectarian groups like the Tehreek-e-Nifaz-Fiqh-Jafaria, the Sipah-e-Sahaba Pakistan and the MQM all emerged during General Zia's rule. The sectarian and ethnic groups which emerged in an organized militant form in the Zia years now threaten the very fabric of society and pose an ever more serious challenge to the state. Zia's policies promoted the growth of sectarianism in a number of ways. The Shia community believed that Zia-ul-Haq's government aimed at the establishment of a Sunni Hanafi state in which the 'Islamisation' of laws was seen to reflect the 'Islam' of the majority community. The 1980 demonstration in front of the government secretariat in Islamabad by tens of thousands of Shias protesting against Zakat and Ushr was a clear indication of their apprehensions regarding Zia's 'Islamisation' project. The selective backing of the Afghan groups resisting the Soviet occupation of Afghanistan again corresponded to a sectarian pattern of preferences that reinforced perceptions on both sides of the divide. By the end of Zia's rule the consequences of his policies were fairly obvious. Over the last decade there has been a major escalation in sectarian tension, the number of sectarian killings and armed sectarian groups. One offshoot of the jehad in Kashmir has been its impact on the sectarian violence in Pakistan. The problem arises when sectarian and religious organizations within Pakistan start training their members under the pretext of Kashmir jehad and then use these young men to kill members of the rival sect. According to one Shia newspaper, Azam Tariq, the Head of Sipha-e-Sahaba, and Masood Azhar the Head of Jaish-e-Mohammed, are great friends and both are old devotees of Haq Nawaz Jhangvi (the founder of Sipha-e-Sahaba). The authorities would never take action against Jaish-e-Mohammed since it was a jehadi organization and was promoting the foreign policy of Pakistan; and Sipha-e-Sahaba by having close links with Jaish-e-Mohammed is abusing the foreign policy of Pakistan to its full advantage against the Shias. The Shias have no help from any of the jehadi groups as almost all of them are Sunni and sympathetic to Sipha-e-Sahaba. It is the Pakistani ISI which is involved in training and arming these mujahideen some of whom are used by organizations like Sipha-e-Sahaba to fight their guerrilla war against the Shias. For reasons known only to ISI it has not formed any Shia jehadi groups in Kashmir. Surely there are enough Shias in Pakistan to form at least one Shia jehadi group! The foreign policy of Pakistan has really cornered the Shias who have been left on their own to defend themselves against the atrocities of these so-called mujahideen.

Most religious parties, since they are generally developed around individual leaders, are faction ridden and split frequently. Until the 1980s Pakistan had only three mainstream Sunni parties, the Jama'at-e-Islami, the Jamiat ul Ulema-i-Islam, and Jamiat-Ulema Pakistan. At this point a new set of militants entered the scene partly because of socio-economic conditions, partly through the factionalising of the existing politico-religious parties. The Jamiat al Ulema-i-Pakistan, a Barelvi religio-political party is now divided into five groups and all of them are prominent in the country. Jamiat al Ulema-i-Islam was also split into three factions. The Sipah-e -Sahaba is also an offshoot of the JUI. Some other smaller groups also broke away from the JUI. Similarly, the Shia organization the Tehrik Nifaz Shariate Jafaria (TNSJ) has given birth to Sipah-e-Mohammad. Most of these groups are also directly or indirectly linked to some terrorist groups fighting in Jammu and Kashmir. The leaders of the three Sunni political parties act almost as patron saints of the terrorist groups irrespective of their affiliation.

Most of the militant groups in Jammu and Kashmir owe their origin to the Islamic parties in Pakistan. Reports have suggested that General Zia-ul-Haq, the late military ruler of Pakistan, gave Rs 50 billion to jehadi groups to start militancy in Jammu and Kashmir. The agenda of the jehadi groups, however, kept changing as the jehadis began pocketing the money. A Pakistani Urdu daily quoted former Prime Minister of Pakistan-occupied Kashmir (PoK) Sardar Abdul Qayyum Khan as saying that during the 1980s, when the Afghan war was on, Pakistani generals and the Inter-Services Intelligence (ISI) made a lot of money through drug-rackets. A large part of this money was subsequently used for organising militancy in Kashmir, he said. Sardar Qayyum, who has been much criticised in Pakistan for openly opposing jehadi terrorism in Kashmir, said General Zia gave the money to start "disorganised" jehad. All the terrorist groups carry names related to Islamic jehad or movements; however, intense rivalry prevails among them including open fighting which could be called turf war. The notorious terrorist group the Jaish-e-Mohammad led by Masood Azhar was built up by forcibly destroying another older terrorist group. However, the Pakistani agency, the ISI, has been responsible for planning their operations, training them and inducting them into the state of Jammu and Kashmir.

Once the Soviets withdrew from Afghanistan in 1989, the ISI's attention was turned to Kashmir where under the directive of General Zia-ul-Haq it began the process of Islamisation and revolt. The Jama'at-i-Islami of Jammu and Kashmir, which is an independent party affiliated neither to the Indian Jama'at-i- Islami of India nor to that of Pakistan, which had a long standing enmity with the ruling National Conference, was activated and a new Islamist political front called the Muslim United Front (MUF) was formed. The MUF provoked violence during the elections while making allegations that the ruling National Conference was bent on obstructing fair elections. The elections were denounced as rigged and thousands of Jama'at supporters demonstrated in the streets in various towns of Kashmir. Hundreds of ISI agents who indulged in baseless propaganda against the National Conference and India were inducted into the Valley. Scores of unemployed young men and volunteers were taken to Pakistan for training in Pakistan and sent back with guns and easy money. During the late 1980s and early 1990s, the ISI was mainly focused on Kashmir and Punjab in India.

The results of the Pakistan election held on 10 October, 2002, for the National Assembly and the provincial Assemblies show that the combining of the religious parties called the Mutahida Majlis-e- Amal (MMA) has made a good showing with 45 seats in the National Assembly comprising the six parties; five of which were the main ideological mentors of the Taliban and also those of the terrorist outfits fighting in the Indian state of Jammu and Kashmir. In the provincial Assemblies of NWFP and in Baluchistan, the MMA have emerged with a dominating position to form governments in the provinces.

The 9/11 terrorist attack on the World Trade Centre in New York and on the Pentagon in the United States was a watershed in the growth of the jehadi terrorist movement throughout the world. There was little doubt that the hand behind the dastardly attack was that of the terrorist Osama bin Laden and his al-Qaida terrorist organization. Osama had been living in the Taliban controlled Afghanistan which refused to hand him over to the United States. Pakistan's General Musharraf attempted to intercede but to no avail. Later reports have indicated that General Mahmood Ahmed, the then Director of the ISI, who had led the Pakistani delegation to Kandhar to persuade the Taliban supremo Mullah Omar to hand over Osama to the United States did not even mention this demand to him during his visit. In response to the terror attacks, Washington declared war on international terrorism and naturally, the first target was Afghanistan. In fact, it was a one-sided war in which the Taliban were no match for the mighty superpower. The few weeks, war exposed, whatever else it might have achieved, the extent of Pakistan's involvement in propping up the Taliban regime. Although it was well-known but if any proof was needed the thousands of corpses which littered the hills and valleys of Afghanistan were evidence of the disaster that had fallen on the Afghan and Pakistan jehadis. It also marked the collapse of the 20-year old Pakistani Afghanistan policy. The swiftness with which the Islamabad regime took a U-turn and joined the United States war against international terrorism does not in any way absolve the Pakistani establishment for the criminal responsibility for the costly and bloody misadventure. This does, however, mean that there was no genuine change of heart or realization of the folly of their policies, but that Musharraf had to accept the inevitable and there is evidence that he was forced by circumstances but he resisted all the way. First, he wanted Washington to give more time for talks with the Taliban, then he talked of the moderate Taliban replacing Mullah Omar and his cohorts, then he denounced the Northern Alliance as bandits, he wanted the Americans to declare a Ramzan ceasefire and lastly, he pleaded with Washington not to allow the Northern Alliance to enter Kabul.

The rapid collapse of the Taliban came as a surprise to everyone, though no one expected them to have the capability for prolonged resistance. The alacrity with which General Musharraf jettisoned the Taliban was also no less a surprise. Even Pakistani writers have expressed shock both at the speed with which he agreed to the conditions which were imposed upon Pakistan which would have been humiliating to any self-respecting nation. Musharraf was able to control the mob protests launched by the religious parties against the US attacks on Afghanistan and his surrender before Washington. Fearing disaffection in the armed forces Musharraf had taken care to reshuffle the entire top leadership of the army; some among them were those generals without whose support he could not have safely landed from the aircraft which had been refused permission to land at the Karachi airport on 12 October, 1999. The jehadis in Pakistan could not have forgiven him for joining with the United States in destroying the Taliban and the al-Qaida. The world community knew very well the activities of the jehadi groups not only in Kashmir but also within Pakistan. Given the fact that Pakistan was a nuclear power and the danger that some day a mad Mullah may have his finger on the nuclear trigger could not be entirely ruled out. General Musharraf in several well publicized TV and Radio addresses to the nation has promised to curb the jehadi forces; to this end he has banned some of the terrorist groups and arrested among others the top leaders of the two major terrorist organizations Lashkar-e-Toyaba and the Jaish-e-Mohammed. The government's move to ban the display of weapons and the collection of funds for jehad in Kashmir has not made much headway. What is more difficult, even if he has the will to do it, is the necessity to curb and eradicate the links of the Pakistani Army with the Taliban and the al-Qaida. There are still credible reports about the ISI having contacts with the fugitive Taliban and the al-Qaida operatives. Hundreds of the al-Qaida and Taliban cadres and leaders have found sanctuary in the border areas of Pakistan. This could not have been possible without the Pakistani Army turning a blind eye to this movement.

The Taliban have been defeated and Osama bin Laden and the al-Qaida along with Mullah Omar are on the run. A new regime headed by Hamid Karzai has taken over in that country. Yet the war in Afghanistan is not over. There is no gainsaying that the Karzai government is dependent on American protection. This was confirmed after Karzai replaced his Afghan security guards with American army men. It is only symbolic of the precarious situation of the Karzai regime. The warlords have become active again with their internecine wars. The economic support that the war ravaged country sorely needed has still to start coming. The western powers which participated in the demolition of the Taliban have no concrete plans to rebuild the country. The nation building task certainly cannot be undertaken by foreigners. It is suspected that once Washington is done with Osama and Mullah Omar they will withdraw just as they had done after the withdrawal of the Soviet forces in the late eighties. The American attention already appears to be focused on dealing with the Saddam regime in Iraq. Here lies the basic vagueness of the United State's policy of fighting against terrorism.

Terrorism is the product of specific social, political and economic causes; it cannot be eradicated by military means. According to G.H. Jansen terrorism or what is also called militant Islam is the result of the attempt by the national leaders to preserve the status quo of semi-feudalism; it is considered a response to the West's military, economic and cultural onslaught on Islamic societies. Jehadi terrorism has some specific features which are different from the terrorism which is the creation of economic deprivation, ethnic or cultural oppression. Jehadi terrorism is inspired by a particular interpretation and understanding of religion. In the ultimate analysis the roots of jehadi terrorism may also lie in some social, economic and political factors. Most

Muslim countries have a long history of colonial domination and imperialist exploitation. The present international situation intensifies the alienation of the Muslims in many countries, a feeling which is often encouraged by local vested interests about the existence of a system in which there is injustice and oppression of Muslims. The United State's moral and material support to Israel in its fight against the Palestinians, the planned attack on Iraq, the killing of hundreds of innocent Afghans during the relentless bombardment of that country are all perceived as an American/Western/ Christian aggression against Islam. No wonder many people around the world were surprised by the mob sympathy that was seen in many Muslim countries for the Taliban in spite of the horrible human rights record of the regime. These subjective perceptions also lead to demonisation of, for example, Saddam in the West and demonisation of the West in Muslim countries.

The rise of jehadi groups in Pakistan is related to the use of Islam by the Muslim League in the pre-independence period for mobilizing the Muslims for the demand for Pakistan as a separate homeland for the Muslims. After Pakistan came into existence, the Constitution makers could not find a consensus on what political system they wanted. From what Jinnah had said before independence it appeared he wanted a democratic moderate Muslim Pakistan. However, the religious parties clamoured for an Islamic state. Through the ups and downs of the history of Pakistan the religious elements continued to agitate for the Islamisation of the country but they did not succeed. The religious parties had street power, but it could not be translated into electoral strength; there were not many elections in any case in Pakistan. There was a brief interregnum during the military rule of General Zia-ul-Haq in the eighties when the religious parties believed that he might fulfil their dream of an Islamic state. He, however, did not do more than some cosmetic measures of Islamisation like the implementation of the Islamic penalties, Hudood ordinance, Shariat Court benches and public flogging, etc.

There was the constant refrain about Islamic laws, about which Justice Mohammad Muneer had remarked that the common man believes that Pakistan was an Islamic state which it was not. It was only after the Afghanistan imbroglio was declared to be jehad that in the late eighties the Pakistan sponsored terrorist campaign was called a jehad. The Pakistani state had been dinning into the ears of the Pakistani people that the state of Jammu and Kashmir rightfully belonged to it and the country had been unjustly deprived of it and therefore, many people in that country came to believe that it was a just war. Since it was being fought in the name of Islam as it was made out to be a struggle in defence of the Muslims of Kashmir against Hindu India, the jehad was accepted by the people of Pakistan. The evolution of the jehadi groups has been given in the earlier part of this Chapter. The 9/11 attack and the retaliatory action by the United States and sudden collapse of the Taliban which was followed by the action taken by the Pakistan government against the militant outfits in the country had greatly demoralised the fundamentalist forces. However, virulent anti-American sentiments prevailed in the country. The large-scale casualties among the Pakistani Taliban, the flow of Afghan refugees who were victims of the relentless US aerial bombardment also aroused the anger of even those people in Pakistan who were not sympathetic to the Taliban or to al-Qaida. It was the direct result of these developments that the religious parties combine MMA have for the first time in the history of that country been able to win almost 20 percent of the elected seats in the National Assembly in the recently held election. It is also likely that the ISI might have made their contribution to the good showing of the MMA group, but the importance of the other factors cannot be minimized.

It is likely that this time, the MMA parties will be in the government that is going to be formed shortly. None of the MMA parties have experience of government except the short tenure of the Jama'at-i-Islami which was in the civilian government under General Zia in the late seventies; this was not an elected government and the ministers had practically no powers. The new government in which MMA is likely to share power with some other party will only strengthen the fundamentalist forces. Though the MMA Ulema appear to be more sophisticated than the Taliban and many of them speak English, the difference between their social and political views from those of the Taliban is only one of degree. Many of these parties have been involved in attacks on the rights of women and whatever may be their declarations about their commitment to rights of the minorities they would not grant equal rights to non-Muslims. Throughout the history of Islam there has always been a section which stands for a liberal view of Islam and another holding hard line views. Similarly, given the present social, economic and political situation in the country it is difficult to conceive of a time when there will be no jehadi elements in Pakistan whatever may be their strength, number or following.

5

Inter-Services Intelligence:

Pakistan's Long Arm of Proxy-War and Jehad

Maloy Krishna Dhar

The Inter-Services Intelligence (ISI) of Pakistan enjoys a unique status in the infrastructure of the Pakistani establishment. It is not an ordinary intelligence apparatus of the state. Over the years it has assumed the singularity of a 'state within the state' discharging three important tasks: controlling the internal civil and political affairs in Pakistan, promoting multinational Islamist jehadist movements in tandem with organisations like the al-Qaida-al-Sulbah and attending to the most strategic task of destabilising India by waging proxy-war and by exporting jehadist movement.

The story of the ISI can be better understood against the background of its collaboration with the CIA, French SDECE/DGSE and Saudi Intelligence during the Cold War bonhomie and Afghan imbroglio. The canvas of study is very vast and the ingredients are interconnected with the evolution of global Islamist terrorism, which is now spearheaded by al-Qaida-al-Sulbah and its supremo

Osama bin Laden. However, from the Indian point of view understanding the ISI would require a quick glancing over the events triggered off by the direct attack on the USA on 11 September, 2001, and the attack on the Indian Parliament on 13 December, 2001, and its intricate connectivity with the al-Qaida. For reasons of brevity the intricate connectivity between the CIA and the ISI is being kept outside the scope of this study.

Some strategic thinkers and political leaders claim that 11 September, 2001, has changed the history of the world. Some Western *pundits* have even claimed that the Islamist terrorists had initiated a global war against democracy and secularism by attacking the very heartland of the modern world order. Exaggeration apart, there is no doubt that with the synchronised attack on the targets in New York and Washington, which symbolise the seat of the only surviving superpower of the post-Cold War era, the Islamist forces have shifted the centre of gravity of the 'civilisational war' into the inner core of the symbol of the new world order, which is arrogant, jingoistic and intolerant.

Some analysts have even gone to the extent of comparing the al-Qaida attack on the US with the cataclysmic events like the First and the Second World Wars. However, they do not speak so loudly about the geo-political changes architectured by the Islamist terrorists by attacking the symbol of the second largest secular democracy in the world, India. 13 December, 2001, is as important as 11 September, inasfar as the multinational Islamist attacks on the regional and global targets are concerned. If the al-Qaida attack on the US targets on 11 September, was a challenge to the 'western power', the dastardly ISI engineered attack on the Indian Parliament on 13 December, was a calculated assault on the only true secular democracy between Rome and Tokyo, which has managed to survive the vicissitudes of the historic changes that have taken place between the collapse of the post-industrial revolution colonial powers and the Soviet bloc.

Indeed, the so called 'reformist' Islamist forces have initiated a new war against the existing world order. Globally it is directed against the Christians and the Zionists and the most important regional targets are Hindus, predominantly Christian Philippines, and the Muslim dominated constituents of the Russian Federation. To the neo-Islamic reformists 'reform' means pushing back Islam to the 7th century, when it was directly piloted by the Prophet (pbuh). These forces are firm believers in the resurrection of Islam in its purest form and re-building the hubs of Islam, which were established between the eighth and fifteenth centuries: the African hub, the Middle Eastern cradle, the Sub-continental hub, the South East Asian hub and the Central Asian hub. Islamist protagonists like Osama bin Laden, who prefers to imitate the symbols of the Prophet (pbuh), do believe that Islamic hubs can be stretched into the heartland of Europe, a task that could not be completed by the early warriors of Islam. He believes in the revival of the Caliphate.

The collapse of the communist monolith has created a Unipolar World Order that does not brook challenge from any other 'ideological and civilisational force'. This neo-imperialism and the collapse of the Soviet bloc have, however, given rise to an emerging world force with incalculable potentiality, the force of purist Islam. The ideological resurgence of this force is yet to be fortified by the concurrent emergence of an invincible singular state-power backed by superior military machine. The emerging force is yet to break the barrier of nationalities, ethnicities and cultural diversities. Yet, it thinks that religion is the most potent force to forge the unified field of nationhood, cutting across the barriers of the continents and seas.

This new force has taken upon itself a new strategy of war, the War of World-wide Organised Terror against the *jahiliya* (non-believer) forces. Such wars, the Islamist protagonists believe, would weaken the enemies of the Faith and re-establish the common bondages in the Ummah leading to the restoration of the glory of Islam. These neo-Islamist forces have made their presence felt in Washington, Algiers, Cairo, Riyadh, Kabul, Manila, Grozni, Delhi, Dushanbe, Bishkek and Urumqi, etc. That the world, dominated as it is by the United States of America, the only superpower, waking up to the reality of a conflict situation with the Islamist jehadist is a passage from history in the making.

The West, basically defined as the US and its strategic allies, politico-economic partners and security collaborators, is not new to the threats from terrorist outfits of different hues. The ideologically fired urban terrorists, narco-terrorists and terrorists born out of social frustration etc., had ravaged urban Europe for over two decades between 1960 and 1975. But the threat from Islamist jehadists spearheaded by al-Qaida, the prime multinational terrorist group of the twentyfirst century...confronts the world with a new kind of threat (*Inside Al Qaida*-Rohan Gunaratna). It has transformed the weapon of 'terror' as an instrument of protest to a global war-machine with a view to restore the glory of Islam by humbling the 'corrupting civilisational forces of the West and its surrogates'. Ironically enough the CIA had provided both the ISI and the al-Qaida with the 'ideological, technical and financial sinews' of the new global war in its bid to humble the Soviet Bloc.

While the ISI was conceptualised as a routine intelligence gathering and coordinating body of the Pakistani Armed Forces the al-Qaida-al-Sulbah (The Solid Base) was conceptualised by Abdullah Azzam, a Palestinian-Jordanian ideologue and Islamic scholar, way back in 1987 as a tool of spreading worldwide jehad. He had defined the philosophy of floating the organisation in the following words: "Every principle needs a vanguard to carry it forward and, focussing its way into society, puts up with heavy tasks and enormous sacrifices.... There is no ideology, neither earthly nor heavenly, that does not require such a vanguard that gives everything it possesses in order to achieve victory for this ideology. It carries the flag all along the sheer, endless and difficult path until it reaches its destination in the reality of life, since Allah has destined that it should make it and manifest itself. The vanguard constitutes Al-Qa'idah al-Sulbah for the expected society'. (*Al Jehad*, April 1988, a principal journal of the Afghan Arabs).

The al-Qaida was born out of an ideological compulsion. The ISI, however, gathered the moss of ideology when the agency was pitted against Pakistan's strategic and ideological enemy, India, and later the common global enemies, the Zionists and the Christians.

After the momentous events of the Iranian revolution and the Russian intervention in Afghanistan, the Islamist movements manifested with renewed vigour in the Middle East, South East Asia, Africa, the Caucasus, the Balkans and in parts of Western Europe. The al-Qaida symbolised the global Islamist thrust. Its collaboration with the ISI, which had an established track record of carrying out sabotage, subversion and proxy-war against India had endowed it with a broad-spectrum ally in spreading jehadist terror.

Azzam and Osama bin Laden co-founded Maktab al Khidmat lil Mujahidin al-Arab (MAK- Afghan Service Bureau) in Peshawar way back in 1984. The al-Qaida operated hand in glove with the US and its allied forces under cover of the MAK. Even before 1989 the MAK infrastructure was converted to the al-Qaida building blocks and the trained Arab and other mercenary forces along with the ISI trained Islamist Mujahidin were deputed to several hubs of conflict between the Islamist and *jahiliya* forces: Kashmir, Bosnia-Horzegovina, Chechnya, Mindanao, Tajikistan, Uzbekistan, Somalia, Indonesia, Georgia, Nagarno-Karabakh, Azerbaijan, Yemen, Algeria and Egypt.

The Islamist jehadists were transformed into 'Islamist Rapid Strike Forces' (IRSF) under the very nose of the CIA and the ISI. While Azzam provided the theological and ideological fundamentals of the al-Qaida, the arrival of another Egyptian in Osama's life, Ayman Muhammad Rabi'al-Zawahiri of Al-Azhar mosque, finally turned the Arab millionaire to a 'global Islamist terrorist' from a CIA-ISI moulded Mujahidin.

While the intelligence machineries of the USA, France, West Germany, Pakistan, Saudi Arabia and Sudan etc., played along the 'inherent ambitions' of Osama bin Laden, the Inter-Services Intelligence (ISI) of Pakistan protected and promoted its strategic and tactical linkages with the global terror-mastermind, till after 11 September, 2001, when the Pakistani establishment was left with only two options: either to align with the USA or to face its military wrath.

In a way, the al-Qaida strike against the USA is something like a 'blowback' of CIA's Afghan episode as the Iranian revolution was another earth shaking 'blowback' of CIA engineered assassination of Muhammad Mussadegh and installation of the corrupt Pehlvi regime. That historical experiment by the CIA had finally ended up in Ayatollah Khomeini's Islamic revolution. Blowback, in CIA lingo, is adverse fall-out of covert politico-terrorist action carried out by the agency at the behest of the White House.

The Inter-Services Intelligence played dual roles in propping up the al-Qaida. It helped the Arabs to get closer to the Pakistan trained Talibans and it provided the jehadist cadres with strategic and tactical support to fight Islamist war in theatres outside Afghanistan. Direct ISI and al-Qaida collaboration in Kashmir came to notice after Brigade 055 of Oşama had succeeded in humbling the Northern Alliance and he was considerably free to pay attention to the 'oppressed Kashmiri brethren'. Pakistan, like the USA, has been an important promoter and collaborator of the al-Qaida.

Only a few months before the 9 /11 attack General Pervez Musharaf said in an interview, " The Western demonisation of OBL (Osama bin Laden), as he is known in Pakistan, made him a cult figure among Muslims who resent everything from the decline in moral values... America's lack of support for Palestinians being killed by Israeli occupation forces, to what Russia is doing to Muslims in Chechnya, what the West did to Muslims in Bosnia and Kosovo, India's oppression of Muslims in Kashmir...It is a long list of complaints that has generated a strong persecution complex that the OBL cult figure has come to embody. He is a hero figure on the pedestal of Muslim extremism" (Arnaud de Borchgrave-interview in *The Washington Times,* 21 March, 2000).

However, Pakistani collaboration with Osama was halted, albeit temporarily, after the US intervention in Afghanistan. Musharaf and his generals were left with very little option but to re-tie the not so ancient knot with the USA and its intelligence machineries.

Even Musharaf had found it difficult to rein in the ISI, which continued to maintain linkages with the Taliban and al-Qaida leaders. The Indian intelligence fraternity had finally convinced the USA that the ISI chief was involved in transfer of funds to the 11 September strikers. That is what ultimately forced Musharaf to sack Lt. Gen. Mahmood Ahmed and replace him by Lt.Gen. Ehsan-ul-Haq on 8 October, 2001. It is worthwhile to mention that Mahmood Ahmed and three other Corps Commanders had forcefully opposed Musharaf's decision to collaborate with the USA.

Ehsan-ul-Haq, a Corps Commander at Peshawar, was well connected with the Mujahidin and al-Qaida forces. He was required to maintain direct linkages with the

Kandhar hubs of the Taliban and al-Qaida. As a former Counsellor to the Pakistani High Commission in New Delhi, he was well informed too about the Indian fault lines and ISI's exploitation of the same. With the appointment of Haq Pakistan sent a friendly message to the USA. But very little changes were carried out on the Indian front, even though the USA had visibly but hesitatingly advised Pakistan to lessen and limit its involvement in Jammu and Kashmir.

On the contrary, India was presented with a devastating blow on the very edifice of its secular democracy on 13/12 at the Parliament building. The perpetrators of the heinous crime derived full support from the Inter-Services Intelligence of Pakistan. India was again at war with Pakistan, an integrated strategic ally of the USA, today and perhaps in years to come.

9/11 might have had challenged the strategic and economic world vision of the only surviving superpower and reasserted the world vision of the Islamist groups, who still envision the feasibility of re-establishment of the Caliphate and re-energisation of the Islamic power-hubs in Asia, Africa and Europe.

But 13/12 has left no doubt in the Indian mind that the Pakistani establishment and its 'third estate' the ISI were no less inspired than the al-Qaida was, to regain for Islam the Indian hub that was lost to the Christian British and later to 'Hindu Bharat'. The killing spree of the ISI in Kashmir and the tragic 9/11 again proved that innocent human lives were of no consequence to the Islamist terrorists. It was also not a consideration when the founding fathers of Pakistan had initiated the infamous 'Direct Action'. Following the same tradition the ISI produced another glaring proof on 13/12 that India was not only vulnerable to proxy-war, which was being waged since 1958, but it was also vulnerable to Hamas and al-Qaida type fidayeen strikes deep inside the civil society and its legal and constitutional edifices.

The al-Qaida is rather a new Islamist force that was born in the cauldron of the Cold War and post-1979 Islamist resurgence. It was another 'blowback' of misconceived US covert operations. The Inter-Services Intelligence, on the other hand, is as old as the CIA is and has mastered the tradecraft of sabotage, subversion, direct military intervention and proxy war to a degree of perfection, as has been achieved by its mirror-brother-in-trade, the CIA. The inter-linkages of covert intelligence and sabotage and subversion operations between the CIA, al-Qaida and the ISI is required to be understood in the context of America's strategic move to turn Afghanistan into Moscow's Vietnam, resurgence of Islamist jehadists and historical abidance of the ISI to the state policy of Pakistan to destabilise India and infuse Islamist fervour and militancy in the second largest secular democracy. Pakistan's direct, proxy and covert wars, according to Pakistani scholars like Dr. Aziz are continuations of the Islamic quest to convert the Indian *Dar-ul-Kafir* to *Dar-ul-Islam*.

It is, therefore, necessary to understand the Inter-Services Intelligence of Pakistan (ISI) before proceeding further to examine the likely impacts of post- 9/11 and 13/12 terrorist actions and Islamist jehad being waged in other parts of the world.

Intelligence establishments are integral parts of nation states. The totalitarian and hegemonistic states, religious ideological and military, use intelligence apparatuses as an extended arm of repression and internal and external state policy, with a view to securing its power bases and destabilising its real and perceived adversaries at home and abroad.

The saga of the intelligence establishments of the former Soviet Union (KGB, GRU), China (Ministry of State Security-Guojia Anquan Bu, 8341 Unit-Central Security Regiment-Second Department) Hitler's Germany (Gestapo) and the Iranian SAVAK, Vezarat-e-Ettella va Amniat-e-Keshvar – VEVAK and Pasdaran-e-Inquilab etc., have been extensively chronicled by the security and intelligence watchers. The exploits of the CIA are replete with innumerable examples of American use of the intelligence apparatus as an extension of its foreign policy almost all over the world. Some murky incidents like the assassination of Allende, Lumumba and Mussadegh have left indelible black spots on the political history of the champion of democracy.

Strong states as well as weak states often use intelligence establishments for securing their respective home bases as well as for adding unorthodox booster to their foreign policies. The use of the political police by regimes ranging from the anachronistic African states to the so-called ideological-revolutionary states form a different saga of blatant human rights violation by the ruling factions.

India and Pakistan inherited a somewhat well-defined administrative and intelligence establishment from the British Empire. The Central Intelligence Bureau, which was predominantly staffed by the whites and trusted Muslim officers, was divided between the two new nations. Ghulam Mohammad, the senior non-white officer of the CIB had taken over the Pakistani part of the Intelligence Bureau (PIB). The Indian Intelligence Bureau, pathetically understaffed and inadequate to the requirements of the internal and external challenges was for all practical purposes, fashioned by an enigmatic personality, Bhola Nath Mallick. As far as building of the edifices and resource bases are concerned he was to the Indian IB what Lt.Gen. Ghulam Jillani Khan was to the ISI.

Inducted to the ISI as a two-star brigadier (a former military attaché in Washington), Jillani had survived the regimes of Yahya Khan, Zulfiqar Ali Bhutto and General Zia-ul-Haq till Lt. Gen. Akhtar Abdur Rahman replaced him. Jillani had fashioned the ISI as the 'third estate' of Pakistan, the first two being the armed forces and the bureaucracy. According to some terse comments by Pakistani journalists the political establishment was rated as the 'fourth estate' and the press-media as the 'fifth estate', which were often made to play surrogate to the 'third estate'.

The political establishment of Pakistan, the 'first estate' in a secular democratic country, as envisaged by the Qaid-e-Azam Mohammad Ali Jinnah was hijacked by the military and bureaucratic establishments headed by the civilian and army duo Ghulam Mohammad and Iskandar Mirza. They relegated the political establishment to the position of 'third estate'. General Ayub Khan's coup in 1958 transformed the political history of Pakistan for all time to come. The armed forces were foisted permanently on a nation, whose democratic aspirations were jackbooted by them.

Some scholars have averred that the Inter-Services Intelligence, as a second hub of intelligence apparatus, was conceived after the alleged failure of the PIB to cater appropriate intelligence about the Indian Army's deployment and political determination of the Indian leaders to pit the entire nation against Pakistani aggression in Kashmir in 1948. Such assumptions do not reflect the truth.

Jinnah was, by and large, a British-bred democrat and he relied on the British iron-frame that he shared with his friend turned foe, Jawaharlal Nehru. His passion for Kashmir was not simply based on religious affinity of the majority of the people. His calculations were based on strategic inputs that he had received from his British mentors and the bureaucracy that he had inherited. On the other hand, Nehru's passion for Kashmir was emotional and the Indian National Congress had never adopted a strategic and geo-political approach towards Kashmir, a Muslim majority state ruled by an unstable Hindu king. Nehru had put all his eggs in the Abdullah basket and had not taken into consideration that geo-politically Kashmir was going to play an important role in the post-Transfer of Power and Cold War era and it was necessary for the Indian National Congress to cultivate the indecisive and misguided king. He did not pay adequate political and strategic attention to the Gilgit Agency and the Northern Territories of the Kingdom of Kashmir. These strategic areas were gobbled up by Pakistan, under British advice even before the 1948 war.

Jinnah had utilised his existing intelligence machineries to mobilise, train, arm and deploy the so-called tribal volunteers. The Pakistan IB and the rudimentary elements of the Military Intelligence had played their cards well. On the other hand, the Indian intelligence had fumbled and had failed to warn and motivate the political leadership about the necessity of augmented military preparations against the well-planned Pakistani thrust in Kashmir—the entire Kashmir, inclusive of the Northern Territories and Gilgit Agency.

Jinnah would have not initiated any action to let down Ghulam Mohammad, the first Director of the PIB. Mohammad had done a better job than his Indian counterpart. Jinnah and his political establishment were aware of the need for strengthening the armed forces and its intelligence prowess. He and his political successors did not intend to weaken the PIB by floating the ISI and fashion it after the CIA, which was created in 1947. The initial political liberal democrats would not have liked the idea of endowing the bureaucracy and the military establishment with hegemonistic powers at the cost of political freedom that was earned by the Muslims of the sub-continent over mountains of dead bodies and rivulets of human blood.

The Inter-Services Intelligence Directorate was conceived, way back in 1948, as a nucleus inter-services co-ordination module, by Major General R. Cawthorne, a British Army officer, who had opted for the Pakistan Army on the eve of Transfer of Power, and served as the Deputy Chief of Staff of the new state. The Kashmir war episode had inspired a section of the Army officers that the political leaders had mishandled the operation, did not fully support the Kashmir war commander (Gen. Akbar) and did not commit the Punjab Boundary Force under Maj. Gen. Rees to the Kashmir war efforts. The disparate units of the Pakistan Army, active strength 30,000 odd, did not give good accounts of co-ordination, planned offensive and superior logistical supplies. But for the logistical difficulties faced by Delhi and political vacillation and miscalculation, the so-called Azad Kashmir Forces would have been cleared out from the entire Kashmir Valley in just another 30 days. But India under Nehru fumbled and stumbled at the doors of the UN, instead of allowing the army to reoccupy Muzaffarabad.

The Kashmir war debacle and lack of co-ordination between the army units on the one hand and the political leadership on the other had prompted military brains like General Rees and Major General Cawthorne to conceptualise the Inter-Services Intelligence as a pivotal force to cater to military requirements, long term strategic planning, inter-agency co-ordination, grooming and training of military attaches posted to Pakistani diplomatic missions and to establish a working relationship with friendly foreign military intelligence agencies, etc. Inspiration for the structural format was drawn from the M15 and M16, the prime British intelligence organisation formed way back in 1909, at the behest of the Committee of Imperial Defence. It is said that an operative of M16 had also pitched in support for Cawthorne, as the dying Empire still longed for strategic geo-political control on the sub-continent, Afghanistan, Tibet region of China and the Soviet Republics in Central Asia.

The father figure of the ISI was Lt. General Ghulam Jillani Khan, who fashioned the outfit as a virulent fighting machine against Pakistan's arch enemy, India, and other geo-political adversaries. Following is the line up of leadership of the ISI from the period democracy was hijacked by the armed forces:

1. Brig. Riazat Hussain	1958 onwards
2. Lt.Gen. Ghulam Jillani Khan	1969 to early years of Zia-ul-Haq
3. Lt.Gen. Akhtar Abdur Rahman	Zia regime till March 1987
4. Lt.Gen. Hamid Gul	March '87-May 1989
5. Lt.Gen. (Retd) Shamsur Rahman Kallue	May'89-August1990
6. Maj. General Assad Durrani	Aug '90-March 1992
7. Lt.Gen. Javed Nasir	March'92- May 1993
8. Lt.Gen. Javed Ashraf Kazi	May'93-June 1994
9. Lt.Gen. Nasim Raja	June'94-1996
10. Lt.Gen. Ziauddin	1996 - sacked by Musharaf in 1999. His retirement benefits were reportedly denied.
11. Lt.Gen. Mahmood Ahmad	Dismissed by Musharaf under American pressure for alleged complicity with the Taliban. India, it is reported, had supplied supporting material to the USA.
12. Lt. Gen Ehsan-ul- Haq	8 October, 2001. He was the Corps Commander at Peshawar. He was formerly posted to the Pakistan High Commission in Delhi in the rank of Counsellor.

Like most other military controlled intelligence organisations the ISI did not prefer staffing its corps of officers and operatives from amongst the civilians. A few civilians inducted at the initial stages to man the desk jobs were eased out in 1956 after Ghulam Mohammad and Iskandar Mirza initiated the process of combined military and bureaucratic stranglehold on Pakistan. The present estimated strength of the ISI, about 18,000 is mostly drawn from the Army, Air Force and Navy, with a minor sprinkling of civilians.

Following are the broad divisions of the functional structure of the ISI:

1. Joint Counter-Intelligence Bureau (JCIB)	Responsible for Counter-Intelligence activities and operations.
2. Joint Intelligence Signal Bureau (JISB)	Generates and denies Signal Intelligence and liaises with the Signal Corps of the Armed Forces.
3. Joint Intelligence Bureau (JIB)	It handles political matters. A section is assigned to study and assess Indian political developments.
4. Joint Intelligence Finance (JIF)	It manages budgetary and non-budgetary funds of the ISI, evaluates and approves critical operations.
5. Joint Intelligence Technical (JIT)	It is responsible for technical, including ElInt, PhotoInt, ImageInt, SatInt, etc.
6. Joint Arms Direction Group (JADG)	This wing is responsible for planning co-ordination in exercises and in procurement of weapons from unconventional sources, besides periodical evaluation of joint exercises.

7. Joint Intelligence Miscellaneous (JIM)	It oversees forward intelligence tasks, sabotage and subversion operations in foreign countries. Three sections are devoted to India.
8. Joint Intelligence North (JIN)	It is the hub of operations in Kashmir and other "special operations" inside India.
9. Foreign Liaison Section (FLS)	Responsible for liaison with friendly foreign intelligence services.
10. Inter Services Federal Intelligence (ISFI)	It supplements the intelligence efforts of the provincial governments and often works as the direct arm of the political/military bosses in internal political matters.
11. Public and Service Groups (P&SG)	It functions in close liaison with the Joint Chiefs of Staff Committee and maintains media liaison. The post-holder is generally close to the Chief of the Army Staff and the top executive. The position holder is handpicked.
12. Joint Intelligence X	Its exact functional charter is not known. It is said that this wing is responsible for Intelligence Estimate, Threat Assessment and Formulation of Highly Sensitive Operations, including Assassination, in collaboration with the JIB, JIM, JIN and ISFI.

The Joint Intelligence Finance manages the central command of the ISI and its personnel policies. Besides managing the human and asset resources almost all the top intelligence and dirty-tricks operations are evaluated and cleared by the JIF. There are reliable inputs that this wing of the ISI also manages like the Drug Money, and operates several frontal financial organisations inside Pakistan and in some foreign countries like Bangladesh, UAE, Kuwait and Nepal, etc.

Inter-Services Federal Intelligence, though officially responsible for inter-services co-ordination, is known to have been used extensively for internal intelligence, especially in suppressing political rivals, in tandem with the Joint Intelligence Bureau.

Joint Intelligence Miscellaneous mainly looks after forward external intelligence in targeted countries. It is concerned with forward intelligence thrust inside India, infiltration of trained agents, terrorists and Islamist jehadis inside India. It also supervises some assigned operations from third country bases in conjunction with the JIX and JIN.

The JIN is especially responsible for all operational responsibilities in Jammu and Kashmir, starting from recruitment of the terrorists, their training, arming and infiltration in the target areas. The Special Services Group (SSG), a US/UK trained commando force, expert in high altitude warfare, pitches in with the ISI in these fields of operations. The JIN is also responsible for floating and sustaining fundamentalist jehadist organisations, which front the ISI in its clandestine proxy-war activities. Brigadier Abdullah, in charge of JIN operations in Kashmir, was, at one point of time, shifted to Muzaffarabad for augmenting the so-called Mujahideen thrust inside Indian Kashmir. After 9/11 and 13/12 Pakistan claimed that Brig. Abdullah was withdrawn from Muzaffarabad. This hollow gesture was aimed at misleading the USA, which had advised Pakistan to tone down its interference in Indian administered Kashmir. President Musharaf has done very little to slow down the activities of the JIN and its army of Mujahidin, Taliban and al-Qaida collaborators. Recent reports indicate that the J/N has inducted the services of about 5o former Taliban and al-Qaida jehadists for carrying out mindless killing of innocent civilians. Reports also indicate that it has doubled the daily allowances of the jehadists and has revamped and reconstructed the training camps in POK, Punjab and the areas of Gilgit Agency, adjacent to J&K border.

Both the JIM and the JIN, it is reported by knowledgeable sources, had established strategic linkages with the Islamist terrorist/Mujahidin groups, including Mujahidins from the al-Qaida ranks with a view to striking deep inside India. The hijacking of IC 814, attack on the Red Fort and attack on the Indian Parliament, it is reported, was masterminded by the JIM, in tandem with the terrorists of the Jaish-e-Muhammad, Hijb-ul-Mujaheedin and Lashkar-e-Toyaba, whose ranks were trained by the al-Qaida in eastern Afghanistan camps. It is now confirmed that Osama bin Laden was in constant touch with the IC 814 hijackers once they landed at Kandhar.

The Joint Intelligence Signals, located at Malir cantonment, Karachi, is responsible for interception and analysis of signal intelligence and breaking of codes. It also supplies the ISI operatives in India and other foreign countries with low to high-grade cipher materials.

The Joint Intelligence Signals had assumed greater responsibilities as the Cold War ally of the USA. Being a member of the SEATO and CENTO Pakistan had received sophisticated monitoring equipments and listening devices. Besides offering operational platforms to the USA, Pakistan was helped by the Central Intelligence Agency (CIA), Defence Intelligence Agency (DIA), U.S Army Signal Centre at Fort Gordon and National Imagery and Mapping Agency (NIMA) etc., to strengthen its signal intelligence prowess.

It is reported that the JIS has its listening and observation posts at Peshawar, Parachir, Bada Bier, Karachi, Quetta, Lahore, Hyderabad, Thatta, Gwadar, Qila Ladgast, Gilgit, Skardu, Chitral and Manshera, etc. Besides operating radio signals, some of these units are equipped with sophisticated equipments to monitor the footprints of Indian satellite communications and monitoring other Electronic intelligence operations originated by India, Iran, and the former USSR republics in Central Asia. The satellite imagery capabilities of Pakistan have recently received sophisticated equipments from China and the USA. Some French equipment has also been acquired during the last two years. The Cold War supplies of US equipments for monitoring SigInt and ElInt from the former Soviet Union and China are still in place and some of these equipments have recently been replenished as part of the package of US forays in Afghanistan. The Joint Intelligence Signals was supplied with super-fast computers and software to break and read the cipher traffic of the Soviet Union and China. In the recent past it has received from the USA digital analysers for code breaking. That is how the ISI enjoys an edge over its Indian counterparts.

The Joint Intelligence Bureau is theoretically responsible for monitoring developments in neighbouring countries, affairs of Pakistan's military attaches posted in missions abroad and activities of guest military attaches on home turf. The JIB also acts as the political wing of the ISI. Several Directors of the ISI have deftly manipulated the internal political events in Pakistan. Notable amongst them are Lt. Gen. Ghulam Jillani Khan, Lt. Gen. Hamid Gul, Lt. Gen. Javed Nasir and Lt. Gen Ziauddin. Pakistan's political history is replete with military coups and installation of puppet civilian governments.

A section of the foreign media reported that Pervez Musharaf had recently abolished the JIB. A spokesman of the military regime promptly denied this. In fact, General Musharaf has adopted certain diversionary tactics and operational camouflages to cover up the activities of the JIB. This mild course correction was necessitated by recent Pakistani bonhomie with the USA and its free-world allies. President Musharaf is a defter manipulator than his predecessors in uniform. His deemed actions against the jehadists are aimed at consolidating his grip on the armed forces and the 'street warriors of Pakistan'.

The internal political operations of the ISI transcended the defined intelligence parameters assigned to the PIB. More than a quarter century of military dictatorship had empowered the ISI to work as the 'third estate' of the establishment. On several occasions it abrogated the role of the 'second estate' as well, pushing the bureaucracy to the third position.

The ISI's involvement in internal political matters has been well documented by several Pakistani and foreign authors. Some of the interesting reading material has been recorded by John Kaniyalil, *The Master Manipulator;* Brig. Tirmazi, *Profiles of Intelligence;* Lt.Gen. Gul Hassan, *Memoirs;* Zulfikar Ali Bhutto, *If I Am Assassinated*; Benazir Bhutto, *Daughter of the East,* etc. The list is fairly long.

Democracy eclipsed in Pakistan with the assassination of Liaquat Ali Khan. The later democratic totems were hated for their inefficiency and also for being Bengalis. The Punjabi triumvirate of Ghulam Mohammad, Choudhri Mohammad Ali and Iskandar Mirza (had Bengali blood in him) had started involving the ISI in internal political manipulation, as they did not have sufficient faith on the overly policed staffed PIB. This trend was capitalised on extensively by President Ayub Khan. He was the first Pakistani leader to involve the ISI with the ethnic insurgencies in North East India. Former president Iskandar Mirza in an interview admitted this fact to the Pakistani High Commissioner in London, (*Memoirs of Gul Hassan*). Ayub Khan was the first president to set up a review commission on the functioning of the intelligence outfits of Pakistan mainly with a view to tighten his stranglehold on the establishment.

Its not that Pakistan is the only country that uses intelligence machineries for political purposes. Established democracies like the USA and UK apart, developing democratic countries like India too have used their internal and external intelligence organs to protect and promote the political interests of the ruling parties. Any conscientious Indian intelligence officer has not yet candidly revealed such uses of the R& AW, the IB, the

CBI and other enforcement agencies by the political leadership against their adversaries.

But the use of the ISI infrastructure both by the elected governments and the military dictators right from Ayub Khan to Musharaf, with brief interludes of the Bhuttos and Nawaz Sharif, is a mirror reflection of the use of the apparatus and *apparatchiks* of the intelligence and political police by regimes headed by Hitler, Stalin, Mao, Nixon and to similar extent by leaders like Mobutu and Mugabe.

The Pakistani leaders have freely used the intelligence organisations, both the PIB and the ISI, for suppressing internal political dissent. In this regard there is hardly any difference between Z. A. Bhutto and his blue-eyed-boy turned assassin Zia-ul-Haq. In fact. Bhutto was responsible for strengthening the ISI and using it against his political adversaries. After the 1971 war, Bhutto had the option of clipping the wings of the ISI. He did not. Such aberrations happen with solar-regularity, as both India and Pakistan refuse to rein in the intelligence organisations by adopting structural and regulatory Acts and making them responsible and accountable to the representatives of the people and the Constitution of the country (whatever constitution Pakistan may adopt from time to time).

As the early blossoms of democracy in Pakistan withered away and the civil servant/army coterie hijacked the fledgling nation, Major General Iskandar Mirza had started nursing and nurturing the ISI as an instrument of governance. The extra-constitutional rulers urgently needed an extra-legal instrument to perpetuate their stranglehold and to carry out a different kind of war against its umbilical enemy, India, more virulently than the descendants of Ishmael are fighting against the descendants of brother Isaac.

With General Ayub Khan usurping the reins of power in 1958, the ISI received a fresh shot in the arm. Needless to mention that officers from the Army-the strongest wing of the armed forces, the second pillar of the Pakistani establishment, have always headed the ISI.

The Pakistani rulers have had the pleasure and compulsion of contributing to the growth of the Inter-Services Intelligence. Field Marshal Ayub Khan, General Yahya Khan, Zulfiqar Ali Bhutto, General Zia-ul-Haq, Benazir Bhutto, Nawaz Sharif and Pervez Musharaf used the ISI for unleashing proxy-war and sustained sabotage and subversion campaign against India. Zulfikar Ali Bhutto's use of the ISI to crush the Baluch rebellion is no less a gory chapter than the genocide in former East Pakistan.

Contrary to speculations that General Zia-ul-Haq was the mastermind behind honing and sharpening the dirty operational edges of the ISI, it was Pakistan's man of destiny, Zulfikar Ali Bhutto, who had strengthened the military dominated intelligence outfit and legalised its involvement in domestic politics. Bhutto had manipulated the ISI to produce intelligence that had convinced Ayub Khan that Nehru's death and Lal Bahadur Shashtri's tenuous rule offered the best opportunity to invade Kashmir. Pakistani historians and military strategists now recognise the fact that Bhutto had forced the war on Ayub Khan. His manipulation of Lt. General Ghulam Jillani

Khan, Director General ISI, and a few other Generals around Yahya Khan before and during the Bangladesh war, formed part of a cynical conspiracy, leading to Pakistan's break up. It was Bhutto who manipulated the post-71 Pakistan Army to his advantage and upgraded the rank of the ISI chief to three-star Lieutenant General. General Jillani later survived the judicial hanging of his Sindhi benefactor and continued to enjoy Zia's patronage.

Russian involvement in Afghanistan in 1979 had changed the old geo-political equations. Involvement of the US, China and Islamic countries in the new killing fields of Afghanistan had tempted General Zia to involve the ISI as a shadow extension of Pakistan's regular forces in the Afghan imbroglio. He had, in fact, remodelled the ISI to a CIA style organisation, adding to its sinister arsenal the unbridled power to interfere in internal affairs, including affairs of his political and military opponents. Legal murder of Bhutto is a testimony to the sinister capabilities of the ISI, nursed so carefully by the slain Premier himself. Having turned Pakistan into a theocratic state Zia also encouraged the madrasas and tanjims to collaborate with the ISI for breeding and supplying jehadis to the killing fields of Afghanistan and to the new war theatre in Kashmir. The ISI was made to infuse in its ranks more fundamentalist adherents to Zia-brand Islam. Zia had encouraged the ISI operatives and the 'deeni tanjims' to break the barrier between the state controlled and privately organised machines for manufacturing jehadists. His regime was responsible for establishment of direct liaison between Osama and his Arab legion and the ISI and its jehadist 'street warriors.'

From Bhutto and Zia there was no looking back for the most important pillar of the Pakistani establishment. The ISI had turned into a pseudo-political entity under Zia and absence of political parties and democratic process and the Russian presence in Afghanistan had conferred upon it a halo of invincibility. The US and China winked at the growth of the ISI and abetted its growth as an instrument for shifting the tectonic plate of Islamic jehadist movement from the Arab world to the fertile soils of Pakistan, where sub-continental moderate Islam was being replaced by orthodox Sunni Wahabism.

For a brief period Benazir Bhutto and General Hamid Gul, the ISI chief, had differed on the Afghan issue. It was Gul, who had cobbled up the Islami Jamhoori Ittehad (IJI), a coalition of parties, which later replaced Benazir. An expert in the tradecraft of clandestine arming and training of Mujahideen, General Gul had not only masterminded the ISI's Afghan saga, he had also helped the military regime to fashion its strategic thrust in the Indian Punjab and Jammu and Kashmir. The ISI, under him, had replicated the rogue CIA.

Benazir, however, after her electoral victory sacked Hamid Gul and inducted Lt.Gen (retd) Shamshur Rahman Kallue. This had infuriated the Army establishment, as the top brass wanted to install a serving ally. An alarm was sounded that Benazir was sure to curtail the ISI's internal political clout, as the PPP had suffered immensely during the Zia regime, including judicial hanging of her father. She had made an effort, through the Zulfiqar Committee, to curtail the ISI's sphere of influence.

Following her contrived dismissal, Maj. General Asad Durrani was appointed chief of the ISI, who served the tenure of the IJI government, a creation of the infamous intelligence organisation and Army. He was followed by Lt.Gen. Javed Nasir and later succeeded by Lt.Gen. Javed Ashraf Kazi, following the dismissal of Nawaz Sharif.

With the induction of General Nasir, an officer of the Corps of Engineers, the ISI was again embroiled in internal politics and export of terrorism. An Islamic fundamentalist, a member of the Jammat-e-Islam and Tabligh-i-Jammat, the proselytising fraternity, and a Kashmiri to top it all, Gen. Nasir thrived on anti-Indian brine. He brought in qualitative changes in the ISI's involvement with the Punjab and J&K terrorists and finalised the blueprint of escalation of Islamist jehad, in the fashion of the al-Qaida, amongst the vulnerable sections of the Indian Muslims.

His tenure coincided with Benazir's second incarnation, during which, state sponsored terrorism had not only affected Afghanistan and India, it brought an adverse impact on the Pak-US and Pak-China relations too. Besides prolonged cross-border terrorism in India, involvement of Pak trained Mujahideen of Harkat-ul-Ansar, Harkat-ul-Mujaheedin and Lashkar-e-Taiba etc., outfits in Bosnia, Chechnya, Dagestan, Kazakhstan, Algeria, Saudi Arabia, southern Thailand, Myanmar, the Philippines, Xinjiang province of China and even on the US soil had peaked by 1992 end when the USA tinkered with the threat of declaring Pakistan a terrorist state. General Nasir's removal, after Nawaz Sharif's dismissal, was welcomed in Washington and Beijing. Lt. Gen Javed Nasir has now revealed that he had defied the U.N. ban on supply of weapons to the Bosnian Muslims and sophisticated anti-tank guided missiles were airlifted by the ISI. Only on the insistence of the USA, the Pakistan government finally removed Nasir from the top ISI slot on 13th May, 1993 (*South Asian Tribune* published from US).

The multinational operations of the ISI are more fascinating than its internal commitments. The Afghan sojourn of the ISI is a modern day saga of buccaneering in international political piracy, once the sole preserve of the CIA and the KGB. The CIA had pumped in $38 billion and almost the entire amount was canalised through the ISI and a considerable fraction through the al-Qaida. The ISI had managed to divert adequate amounts to its Indian operations.

The Taliban episode is a flagrant violation of international diplomatic fair play, with open encouragement from the USA and several Islamic countries, including Saudi Arabia. Achievements of the ISI in Afghanistan clearly proved Pakistan's capability to escalate Islamist jehad in any theatre. It emboldened the ISI to plunge headlong into the simmering movement in Jammu & Kashmir and turn it into a direct proxy war. Pakistan had always maintained that a spate of renewed acts of terrorism and violence in Punjab and Kashmir, by trained commandos and Jehadist forces would not invite swift retaliation from India inside Pak territory, as the Indian leaders were more adept in filibustering than busting bunkers.

Pakistan also supported Islamist terrorism in the Xinjiang province of China and other Central Asian Republics, as an instrument of its enduring centrality in evolving regional dynamics and deep-rooted economic interests. Pakistan simply tried to pick up the shattered mantle of the Turkish, Iranian and Saudi influences in the Central Asian void, after the breakup of the USSR. It is still in the game. Centrality of Pakistan in breeding and exporting Islamic jehad is now recognised even by its mentor, the US administration.

However, pressure from the US, China and Saudi Arabia and internal compulsions forced the ISI to shift the terrorist training schools from its soil to Afghan territory, especially after Osama declared open war against the USA. The rapidly expanding terrorist training system was integrated with the madrasas in Pakistan and even with selected deeni madrasas in India in Western UP, Bihar, Gujarat, Maharashtra, Andhra Pradesh, Karnataka, Assam, West Bengal, Tamil Nadu and Jammu & Kashmir.

The madrasa-bred warriors, the Talibans (plural of *talib*-student) believe in the ideology of *Ummat-i-Wahidah,* i.e. Islamic nations are one unified organic whole that transcends geographical boundaries. The ISI's resource pool in Indian madrasas is reflected by the illustrative figures of 4,500 in West Bengal, 3,000 in Maharashtra, 2,567 in Assam, 1,835 in Gujarat, 965 in Karnataka, 9,975 in Kerala, 6,000 in Madhya Pradesh, 7,000 in Bihar, 1,780 in Rajasthan and over 8,000 in Uttar Pradesh. A significant part of this vast resource pool has been exploited by the ISI's plan for exporting jehadist terrorism among the vulnerable sections of the Indian Muslims.

This new doctrine of involving the madrasas beyond the borders of Pakistan, including madrasas in Bangladesh and Nepal, is pregnant with the process of manufacturing rabid jehadists. A large number of madrasas in southern Nepal and Bangladesh are also being patronised by the ISI and other ideologues of *Ummat-i-Wahidah*, for training and arming the fundamentalist forces, with financial support from pan-Islamic organisations. Besides strengthening the Islamist bases in these two countries some of the madrasa-bred Talibans are utilised for operations in India. The ISI operations in India have always been an extension of the strategic and diplomatic arms of the Pakistani establishment. The list of ISI involvement in the internal security woes of India is fairly long. We will examine these aspects as we proceed with the functioning of the different branches of the ISI.

In this regard a special mention is required to be made of the Joint Intelligence X. The Joint Intelligence X is tasked with a special responsibility, besides other assignments. It carries out detailed analysis of the existing and developing fault lines in target countries including India and prepares intelligence estimates and project compendia. Systematic study of the fault lines amongst the religious, ethnic and linguistic groups are carried out with the help of distinguished scholars and media personalities. This study material is utilised by the JIM and JIN, after obtaining political approval, for advancing aggressive intelligence, sabotage and subversion operations in targeted foreign destinations.

Like most other intelligence organisations the ISI has put in position a well-defined functional and operational structure.

Director General Intelligence (DG ISI)

(Three-star General)

|

Deputy Director General-Political

(Two-star officer)

|

Deputy Director General-External I

(Two-star officer)

|

Deputy Director General-External II

(Two-star officer)

The number of two-star officers has proliferated over the years and it is estimated that four such officers of the rank of Major General (one each from the Air Force and Navy) have been put in charge of designated divisions. These are reported to be post-Nawaz Sharif developments.

The DDG (Pol) controls the territorial and subject desks and sections, which cover the activities of the political parties, students, labour, Mujahideen organisations, madrasas and religious institutions, tribal affairs, internal surveillance/security duties, VIP security duties, minority affairs and anti-terrorism activities. An officer of the rank of Brigadier generally heads each sub-division. But officers of the rank of Colonels and Majors head some of the lesser units.

Some recent reports, especially after the massive rigging of Musharaf's referendum, had mentioned that the political wing of the ISI was disbanded. This is far from true. The DDG-(Pol) continues to function with full blessings of the military dictator and is said to have been tasked to screen the candidates, eliminate the undesirable aspirants either by persuasion or by force and to ensure that the election returns a rubber stamp National Assembly. Some of the Pakistani newspapers have been brave enough to expose such nefarious tactics of the ISI.

The office of the DDG-External I requires some special mention. It controls the 'foreign operations' of the ISI and presides over the most dreaded wing of the ISI-Counter-Intelligence. It also covers the territorial, geopolitical, economic, strategic intelligence affairs in the Middle East, Africa and other countries. The DDG-Ex I also maintains liaison with the PMO, whenever there is one and with the office of the CMLA/CEO, whatever designation a military dictator prefers to decorate himself with. DDG-External I is a powerful position.

Counter-intelligence is a multi-faceted instrument. Separate sub-divisions cover groups of diplomatic missions on Pakistani soil and carries out human, technical, electronic and signal surveillance etc., against the target missions. This vast sweep of activity includes identification and neutralisation of embassy/mission based foreign agents as also identification, interception, categorisation and final disposal of foreign intelligence agents operating from non-diplomatic bases and hubs. This division has strong presence in Lahore, Karachi, Peshawar and a few other important places, especially along Indian, Iran and Afghan borders. India, as expected, gets special attention of the JCIB.

The JCIB also carries out liaison work with Pakistan based diplomats of the accredited countries and maintains professional linkages with the intelligence agencies of friendly and fraternal countries like the USA, Saudi Arabia, the UAE, Nepal, Bangladesh and China, etc. Some instances of the JCIB outstretching its operational activities into the areas defined for the JIM have been reported from time to time. The JCIB, it is reported, takes up independent operations in countries like Nepal, Bangladesh, Gulf locations and India. Reports of cross-connectivity and friction between the JCIB and the JIM are common. Such conflicts of operational interests have been reported from Nepal and Bangladesh, the countries used by Pakistan for intelligence encirclement of India.

It is alleged that Zia-ul-Haq had turned Pakistan into an Islamic State with a view to perpetuating his personal hegemony on the beleaguered people of the country. It is correct that Zia had promulgated several decrees to give a distinct Islamic character to Pakistan, an Islamist identity, not vastly different from the theological autocracies of the Arabian Peninsula. Some of his ordinances included: Hadood Ordinance, Qazaf Ordinance, Zaqat Ordinance, Usher Ordinance, Federal Shariat Court, Ramzan-e-Mubarak Ordinance, Compulsory Arabic News in PTV, Majlis-e-Shora (in place of National Assembly), etc.

But the essentiality of the Islamic character of Pakistan did not start with Zia. It started way back in the late 19th century and culminated in the creation of Pakistan. The movement was spearheaded by the Urdu speaking Muslims of the United Provinces, Bihar, Bengal, Maharashtra etc., and not the Sindhi, Punjabi and Pushtun speaking Muslims of the present geographical entity called Pakistan. Zia, a Jalandhari Punjabi Muslim, was the first to initiate the steps to link up Pakistan with multinational Islamism, which incidentally coincided with the arrival of another multinational Islamist movement on Pakistani soil; the al-Qaida al-Sulbah. The two multinational Islamist forces co-existed from 1979 till Musharaf succumbed to the US pressure to turn his forces against Osama bin Laden after the fall of the proxy-government in Kabul.

Osama had reached Pakistan soon after the Soviet intervention in Afghanistan. His meetings with Burhanuddin Rabbani and Abdur Rasool Sayyaf, the two Afghan resistance leaders, were facilitated by the ISI, at the instance of the CIA. Osama's main office in Peshawar at house number 10, street 11, section H1, phase II was also set up by the ISI. The two multinational promoters of Islamist terrorism worked in close co-operation with the CIA, even after the Soviets were humbled. Afghanistan bled under fratricidal tribal wars and later in conflicts between the Pakistan-created Taliban and Northern Alliance forces. Osama's Arab contingents were integrated with the Talibans and the Pakistani regulars, which succeeded in installing Pakistan's proxy-regime in Kabul. This honeymoon continued unabated even after the bombing of the World Trade Centre in 1993, failed attempt to kill President Clinton, Fidel Ramos and Hosni Mubaraq. The US pressure at that point of time had failed to chill the ISI's relationship with the al-Qaida.

The above deviation is aimed at highlighting the fact that al-Qaida is not the only multinational Islamist terrorist outfit. The Inter-Services Intelligence of Pakistan is the original procreator of the multinational Islamist movement that had created/generated scores of terrorist/ Mujahideen organisations to carry out terrorist activities in India, Chechnya, Bosnia-Herzegovina, Kosovo, Indonesia, the Philippines, Malaysia, Xinjiang and in theatres like the USA, Algeria and Egypt. The al-Qaida had pitched in slightly later. The offices of the DDG External I and II directed all these operations. They were directly responsible for floating and patronising the Mujahideen organisations.

Some of the top Islamist Mujahideen organisations promoted/generated/ patronised by the ISI are listed below:

1. Jammat-e-Islami
2. Jammat-ul-Fuqra (established in 1980 by ISI to assist Afghan and Kashmiri Mujahideen)
3. Pasban (a front of the JEI)
4. Hijb-ul-Mujaheedin (trained and funded by Fuqra and associated with al-Qaida)
5. Islami Mahaz
6. Ikhwan-ul-Mussalmin
7. Markaz-Al-Dawah-Wal-Irshad
8. Sipah Sahaba
9. Muslim Mujahideen

10. Al Jehad
11. Jammat Islamiyaa
12. Harkat-ul-Mujaheedin (reincarnation of Harkat-ul-Ansar)
13. International Justice Group
14. Jamait-ul-Mujaheedin
15. Harkat-ul-Ansar
16. Lashkar-e-Taiba
17. Al Faran
18. Al Badr
19. Allah Tigers
20. Jamait-ul-Ulema
21. Jaish-e-Mohammad, etc

Most of these organisations owe allegiance to the Wahabi-Sunni cult of Saudi variety and Deoband-Bareilly-Patna Sharif schools of Islamist theology. Though basically Hanafi by sect the volunteers of these organisations accepted the supremacy of the Salafi pedigree of Osama bin Laden. The ISI and the Jehadist Ummah keep on breeding new organisations keeping in view their operational needs in different theatres. The denominations change as required by political compulsions of the ruling regime in Pakistan and its domestic and international commitments.

Most of these jehadists have been trained in about 8,000 madrasas run by the jehadist mullahs and patronised by the umbrella organisations like the Markaz-Al-Dawa-Wal-Irshad, Arab financiers and foreign funds canalised through innumerable NGOs. The ISI works as the main co-ordinator, on behalf of the Islamist State of Pakistan. The volunteers of the Islamist Mujahideen organisations are also drawn from countries like India, Bangladesh, Malaysia, Indonesia, Philippines, Sudan, Yemen, Somalia etc.

Some of the illustrative prominent training bases of these Islamist forces are located at:

1. Islamic University, Peshawar, Pan-Islamic Institute, on the model of Patrice Lumumba Friendship University in the former USSR.

2. Binnori Town Mosque, New Town District, Central Karachi, mainly training the Talibans for Afghanistan and India.

3. Camps located in the suburbs of Jalalabad, Afghanistan. Destroyed by the US bombing.

4. Khunar Valley camps, Afghanistan. Destroyed by the US bombing.

5. Badr 1 and Badr 2 camp near Khost, Afghanistan (also used by al-Qaida). Presumed to be destroyed by the US bombing.

6. Pabi Camp near Jallozai, Peshawar, Pakistan.

7. Warshak Institute, near Peshawar, Pakistan.
8. Miran Shah camp, near Peshawar, Pakistan.
9. Saada camp, near Peshawar, Pakistan.
10. Muzaffarabad, Jalkot, Biarai, Cherat camps in Pak Occupied Kashmir.
11. Pasrur, Lahore, Kasur, Changa Manga (reportedly scaled down as Punjab thrust has been pushed to the back burner).
12. Muridke camp of the Markaz Al-Dawa- Wal-Irshad and affiliated groups.

Some of these training facilities have either been shut down or camouflaged after the USA moved in a big way following its mission in Afghanistan and against Osama bin Laden. But the camps in Pak Occupied Kashmir (POK) continue to be functional.

Origin of funds for training of the Mujahideen can generally be traced to Saudi Arabia, a few other Islamic countries and drug money generated by the ISI. Several NGOs, affiliated to the government of Pakistan also funnel in foreign funds generated almost all over the world by Islamic fundamentalist groups. Liberal donations are also raised from the Pakistani civil society in the name of Islamist jehad against *jahiliya* India and Zionists and Christian nations, where Muslims are allegedly oppressed. The amount of propaganda literature in support of jehad surpasses the quantity of text books marketed for the impoverished students.

Though Chinese funding and the US assistance have dried up after 1994, some doubts have been expressed that Pak ISI operations in the Central Asian Republics and China are still funded, at a low key, by the USA.

The international commitment of the ISI did not end with the demolition of the Taliban regime and Pakistani collaboration with the USA after 9/11. It may be recalled that the ISI and its proxy Taliban regime had significantly helped Osama in setting up his operations against the Jewish, Christian and all other *Dar-ul-Kafir* and *Dar-ul-Munaifiqin* (irreligious Muslim) countries. Osama's 23 February 1998 declaration of alliance was signed, besides his Arab lieutenants, by Sheikh Mir Hamzah, secretary of the Jamait-ul-Ulema-e-Pakistan, and the butcher of Bengali Muslims Fazlul Rahman, leader of the Jehad movement in Bangladesh. Both these characters are known and identified clients of the ISI.

The highly applauded 055 Brigade of the al-Qaida, though technically integrated with the Taliban Army, functioned in close collaboration with the Pakistani Army officers who masqueraded as Taliban commanders. One Colonel Jamir (a pseudonym), on deputation from the Joint Intelligence Miscellaneous helped 2,000 odd 055 Brigade fighters in advancing the territorial war into the heartland of the Northern Alliance, like Mazar-e-Sharif and Kunduz, etc. Several Pakistani, Bangladeshi, Filipino, Indonesian and Malaysian and a few Indian Kashmiris trained by the ISI were integrated with 055 Brigade. They were deployed for jehad in Central Asia, Russia, the Balkans, Indian Kashmir and a few of them were assigned to work on the blueprint of *Daulah Islamiah Raya*, the Islamist state comprising Malaysia, Indonesia,

Singapore, Southern Thailand, Southern Cambodia, the Philippines, and Singapore.

In this regard the exploits of Jemmah Islamiah in Malaysia, Indonesia and Singapore are worth watching, as the movement is gathering strength and is being increasingly supported by the al-Qaida, the ISI and other international Islamist forces. The names of Hambali alias Riduan Isamuddin, Abubakar Ba'asyir, Omar al-Faruq and Abu Sayyaf, the Moro Islamic Liberation Front (Spanish pejorative for Moor) leaders are uttered with awe by the Muslims of South East Asia, who are being drawn into the vortex of Islamist Jehad. Recent arrests of about 30 Jemmah Islamiah terrorists by the Singapore government indicate that at least two of them, Mahfuh Halimi and Habibullah Hameed, had undergone training in Pakistan and in one of the Al Badr camps of Osama. The heinous Bali bombing incident has proved beyond all doubts that the ISI and al-Qaida bred jehadists are capable of operating in any theatre of conflict.

The ISI's involvement with the Islamic Movement of Uzbekistan (IMU), which is accepted as an umbrella organisation for the Islamists in Tajikistan, Kazakhstan, Kyrgyzstan and a part of Turkmenistan has helped in bringing the divergent ethnic groups under the common bond of Wahabi Islam. Ironically Ferghana Valley, from where the Mughal conquerors came to India, has been selected as the hub of activities of the IMU.

The ISI has also trained the volunteers of the East Turkmenistan Islamic Muslim (ETIM) terrorists, the Uighur Chinese dominated outfit that is struggling for establishment of a Sunni Wahabi independent state.

Unlike the Hun and Hui Chinese of the Xinjiang province, the Uighurs use Arabic as the main language of communication. It is believed that under the Chinese and US pressure Pakistan has put a temporary plug on aiding and abetting the Uighurs, but their tryst with the IMU continues unabated, as the US wants to use the Islamic weapon to weaken Russian hold on the oil and mineral rich Central Asian Muslim countries.

It would, therefore, be seen that the Inter-Services Intelligence of Pakistan is the first promoter of multinational Islamist jehad. It enjoyed the full state backing and support from the USA, Saudi Arabia, France and other Cold War allies of America.

The second Islamist multinational organisation, the Al Qaida-al-Sulbah emerged a little later, first as an Islamist weapon against the Russians and now against the *Dar-ul-Kafir* and the *Dar-ul-Munaifiqin*. This intricate relationship between the ISI and the al-Qaida is important for analysing the worldwide Islamist resurgence, which is often erroneously described as conflict of civilisations.

The Joint Intelligence Miscellaneous (JIM), the JIB and the JIX, as well as the Directorate of Military Intelligence collaborated extensively with the al-Qaida and drew upon its talents to be used by the Joint Intelligence North (JIN) that is entrusted with Kashmir operations. It is rather unfortunate that the US and its so-called allies have singled out the al-Qaida after 9/11 as the prime enemy and have adopted a nauseously indifferent attitude towards the earth-shaking incident of 13/12, for which the ISI multinational was directly responsible. War strategy against worldwide terrorism cannot thrive on hypocrisy and to protect interests of a dominant nation.

The al-Qaida does not operate under state control; but it has immense influence on the Islamic Ummah that is the genetic building block of each and every Islamic country. The ISI works under state control. But its history is replete with evidence of the state being controlled by the ISI. How long would Musharaf be able to hold on the cork that he has very reluctantly put on the smoggy ISI bottle? How long would the USA feign that the ISI jinn has been corked? The FBI has already started accusing unnamed ISI operatives for protecting the al-Qaida fugitives. As far as India is concerned neither the USA nor Pakistan appear to be interested in bottling up the jinn.

The Joint Intelligence Miscellaneous and the Joint Intelligence North direct the Indian operations of the ISI. The Pakistan IB, unlike Indian IB, is not totally barred from conducting operations in selected foreign countries. For Indian targets they are allowed to conduct certain shallow penetration trans-border operations as well as assigned High Commission-based operations.

Territorially the JIM is responsible for conducting forward intelligence operations in India in collaboration with the JIB and the JIX. Deputy Director General External II oversees and co-ordinates these operations. The JIM operations can be categorised into four sections:

a) Home-based operations

b) High Commission/Diplomatic Mission-based operations

c) Third country-based operations.

d) Operations conducted through agencies of friendly third countries

Home-based operations include:

(a) Shallow penetration, trans-border operations, which are carried out through low-level intelligence assets, border smugglers, *sawari* traffic (habitual but illegal trans-border traders). These categories of agents are used to collect tactical intelligence, geographical data, data on communication facilities, defence preparations within 25 km of the international border, deployment of units of the armed forces in the bordering regions, location of radar and missile batteries, etc.

(b) Long-term resident agents trained and infiltrated by the JIM are allowed to 'sleep' for a while with a view to merging with the assigned target area's milieu. They are activated at a later date through instructions conveyed over cell-phone, satellite phone (in case of sensitive areas), e-mail and also coded messages broadcast over the Pakistan Radio and TV at appointed time, date and frequency. In some cases use of innocuous social messages, like *nikah* (marriage) etc., sent over fax at pre-determined PCOs have come to notice. On rare occasions India based trusted 'hawala' operators are also used as communication channels.

The resident agents are assigned specific tasks, which may include defence targets, creation of Islamist modules, engineering of communal violence, selected sabotage and subversion tasks and cloning of sub-agents in assigned areas. These clones carry out assigned propaganda and take part in sabotage and subversion operations.

For example, a Resident agent located at Siliguri Chicken Neck corridor may be directed to clone sub-agents at Dhupguri and Mainaguri etc., amongst the Kamtapuri Liberation Organisation. The same Resident agent may also be required to clone sub-agents at Bagdogra Airbase and Binnaguri Corps formation. Such top-grade residents are trained to merge with the background and operate a widespread network. Some of the favourite areas for locating Long Term Resident Agents (LTRA) are Kolkata, Delhi, Guwahati, Doomduma, Siliguri belt, Danapur, Patna, Kanpur, Jhansi/Babina, Saharanpur, Jullandhar, Amritsar, Adampur, Kota, Jaisalmer, Mumbai, Nasik, Ahmedabad, Bhuj, Kochin, Vishakhapattnam, and Tuticorin, etc. This is an illustrative list.

Some top level Resident Agents are assigned the tasks of infiltrating the Islamic educational and religious institutions with the help of organisations like Jammat-e-Islami, Tablig-i-Jammat, renowned madrasas and even NGOs run by the minority community. This process is used in creating Islamist modules among the vulnerable sections of the minority community and in establishing linkages with the mafia and the underworld, which generally work in tandem with the intelligence operatives on guidance received directly from Pakistan and third country bases. These are labyrinthine processes and require minute analysis and neutralisation by the professional organisations of the state and the central governments.

The trained Residents, some of whom may be serving personnel of the ISI, are normally located closer to sensitive defence locations/formations, ethnic-religious malcontent elements and vulnerable but friendly co-religionist population. The JIM and the JIN have come to notice for planting their serving officers amongst the Punjab and Kashmir terrorists.

The High Commission-based operations are supposed to be very subtle and classical. These are supervised by the ISI operatives posted under cover of diplomats and subordinate ISI operatives working as non-diplomats.

The JIM operatives of the ISI and the Pak DMI operatives in India, operating under cover of accredited diplomatic and non-diplomatic officials, numbering about 30, depend largely on:

a) Sympathetic conscious/sub-conscious friends in conducive religious and social circuits, intellectuals, glitterati and culturatti, media personalities and business groups involved in trading with Pakistan, defence contractors and suppliers, etc.

b) Migrants from West Pakistan, who suffer from ethnic and cultural nostalgia and nurse dreams for the lost paradise.

c) Fundamentalist groups among religious minorities, who are fed on the theme of resurgence of the Ummah, reassertion of Islam on the subcontinent and Che Guevara type spontaneity of Islamic revolution.

d) Socialites and *femme fatales* having access to top target areas and individuals in the government sectors and the defence services.

e) Some resident agents placed in key positions are also guided by the High Commission-based operators.

f) Some itinerant agents, criss-crossing the border through regular and illegal routes remain in touch with non-diplomatic operators.

g) Third country based operatives—Nepal, Bangladesh, Maldives, Sri Lanka, Thailand, Singapore etc., often contact Delhi-based operators with a view to skirt the intelligence operatives of their respective host countries.

h) The undercover officials of the Consular section pick intelligence talents from the passport and visa seekers.

i) Intelligence talents are generated at holy places where the faithful of the Allah regularly congregate.

j) Sub-agents and lower staff maintain regular watch at places of residence and work of the middle and lower ranking defence personnel.

k) Some Pakistani visitors manage to stay back in India and settle down in sensitive locations. They are energised by the Mission-based operatives for penetration of target areas. Recent reports indicate that there are over 11,000 Pak nationals overstaying/missing in India.

These are a few illustrative tradecraft techniques used by the Mission-based JIM/PDMI/PIB operatives.

The initial connectivity with the insurgent groups of North East India was established by the PIB from its Dhaka-based stations. But these operations were taken over by the ISI after 1962. The saga of Pakistani and Chinese collaboration with the Naga, Mizo, Meitei, ULFA, Bodo and Tripura insurgents/terrorists has been adequately exposed and partially neutralised. The ISI collaboration with the insurgents included: provision of safe houses in East Pakistan/Bangladesh, training in guerrilla warfare, supply of sophisticated weaponry, travel and banking facilities and establishing linkages with the Chinese authorities in the early sixties and with various Human Rights groups in the west in the late nineties. Presently these operations are being implemented in collaboration with the DGFI, NSI and BDR of Bangladesh. Friendly elements in the Bangladesh Armed Forces have not failed to offer adequate assistance to the JIM/JIX operatives. In fact, a significant section of the army brass and civilian bureaucrats, still operate as extended arms of the Pakistani establishment.

The JIM has powerful fundamentalist friends in Bangladesh in the Jammat-e-Islami (political ally of the BNP), Islamic Chhatra Shibir (ICS), Islamic Oikyo Jote (third important political force), Al Badr, Harkat-ul-Jehad-al Islami (HUJI) and al-Qaida affiliated al-Jehad. In addition to the above, two groups of the Rohingya rebels (Myanmar Arakan Muslims) operate freely in collaboration with the Bangladeshi and Pakistani operatives. The Rohingyas aspire for establishment of an independent Islamic state in the Arakan region of Myanmar. There are reports of the presence of a sizeable al-Qaida activists inside Bangladesh. These elements are reported to be involved in training the HQJI and ICS activists.

The Islamic Chhatra Shibir(ICS) operates from six territorial divisions and over 200 sub-divisions. It is affiliated to the International Islamic Federation of Students Organisation (IIFSO) and has strong fraternal links with the Students Islamic Movement of India (SIMI). The ICS is liberally funded by the ISI.

The HUJI, with its 15,000 strong contingent, is considered to be the strongest ally of the ISI and the al-Qaida. A large number of HUJI volunteers have been infiltrated in Assam and West Bengal with a view to establishing Islamist modules and to prepare the vulnerable local Muslims for armed struggle. Over the years the JIM and JIX have achieved spectacular success in Assam, where over half a dozen militant and jehadist groups function, often with blessings of civil political groups. It is estimated that the JIM and the JIX have achieved the capability of turning Assam into a volatile communal battlefield.

Bangladeshi HUJI recruits are taken to Pakistan through Nepal and are trained as guerrillas and terrorists. A number of them were assigned to Afghanistan, Bosnia and Chechnya etc., operational theatres of the multinational Islamist forces, i.e. the ISI and the al-Qaida.

Recent involvement of Pakistan trained HUJI elements in violent activities in Kolkata and Delhi against the US and Indian targets prove that the ISI has successfully applied its multinational roles in Bangladesh.

The ISI made strategic advances into Nepal between 1985 and 2001. India's lackadaisical diplomatic relationship with Nepal helped Pakistan in establishing strong diplomatic and economic bonds with the Himalayan Hindu kingdom. That the ISI, especially the JIM and JIX operatives, have been providing support and sustenance to the Sikh terrorists and the Islamist operatives from Kashmir have been proved by several sensational unmasking operations by the security and intelligence operatives of Nepal and India. These included recovery of RDX explosives from the residence of an accredited diplomat, recovery of fake Indian currency and neutralisation of several ISI safe houses in the capital of the kingdom. The 12 June, 2001, issue of *India Today*, a credible weekly, had carried some authentic revelations about ISI activities in Nepal and growing Islamist fundamentalism in the Hindu kingdom.

It is an acknowledged fact that the NSCN (IM) leaders have lived in Kathmandu over several spells and David Ward, a so-called friend of 'Naga Vigil', has used Kathmandu as an operational base. Other terrorist organisations, which have used Nepal as safe bases in Jhapa, Ilam, Tapleganj and Panchthar areas, are the ULFA, NDFB, KLO and the NLFT of Tripura.

The Maoist movement in Nepal has come to notice for strengthening its linkages with the MCC, PW groups in West Bengal, Bihar and Orissa. The Left-Extremist movement in India, which continues to afflict Andhra Pradesh, Jharkhand, and Maharashtra, is steadily developing linkages with the Nepal Maoists. In fact the Coordination Committee of the Maoist Parties and Organisations (CCOMPOSA) was formed in a formal meeting between the Maoists of Nepal, India, Bangladesh and Sri Lanka.

Some recent reports suggest that the JIM and the JIX are pumping in financial resources and weapons to help the Maoists with a view to install a more friendly government and to psychologically de-Hinduise the staunch Hindu population. Reports of clandestine meetings between the Nepal Maoist leaders like C.P.Gujurel (foreign affairs), Krishna Bahadur Mahara (chief of armed group) and Hisila Yani and ISI operatives in Karachi, Dhaka and Patna are required to be treated with utmost care. The linkages of the Nepal Maoists and the Indian MCC and the PW with the Sendero Luminiso of Peru and Revolutionary International Movement (RIM), which enjoys Chinese backing, are also required to be probed deeply.

The allegations of complicity and collaboration between a section of Nepali politicians and bureaucrats with the Inter-Services Intelligence are not without substance. The Indian intelligence community has some tangible evidence that the ISI is using some influential Nepali figures to augment their operations against India and to develop a firmer grip on the kingdom.

Some Pakistani banking and financial institutes operating from Kathmandu have also been used for funding the Indian terrorist groups, especially the Sikh, Kashmiri, ULFA, Bodo and Kamtapuri rebel groups. A Pakistani construction company selected for road construction in Pokhara area had successfully infiltrated the ex-Indian army men living in the neighbouring villages for priming some of them as vital intelligence assets.

The most significant incursion made by the ISI is amongst the growing Muslim population in Nepal Terai area. The latest census figures indicate that growth of Hindu population has gone down by six per cent, whereas the Muslim population in the southern part of the country bordering India has shown an astounding growth of over 15 per cent. Besides progressive procreation, there has been liberal influx from India and Bangladesh.

Growth of population has been accompanied by mushrooming of madrasas (250). Institutions and organisations like Jamia Mohammadia (Tulsipur), Jamia Sirajul-Uloom (Boundhiyar), Jamaitul Banatun Salehat, Jamia Ittehad-e-Millat and Darul-Uloom-Fazi-e-Rahmaniya have taken up the task of spreading radical Islamism. There are confirmed reports of regular visits to these bordering Muslim villages by Kathmandu-based diplomats of Pakistan and other Islamic nations. These institutions and madrasas receive generous funds from Pakistan, Indian Islamic Institutions, Saudi Arabia and other Islamic countries. Recently some units of the HUJI of Bangladesh have taken root in the Muslim inhabited Terai areas of Nepal. Rapid demographic changes along India-Bangladesh and Indo-Nepal borders are intricately linked with the Islamist terrorist activities and growing collaboration between the terrorists and the crime cartels.

Besides the above-mentioned organisations, Nepal Islamic Yuva Sangha, Jamat-e-Islami Nepal (1990), Nepal Muslim Seva Samiti, Jammat-e-Millat-e-Islam, Nepal Muslim Ittehad Association, Muslim Democratic Welfare Association, Jammat-e-Ahle-Hadis are actively involved in promoting 'talibanisation' of the madrasas and forging links with SIMI and HUJI as well as with organisations like Markaz-Al-Dawa-Wal-Irshad and Harkat-ul-Mujahideen. It may be recalled that the key planners of the hijacking of IC 814 from Kathmandu to Kandhar received clandestine support from the HUJI and Pakistan Embassy based operatives. Nepal, indeed, like Bangladesh has emerged as a launching pad for the JIM and JIX operations against India.

The initiatives taken by the Zia-ul Haq regime in fomenting and supporting terrorism in Punjab is a glaring example of exploitation of developing Indian fault lines by the ISI. Masterminded by Zia himself and refined by Joint Chiefs of Staff, the Punjab operations were jointly handled by the JIM and the JIX. The gory saga of training and arming of the Sikh militants was meticulously architectured to maximise the use of the training facilities developed to train the Afghan Mujahideen and al-Qaida cadres in camps in Pakistani Punjab and the Frontier areas. It is intriguing to note that the ISI and the al-Qaida had established a joint training camp at Lawrancepur near Attock for training Sikhs and Kashmiri Mujahideen.

By 1987 the ISI enjoyed a comfortable logistical position to dole out Afghan war surplus and the cached away cash and supplies from the CIA to the Sikh militants. Special training was imparted to fabricate improvised explosive devices and in the use of RDX, Semtex, C4 and sophisticated timing devices. At one point of time the Punjab militants were supplied with Korean and Japanese communication sets and VHF monitoring devices.

Pakistan's strategic calculations were clear about Punjab. India, it knew, would never allow Punjab militancy to traverse beyond the event horizon and the Sikhs, sooner than later would be disillusioned with Muslim Pakistan, with whom they had a historically troubled relationship. The Sikh militant leaders too were aware that Pakistan would not like to go to war with India for creating an independent state of Punjab as India did in the case of Bangladesh. Zia-ul-Haq, a Jullandhari Muslim,. made the serious foray into Indian Punjab, with the help of two other Jullandhari Generals to keep India busy and prevent it from logistically supporting the Kabul regime and factions of the Northern Alliance. It was also a rehearsal for Zia's planned actions in Jammu and Kashmir, which is generally and erroneously referred to as Operation Topac.

Zia had his Punjab blueprint worked out way back in 1978-79 with inputs from some important leaders of the Sikh diaspora and some key leaders of the Sikh Gurdwara Prabhandhak Committee (SGPC), around the same time the Janata Party/Akali Dal government and the Congress were fooling with competitive religious fundamentalism amongst a section of the Sikhs, who blindly believed the falsehood spun by separatist Sikhs like Sardar Kahan Singh (*Hum Hindu nahin hain)* and Kapur Singh, the redoubtable ICS officer. The Indian leaders refused to recognise the infernal power of the fire of fundamentalism that was raging in Afghanistan and Pakistan stoked by the CIA and the ISI. It is sufficient to say that Mr. Bearden of the CIA and Brigadier Youssaf Mohammad of the ISI had guided and directed Brigadier Nasir of the JIM to play a low key proxy-war in the Punjab, as long as the Sikhs were ready to play the game. It is worth mentioning that both Bearden and Mohammad were directly responsible for guiding the Afghan Mujahideen, ISI trained Pakistani jehadists and the Arab force of Osama bin Laden. In short term consideration 'The Bear Trap' in Afghanistan gave tremendous dividends to the ISI and Pakistan. But the 'Punjab Trap' had left too many permanent scars on the Indian socio-political system. The job was well done by the JIM and the JIX. India had suffered the misfortune of losing a Prime Minister, who was trapped in the fault line, due to machinations of her aides.

The JIM and the JIX have achieved another spectacular breakthrough in India. The Iranian revolution and the Mujahideen wars in Afghanistan transcended the concept of nationalism and ushered in an era of multinational militant Islamism. It was different from the national struggle of the Palestinians and simmering growth of nationalist identity amongst the Balkan and Central Asian Muslims. Besides Pakistan's renewed foray into the killing fields of Kashmir, which is the proxy-war area of responsibility of the JIN, the ISI made systematic efforts to inject the jehadist poison amongst a vulnerable section of the non-Kashmiri Indian Muslims. The thrust went beyond the parameters of the oneness of the Ummah. It was directly spawned in the hatcheries of the multinational jehadist identity of Pakistan.

There are some impressions that militant Islam had established a toehold in India after the demolition of the Babri Mosque by a fanatic Hindu fringe and after the retaliatory serial bomb explosions in Mumbai. This observation by the 'secularist' historians reflects partial truth. In fact, the ongoing process of 'Islamisation' of the 'secular Muslims' of India by the pan-Islamic forces did not cease with the partition of India. The fundamentalists loathed the 'assimilistic' tendency in Indian Islam and socio-religious practices of the Hindus polluting their 'khalis' (pure) identities. A section of the Ulema had continued the process of keeping alive the embers of Wahabi fundamentalism even after partition of the country. Pakistan took advantage of this tormented psyche of a section of the minority and launched a new "war". This new 'war' is aimed at transforming 'nationalism' of the Indian Muslims to trans-Arab 'Islamism', the concept of Islam wedded more to the fundamentalist values of Sunni Wahabism of Saudi variety. The hard core Islamists had never ceased to operate once they realised that even in a democratic British India they would be ruled by the 'once ruled upon' Hindus. They were not ready to accept the 'Firengi Raj' to be substituted by the Hindu Raj. That historical mechanism, conceived way back in 1905-06 finally took the shape of Pakistan, and since 1925 the Islamists continued to make conscious efforts to erase the 'Indianness' of the sub-continental Muslims.

Pro-Zia forces in Pakistan pursued this policy with dogged determination. Zia had turned Pakistan into a theocratic state and he fortified the efforts of Islamisation of the Indian Muslims with the help of some of the Afghan veteran Mujahideen organisations and a few freshly spawned fundamentalist jehadist groups that were being readied for the oncoming 'liberation struggle' in Kashmir. Her democratic façade notwithstanding, Benazir Bhutto gave a free hand to the ISI to diversify the 'Afghan veteran' Islamists to infuse militancy amongst the 'nationalist' Muslims in India, Nepal and Bangladesh.

The JIM and the JIX have fully exploited the fault lines reopened by the Hindu chauvinists through their accentuated religion-tinted political activities from mid-1987. Like their Congress predecessors the extreme Hindu fringe failed to recognise that the Afghan experience had infused a new Islamist identity amongst the radical Muslims all over the world and the Indian Muslims were as vulnerable targets as the Muslims of Indonesia and the Philippines were. The geo-political interests of Pakistan coincided with the neo-Islamist thrust propelled by al-Qaida-al-Sulbah and its worldwide affiliates. The 'Hindu forces' did not appreciate that the jehadist thrust from Pakistan could only be contained by balanced and pragmatic state policies and not by re-energizing the 'Hindutwa' forces.

The growth of 'Hindutwa' forces was a historical necessity of the mid-nineteenth century and the period that witnessed rapid engineered growth of 'different nationalities inside the Indian nation'. Assertion of Hindu identity is an essential building block of the nation. But the idea of fighting the Islamist jehadist forces with equally powerful religiously fired political weapon can only give rise to civil turmoil. It cannot fight the enemy that targets the vulnerable sections of the Indian Muslims. Hindu consciousness can at best unify the Hindu society and strengthen the building blocks of the nation. The job of fighting the jehadist thrusts is better left with the secular machineries of the state.

The JIM and the JIX had taken full advantage of this emerging contradiction and due to their untiring efforts the Islamist strain of jehadism has come to root in firmly on Indian soil with possible devastating consequences.

The symptoms of Jehadist infection have been characterised by:

- Rapid growth of linkages with the multinational jehadist forces and proliferation of secret modules and cells.
- Acquisition of ways and means to use violence for reassertion of distinct Islamist identity.
- Rapid retaliatory and pre-emptive response to perceived acts of injustice and offensive actions emanating from the majority community.
- Formation of underground tanjims and armed groups, etc.

This strain of ISI sponsored jehadist virus is different from the one generally described as 'proxy-war'. Pakistan's proxy-war against India had started way back in 1958, in the North East. It had hit the Punjab like a devastating tornado and it is still tormenting the country in Kashmir.

The Indian Muslims, mostly converted from Hindus, had assimilated non-Islamic social, cultural and religious practices of the respective provinces they inhabited. The Muslims of Bengal, Maharashtra, Bihar etc., had assimilated several social practices and despite Islamist propaganda continue to be Bengalis and Maharashtrians first and Muslims next. Pan-Islamism dreaded these polluting factors more than 'firengi' influence. These forces had never ceased working on purification of the sub-continental Muslims out of such impurities.

Pakistan's efforts to inject 'Islamist' militancy have traversed beyond the pan-Islamic efforts of unifying the Ummah. The JIM and the JIX, in collaboration with the fundamentalist organisations, have penetrated the madrasas where Middle Eastern brand of fundamentalism and jehadism are taught more than any other secular or vocational subjects.

Attacks on Hindu temples in Gujarat, Jammu, Uttar Pradesh and violent incidents in West Bengal, Tamil Nadu, Karnataka, Andhra Pradesh, Gujarat, Rajasthan and in Delhi are symptomatic of the 'Islamist' war against the *Dar-ul-Kafir* and *Jahiliya* Hindu society. This new war is aimed at rekindling the religious fault line that had resulted in the division of the country and it now aims at creating ripples and waves of a 'second two-nation' movement.

History is often made in a second and very often it takes several decades to peak the events up that generate devastating tectonic forces leading to assertion of 'new national identity'. This has happened in the Balkans and the same process is bursting forth in the Central Asian Republics. The Pakistani establishment and the ISI have researched well on these intelligence operation projects, for which they draw support from whichever government happens to be in power in Islamabad and international Islamist organisations like the World Muslim League and al-Qaida-al-Sulbah. These operations are carried out by Pakistan-based Mujaheeds and Mujaheeds recruited from the madrasas and over 5,000 Islamist modules set up all over India and Islamist associates in Bangladesh and Nepal.

The above narration is not an assertion of an article of faith; it is a candid admission of facts, which are very often not discussed in the name of the Holy Ghost of secularism. Countries like India where the Muslims constitute an integral part of the secular democratic system are most vulnerable to the Islamist and Jehadist thrusts of the type espoused by the Pakistani establishment and the al-Qaida. Similar tectonic fissures are being infused amongst the traditionally secular Muslims of Malaysia, Indonesia, Singapore, Thailand and the Philippines. The symptoms of the most important dimension of ISI operations in India are palpably perceivable and visible. These symptoms are not a part of the proxy-war. These are integral parts of the ISI's multinational and geo-political role in South and South East Asia.

Enlightening the Indian masses on this emerging trend should form a part of the psychological warfare against the jehadist expansionism of Pakistan and its associates. It is high time for the Indian social scientists, the political breed and politicised religious fringes to understand the intricacies of the corrosive changes that Indian Islam has undergone in the wake of Zia-ul-Haq's transformation of Pakistan to a theocratic state and the Afghan experience and exposé to competitive religious dogmatism and fundamentalism. Islam in India has started gathering the storm particles sown by the ISI and other pan-Islamist forces. The same trend has been noticed amongst the alleged impure Muslims of Bangladesh, Malaysia, the Philippines and Indonesia. Only good political, economic and social management can dissipate these contaminated storm dusts.

The most dreaded arm of the ISI, the Joint Intelligence North, has played havoc with the Indian security umbrella in the state of Jammu and Kashmir. It is claimed by some Pakistan watchers that President Ayub Khan had created special operations cells in the ISI to handle the Naga and Mizo insurgents and for Kashmir affairs before the 1965 war. Ayub Khan had carried out reorganisation of the PIB and the ISI and the JIN had come into existence after the review by the Sheikh Committee.

It should be interesting to note that Pakistan had appointed six committees to review the functioning of its intelligence agencies:

a) Ayub Khan appointed Lt.Gen. K. M. Sheikh Committee-1960;

b) Ayub Khan appointed Fida Hussain Committee-1967;

c) The CMLA appointed G. Ahmed Committee-1971;

d) Z. A. Bhutto appointed Rafi Raza Committee-1974;

e) Zia appointed Sahibzada Yakub Khan Committee-1981; and

f) Benazir appointed Zulfiqar Ali Khan Committee-1989.

Some of these review operations were carried out to strengthen the intelligence edifices and to cater to the domestic political and military needs of the rulers. Zulfikar

Ali Bhutto and Benazir had tried in vain and rather a little late in the day to rein in the powerful 'third estate' of the establishment. By that time the ISI had transcended beyond the reach of any political government that Pakistan might have intermittently had. In the recent past Pervez Musharaf has carried out certain cosmetic changes to reassure his fidelity to the USA and to secure his own position. But Ayub Khan's first review had added new dimensions to the ISI and it was directed to take over the operations in India's North East. They did not do a bad job.

The 1965 war experiences and internal political turmoil had propelled Ayub Khan to re-examine the loyalty and effectiveness of the ISI. Zulfikar Ali Bhutto had tinkered with the ISI well before the 1965 war. Near complete mobilisation of the ISI to monitor domestic political problems had incapacitated the organisation to collect and collate cogent and reliable intelligence about Indian preparedness and resolve to face another Pakistani attack, soon after the Kutch skirmish. For the first time the Indian Intelligence Bureau excelled over its Pakistani counterparts, the Joint Intelligence Bureau and the Pak DMI. It is also said that raging rivalry between the ISI and the DMI had resulted in poor intelligence input.

However comic it might sound, it was Yahya Khan and later Zulfikar Ali Bhutto, who initiated the process of 'proxy-war' in Kashmir by way of encouraging the JEI network of Indian J&K and Pak Occupied Kashmir to set up strings of madrasas to spread true 'Islamist' ideology amongst the 'Sufi' Kashmiris. The aim was to destroy the so-called 'Kashmiriat' of the Valley Muslims and to convert them to Sunni Wahabism. The first group of 'Kashmiri

Talibans' were churned out of these madrasas, well before the madrasas at Binnori, Peshawar, Quetta and Muridke etc., had started churning out 'Afghan Talibans' and Pakistani Mujaheeds. Bhutto had deftly used JIN and JIX to penetrate the nascent malcontent element like the JKLF. The JIN and supporting groups from the SSG and Pakistan Army directly supervised this programme in collaboration with the frustrated political elements of the Vale of Kashmir and Pakistani jehadist organisations, which had started sprouting by 1978 to fight the Russians in Afghanistan. The seeds of proxy-war in Kashmir sown by Yahya and Bhutto had fully sprouted under the theocratic dictator Zia-ul-Haq.

Despite availability of convincing intelligence that Pakistan had initiated the 'talibanisation' process the political governments of Delhi and Srinagar had closed their eyes and minds and continued to tinker with the delicate political situation in the state of Jammu and Kashmir. They did precious little to neutralise the jehadist madrasas, open interference by the JIN and Pakistani Army agents and blatant subversion of the Kashmiri youths. That the ISI would emulate its Afghan experiment in the Punjab and Kashmir was not taken seriously, though the intelligence community and the armed forces did not dither in maintaining vigil. Government responses were limited to police action that was void of political, economic and diplomatic contents. The JIN, like the JIM, took complete advantage of the existing fault line in Kashmir widened by the short sighted and petty political manoeuvres of Delhi. The subversion and talibanisation process in J&K was given the shape of total proxy-war by 1989.

The jehadist organisations mentioned in earlier paragraphs were crafted by the ISI during the Zia regime and nourished and motivated by the subsequent regimes for fighting the Russian forces. With the Russian target vanquished, these very organisations were revitalised with the help of the JIN and the JIX for carrying out jehad against India. The low-key proxy-war in Kashmir was given a strident military shape around 1988 and it continues to rage virulently, though Pakistan is aware that Afghanistan type jehadist war cannot win Kashmir for it. But the war of 'thousand cuts' spearheaded by the ISI supported jehadists have often been blended with direct military actions. That is how Pervez Musharaf indulged in brinkmanship in Kargil in 1999. Musharaf's Kargil gamble was bolstered up by ISI trained Hijb-ul-Mujaheedin and Lashkar-e-Toyaba jehadists.

The Kargil episode indicated that the Indian civil and military intelligence apparatuses had failed to appreciate that Pakistan could combine its proxy-war with a limited direct military thrust as it did in Afghanistan. This chapter of joint ISI-army action was lifted out of the text of the CIA-ISI-al-Qaida-Pak Army's final thrusts in Afghanistan. In fact, Kargil was a sophisticated re-screening of the 1948 'tribal thrust' into Kashmir. The JIN, JIX, SSG and the military intelligence had planned these operations jointly well before February 1999, during the regime of Nawaz Sharif.

The proxy-war as a weapon of bleeding India and weakening it from within has paid large dividends but has not won Kashmir for Pakistan. The military establishment is aware that threats of direct war and nuclear blackmail are not going to internationalise 'the nuclear flashpoint' in Asia. Despite its 'anti-terrorist alliance' with the USA, Pakistan has failed to derail the bilateral character of the 'dispute', which in the Indian view can be discussed in the light of the Simla Agreement and Lahore Declaration, only after abandonment of the proxy-war by Pakistan.

The fond hope of Pakistan that the 5,000 odd jehadist modules inside India, set up by the ISI and its jehadist fronts would be able to initiate Mindanao, Sulawesi and Ambon type internal rebellion and civil strife has not gathered momentum. Though certain areas in India, according to ISI think tanks, have reached 'mature state of preparedness for violent jehad', the Indian Muslims, by and large, have refused to be trapped by the 'Islamisation and Jehadist' thrusts of Pakistan. They have retained the 'Indian' identity of Islam, which is secular and assimilative in nature. They have come to respect that religion and state are two different things.

This realisation has now propelled the ISI planners to fall back on fidayeen missions in Palestinian and al-Qaida style. The JIN planned fidayeen attacks in Kashmir and Jammu region have added a new tactical twist to the proxy-war.

This strategy has been extended to the heartland of India as exemplified by fidayeen attacks on the Red Fort, the Parliament House and Akshardham temple in Gujarat. Such fidayeen attacks on the religious and political symbols of India are likely to increase adding sharp edges to the twin objectives of the ISI i.e. widening the communal cleavage and enlarging the arches of the second coming of the 'two-nation' demand.

Long before the Kargil episode, the ISI had diverted the Afghan and other Arab mercenaries to Kashmir to give a decisive edge to the proxy-war. Therein comes the al-Qaida connection of the ISI trained Mujahideens. Osama bin Laden had maintained extremely useful operational relationship with the Pakistan-based Mujahideen groups. This became clear after the US bombed Osama's dens with cruise missiles in August 1998. Of the 20 odd jehadists who died in the US bombing nine were Hijb-ul-Mujaheedin volunteers. Evolved out of the Harkat-ul-Ansar one small branch of the HUM, the Al Faran had kidnapped five foreigners and killed them like another offshoot had killed Daniel Pearl in January 2002. A breakaway faction of the HUM, Jaish-e-Mohammad was responsible for the hijacking of the IC 814. All these elements had fought in Afghanistan side by side with the Afghan Arabs of Osama and the Taliban Afghans.

Pakistan may crouch behind its freshly struck alliance with the USA and decry Indian allegations of firm linkages between the ISI and the al-Qaida. The linkages between Mir Aimal Kansi, the Pakistani who killed CIA officials, are well documented. A sinister collusion between the ISI and the Taliban had prompted the Salafi leader Osama to agree to train Sunni Wahabi sect outfits like the Sipah-e-Sahaba (Army of Prophet's Companion) and Lashkar-e-Janghvi in urban guerrilla tactics for attacking the Shia minority. The Sipah-e-Sahaba has taken part in Kashmir jehad and its forces had joined Brigade 055 of Osama to assist the Islamic Movement of Uzbekistan (IMU).

The main ISI sponsored jehadist groups like the Harkat-ul-Mujahidin, Jaish-e-Mohammad and Lashkar-e-Taiba (the military wing of Markaz-al-Dawa-Wal-Irshad) have received training in al-Qaida camps.

After June 1999, about 200 soldiers of Osama's Brigade 055 were deputed to Kashmir (Mark Hoselball and Daniel Klaidman-"Periscope: Calling al-Qaida Questions about Iran", *Newsweek,* 25 February, 2002). These forces fought alongside the prime proxy-war agents of the ISI in the Vale of Kashmir and especially in Hindu majority areas of Jammu with the prime objective of causing Hindu exodus. Some of the Brigade 055 terrorists had taken part in the Kargil adventure too.

It is intriguing to note that at Kapran camp in Anantnag district, established by the Harkat-ul-Jehad-e-Islami, al-Qaida veterans had trained the local Mujahideen groups. Some of the captured terrorists like Muhammad Ismail and Waqar Shah had revealed during interrogation that the al-Qaida had trained the Kashmiri militants and their Pakistani compatriots at Yawar camp in Afghanistan. Some other arrested terrorists like Jabed Akhtar Abbasi admitted that while on training in Afghanistan they were addressed by Osama bin Laden. Omar Sheikh, the British national of Pakistani origin, now being arraigned for the murder of Daniel Pearl, was trained by the ISI and the SSG instructors as well as the al-Qaida Arabs for carrying out terrorist attacks in India. There are scores of such instances of close cooperation and coordination at the ideological and operational level between the ISI and the al-Qaida. Pervez Musharaf's tactical turnabout cannot obliterate the recorded history, though the USA may develop convenient amnesia to suit its geo-political and hegemonistic interests.

While the HUM and organisations like Tehrik-e-Jehad maintain offices in Muzaffarabad, the Lashkar-e-Toyaba runs its affairs from Islamabad. The LET had deputed hundreds of volunteers to Afghanistan. After the Afghan mission these Mujahideen were placed at the disposal of Brigadier Abdullah of the JIN, who had set up a special operational office of the JIN at Muzaffarabad. The Mujahideen were recruited from the training camps of the respective terrorist outfits and from the madrasas with adequate financial incentive. Most of these Mujaheeds acted as contract mercenaries. But a large number of them were motivated to act as fidayeen, with assurances of financial help to their families and secured slots in Allah's heaven.

The ISI's tryst with proxy-war in Kashmir has succeeded to a considerable extent in generating 'Afghan Jehad' type religious fervour amongst a section of the 'talibans' recruited from madrasas and training facilities of the 'tanjims'. These elements are still inspired by the 'shaheeds' of 9/11 and 13/12. In case Musharaf fails to turn them on against India there are distinct possibilities that these 'street warriors of the Allah' will take on the US-friendly regime in Islamabad and try to infiltrate the establishment machineries. Therefore, the possibility of reduction in Musharaf's proxy-war and jehadist thrusts appears to be remote.

The ISI, described as a state within the state, is in fact an extension of the state-arm of Pakistan; as the CIA used to be the White House's undeclared military arm for South American operations and operations against the Soviet Block countries. It functions under close supervision of the Pakistan Army High Command and the person in whom the state power remains vested from time to time. Some experts have aptly described the ISI as the 'third estate' of the Pakistani establishment, which works as an extended arm of the state policy of the rulers of the day, often usurping the political role of the civil society, carrying out proxy-war on behalf of the conventional armed forces and substituting diplomacy by sabotage and subversion. The ISI is an integrated part of the armed forces, which in collaboration with the jehadist fringe of the political and civil society has emerged as deadly an organisation as the al-Qaida is. The spy organisation has acquired four distinct areas of operational expertise: internal political operations, promotion of sectarian war, regional proxy-war and jehadist activities and multinational jehadist connectivity. The Pakistani spy organisation has amassed as much power as the CIA and the KGB wielded in their heydays during the Cold War.

India is the prime target of the Pakistani establishment and the ISI. The entire internal security and external defence preparedness are required to be pitted against multi-pronged offensives of the ISI like classical espionage activities, sabotage and subversion, intelligence encirclement from third country bases, exploitation of the ethnic-religious fault lines, proxy-war and infusion of Islamic jehadist modules with the long-term objective of dividing India once again on religious lines. Different wings of the ISI coordinate these activities as specialised operations projects. Free collaboration between one or more wings of the ISI in its India-centric operations has been clearly identified.

All such operations sponsored by the Pakistani establishment cannot be carried out without steady financial support from the government. The defunct Bank of Credit and Commerce International used to work as a conduit of terrorist funding. It used to recycle ISI generated drug money and finance its jehadist operations against India and other targets. The prestigious Habib Bank too worked as a front realtor of the ISI. However, under international pressure drug production in Pakistan has considerably reduced, though the Afghan tunnel is still wide open, notwithstanding Pakistan's open alliance with the USA.

The Mehran Bank scandal that came to light in 1994, in which Habib Bank too was implicated, had exposed the involvement of the ISI in bringing about internal political changes. General Mirza Aslam Beg, Air Chief Marshal Asghar Khan and other Pakistani luminaries have substantiated these charges. Pakistani banks and financial institutions located in the Gulf countries, Nepal (Himalayan Bank) and Bangladesh also generate black money for directing different ISI projects in India. Some of the suspect Bangladesh banks are: Habib Bank Ltd, Ansar VDP Unnayan Bank, Arab Bangladesh Bank Ltd, and Al Baraka Bangladesh Bank Ltd.

Besides recycling drug money, the ISI has invested wisely, in al-Qaida style, in different front companies and establishments. Over a dozen Leasing and Finance Companies front the ISI in Islamabad, Lahore, Karachi and Peshawar. At least two undercover construction companies are owned by the ISI.

A couple of NGOs floated by the ISI also obtain foreign donations, which are used for funding operations inside India. At one point of time, before Osama decided to attack the US establishments in Africa, the ISI used to receive liberal funding from the al-Qaida for sustaining operations of the organisations like Hijb-ul-Mujaheedin, Lashkar-e-Toyaba and Jaish-e-Mohammad.

The state machinery had turned a blind eye to donations exacted by the Mujahideen organisations from Pakistani citizens, especially on *Jumma* prayer days, during Ramadan and as forced *Zaqat* (voluntary donation) from well to do citizenry. Such fund collections are facilitated by the madrasas and tanjims floated by the terrorist organisations.

Funds are also received from Islamic nations and the Muslim diaspora in the western hemisphere by the religious institutions and the NGOs affiliated to the jehadi tanjims. Similarly some of the minority educational, religious organisations and NGOs in India receive liberal foreign funds, which are diverted to the cause of militant activities and are not spent to uplift the economic conditions of the Muslim masses.

The US had recently brought to the notice of the authorities of the Revival of Islamic Heritage Society of Kuwait that its Pakistani branch was funnelling funds to the jehadists. The ***Observatoire Geo-politique des Drogues***, an independent anti-drug research institute, had also pointed out that the ISI was using drug money to promote jehad in India and even in Xinjiang, China.

Some observers feel that the following NGOs are cooperating with the ISI for canalising funds to the jehadists:

The Millie Yekhjehti Council
Islamic Relief (Neelam valley AJK)
Islamic Relief Agency-Pakistan
Islamic Foundation
Pakistan Community Development Programme
Sarhad Rural Support Organisation
Taleem Foundation

The ISI uses the 'hawala' (non-banking private) channel to fund its operations in India. Some complicated channels were recently busted which connected the ISI with London-based operatives like Ayub Thakur and several Gulf-based banking organisations. The trails of funds that were involved in recent Kolkata incidents indicate that the long arm of the ISI and mafia connectivity span over the seas and continents. Kidnapping for ransom has been perfected as a tool of fund generation by the ISI trained operatives in India, Nepal and Bangladesh. ISI linkages with the mafia and the underworld that came to surface after Mumbai serial bomb blasts indicate mutual financial transactions generated out of drug and human trafficking and patronisation of protection monopolies. Some of the Islamist modules operating in Tamil Nadu receive regular funds from the South East Asian conduits operating from Nana Road, Bangkok, and Johor area of Malaysia. Similarly Gulf-based ISI sources and fronts have come to notice for funding jehadist projects in Kerala, Karnataka, Maharashtra and Gujarat.

Incidentally, it may be mentioned that Hijb-ul-Jiahd-Islami and the Islamic Chhatra Shibir of Bangladesh have emerged as conduits of funding some of the ISI operations controlled from Dhaka, Sylhet and other covert stations for the insurgent groups in the Indian North East.

The military regime, it is understood, had allocated an amount of Rupees (P) 140 crores alone for operations of the JIX, JIM and the JIN inside India in the financial year 2000-2001. As long as the Pakistani state uses the ISI as an extension of its military tool against India funding is not going to pose any problem.

Analysis of a couple of recent fidayeen operations deep inside India indicate that the ISI has started emulating the classical training manuals of the al-Qaida. The following features are palpably discernible:

- Jehadi modules have been split into cell formations, each one not exceeding 5 to 7.

- Communications between the cells and the modules are carried out on command from the master co-ordinator in the JIM/JIX or designated 'Resident/Sleeper' inside India.

- Use of cell/satellite phones have been limited to essentials after recent Indian success (rather well publicised) in signals monitoring.

- Safe accommodation for the actual operatives is rented by reliable local contacts of the concerned cell in the target operational area. Hindu names are preferred over Muslim identity.

- Collaborating cell members or sympathisers purchase old/used cars in fictitious name.

- At present long 'sleeping' period is not allowed by the ISI for the fidayeen directly sent from Pakistan.

- Local cells conduct survey of the target area and detailed maps/photographs are transmitted over the Internet. On selected occasions such materials are sent to the ISI HQ through diplomatic bags.

- Funds are provided at a location near the target to be attacked, through hawala operators and cell conduits.

- Arms and explosives are no more carried from Pakistan directly. These are cached with the local cells or are obtained from stores built up over time at selected places, like safe havens in western Uttar Pradesh, bordering villages in West Bengal, Nepal-India bordering villages, mafia collaborators and in selected madrasas. Certain pockets in Delhi and National Capital Region towns are also used as arms caches.

- Fidayeens normally travel through Bangladesh/Nepal directly from Pakistan. Often selected groups are infiltrated through LoC, Gujarat and Rajasthan borders.

- The ISI has adopted the policy of selecting most sensitive targets, vulnerable places and important individuals. It would not be surprising if the fidayeen groups were directed by the ISI to target India's nuclear facilities, offshore oilrigs and major infrastructures. These are very vulnerable and probable targets.

The above rules of the game are reviewed from time to time and commands are conveyed over secured channels of communication. The JIM and the JIX have almost perfected the tactical and strategic inputs for delivering deadly blows anywhere inside India, at any target chosen by the Pakistani establishment; be it a temple or a Very Important Person. The strategy is to build up continuous heat by such fidayeen attacks with the following objectives:

a) To scuttle diplomatic normalisation process and to keep the ambience of confrontation at the maximum boiling point.

b) To keep the world capitals aware of the 'possible nuclear flashpoint' over Kashmir.

c) To spread the jehadist movement deep inside India and to allure the Indian Muslim youths to join the 'modules', 'cells' and to embrace the honourable life of a martyr. This is done by wide circulation of Jaish-e-Mohammad, Lashkar-e-Toyaba, Harkat-ul-Mujaheedin and al-Qaida audio/video tapes and printed materials amongst the target population.

d) To generate communal conflagration and matching reprisal from Hindu fundamentalists.

e) To bleed India 'inside each home' with a view to retarding its political and economic progress.

The other areas that have been troubling the Indian intelligence organisations are the progressive use of sophisticated information technology by the ISI operatives.

The age-old clandestine wireless communication and even PSTN/ISD telephones have yielded to cell-phones, satellite phones, fax and Internet communications. The Punjab and Kashmir militants used the VSNL ISD facilities widely. The technical facilities available to the Indian agencies were rudimentary even for keeping track of those 'gateway cleared' calls. Proliferation in mobile phone providers and their collaboration with multinational companies has offered almost unhindered communication facilities to the ISI linked Indian and Pakistani operatives. In addition to the ISI, the international mafia cartel based in Pakistan, Gulf countries, Thailand, Malaysia and Singapore have jumped into the fray of multinational terrorism to facilitate drug and human trafficking. Their communication facilities are often used by the ISI.

The use of Internet for communication between the ISI and its India based operatives and collaborators has thrown up another challenge. In addition to the regulated Indian ISP facilities some of the cable net operators have started directly downloading ISP facilities provided by foreign companies. Such down-loaders and distributors have proliferated over the last two years. It is next too impossible to keep track of these directly downloaded broadband ISP facilities. It is reported that some of the ISI backed jehadist operations use 3′ diameter dish-antenna to intercept KU band signals for 'non-interceptable' Internet communications. Such contraptions can be installed at an affordable cost of Rs. 2 lakhs.

Immense quantity of high-speed computer facilities and faster analysing capabilities are required to identify clandestine Internet communications. Software used for interpreting Internet coding system are in short supply and Indian software researchers have so far not developed foolproof technology that can block transmission of Internet traffic by the preventive agencies from certain individuals and organisations linked to terror masterminds. The data pool is vast and it is almost beyond the capability of the presently available technology to cope with these threats emanating from ISI and its mafia conglomerates. The India based servers are 'slaves' to the master servers mostly located abroad and the WWW facilities have proliferated even beyond the capability of advanced organisations like the CIA and the FBI. The Internet browsers are beyond tampering by the enforcement agencies. However, some limited cooperation between the Indian and the US/UK agencies have started yielding some results. Proliferation in WWWeb Pages and use of codes in such Web Pages have thrown up serious problems even to the FBI and the CIA. Recent listing of Web Pages suspected to be used by the multinational terrorist organisations, including the al-Qaida, HuM, LeT, JeM of Pakistan and Jemmah Islamiyah of Indonesia and MLF of the Philippines indicate that coded communications over the Internet are undergoing periodic innovations. This worldwide connectivity between the Islamist jehadi organisations has enhanced their multinational character. On the other hand, there has been a proliferation in Web Pages maintained and updated by the jehadist organisations, for which there exists a vast clientele. These are ready tools for propagation of jehad and communication through coded messages.

While the multinational jehadists have walked into the realm of breaking into the WWW sites of different government and security agencies, the enforcing authorities have not yet gone for acquiring technology to 'bug' the suspected jehadist WWW sites. More research is necessary in this direction. Synchronisation of ImageInt and SatInt with the GPS systems of the operating master computers and online international data networking should be the immediate target to combat increased technological advances made by the regional and multinational jehadist forces. Speedy communication alone can thwart some of the nastiest terrorist strikes.

Use of mind-boggling fidayeen type violence against soft religious and civil targets is no more confined to the Palestinian terrorists. The ISI sponsored attacks on soft religious and civil targets in India and similar targets inside Pakistan have proved beyond doubt that the Inter-Services Intelligence of Pakistan, the Al Qaida-al-Sulbah and their affiliates all over the world have adopted wanton violence as a tool for spreading Islamist jehad. The attack on the World Trade Towers on 9/11 and the attack on the Indian Parliament on 13/12 are linked incidents. The thin film of difference between the al-Qaida and the ISI has been exposed by the events inside Pakistan even after Pakistan volunteered to be an ally of the USA in its fight against global terrorism.

The Pakistan government has officially distanced itself from Lashkar-e-Toyaba, Jaish-e-Mohammad and Hijb-ul-Mujaheedin organisations under Indian and US pressure. However, most of the important leaders arrested after the collapse of the Taliban regime are being freed almost on a daily basis. There are several pro-jehad elements among the higher echelons of the armed forces. They are expected to allow Musharaf to adopt a pragmatic course of calculated support to the USA, but they are not likely to leash the jehadists' operations in India.

The jehadist fronts in Pakistan do not enjoy majority. They cannot win any free election. But they have immense influence on the mass psychology of the impoverished Pakistanis who have been constantly fed on the themes of jehad and anti-Indianism. Therefore, if now that the farcical elections are over and Musharaf has put on a legalised crown, the jehadists will be given 'elasticity' to resume their activities more devastatingly inside Kashmir and selectively elsewhere inside India. He will have the advantage of a 'political government' buffer between him and the jehadists. The strategist of Kargil and an admirer of Osama, Musharaf cannot be expected to renounce violence and terror altogether. The military regime in Pakistan is most likely to stonewall the civil society and political governments with increased support from the jehadists. There are clear indications that the pro-al-Qaida groups have started clamouring against the US intervention in Pakistan. They are not likely to remain contented with in sops offered by General Musharaf. Though the FBI and the CIA have set up several offices inside Pakistan and the ISI is said to be working 'under US supervision' it can be safely deduced that the Pakistani establishment is not likely to reduce its proxy-war forays and jehadist/fidayeen attacks against India. Pakistan's visible efforts to protect the US interests in Afghanistan and Pakistan have been restricted to 'limited tactical manoeuvrability'. The military rulers are aware that the White House needs them as direly as they need American benevolence to tide over the looming economic disaster. Neither the USA nor Pakistan is new to such 'strategic bed partnership'. The US buggy of relationship with India and Pakistan is mounted on parallel tracks. Pakistan enjoys a different strategic privilege. While fulfilling its tactical commitment to the

USA Pakistan can afford to carry on its regional jehad. A temporary plug on the multinational dimensions of the ISI and the jehadist organisations should be evaluated only as tactical 'resilience'.

The JIN has kept up its operations at an escalated level inside Kashmir, though it is reported that Brigadier Abdullah has been shifted out of Muzaffarabad. It makes little sense. The quantum of infiltration may wax and wane periodically but the proxy-war and the fidayeen attacks are going to be the principal weapons of Pakistan's Kashmir policy. Recent election related violent incidents clearly point out that despite the FBI and CIA presence in Pakistan, the ISI is not interested in downsizing its India operations. The USA thrives on 'perpetual war-economy'. It seeks out war on some pretext or the other. Therefore, the USA is likely to turn opaque eyes to Pakistan's 'small wars' against India, till such wars lead to a nuclear flashpoint.

Some recent trends indicate that the establishment planners of Pakistan have evolved some common and co-ordinated programme for the JIM, JIN and the JIX for carrying out jehadist war deep inside India, with a view to initiate large scale communal conflagrations, larger than the one recently witnessed in Gujarat. Maharashtra, Gujarat, Uttar Pradesh, Bihar, W. Bengal and Assam continue to be on the priority list of the ISI. This sinister plan is likely to assume greater momentum as India walks down to the next Parliamentary polls in 2004.

The prognosis, as far as India is concerned, does not appear to be encouraging. The ISI carries out four types of operations in India: classical forward intelligence, collaborative proxy-war as in the North East, direct proxy-war as in Kashmir, and promotion of multinational Islamist Jehad amongst the targeted segments of the Indian Muslims.

Pakistan has drifted away from the concept and character of sub-continental Islam. It has adopted Middle Eastern Islamic character and has assumed a multinational role in promoting Islamist jehad in the identified Islamic hubs in the sub-continent, South East Asia, Central Asia and Western China, Africa, the Middle East and pockets in Europe. Ingestion of multinational Islamist jehad amongst the Indian Muslims has become a state policy with Pakistan, though Kashmir continues to be the flashpoint of the sub-continental conflict. The ISI continues to enjoy the 'third estate' status in Pakistan and the Pakistani establishment is not likely to plug out from multinational Islamist jehad policy, even though it is tactically cooperating with the western powers.

Some scholars like to characterise the growing Islamist thrust as a conflict of civilisations. Huntington is correct when he points out that 'Islamic resurgence' is a civilisational landmark of the twentieth century. It is difficult to diagnose if a fresh civilisational conflict between the Islamists and the Zionists and the Christians is on the anvil. The real character of the prognosis would emerge only with time.

However, as far as India is concerned, Kashmir is a mere visible unsolved political issue between the two countries. Pakistan intends to use Islamist jehad as a catalyst for aggravating the perceived civilisational conflict between Hindu India and a greater Muslim Pakistan.

Fortunately the vast majority of the Indian Muslims continue to believe in the assimilated values and have not yet succumbed to Pakistani machinations. It now depends on the political governments and the greater civil society to stand in solid phalanx by the side of the minority and refurbish the secular values, which alone can defeat the machinations of the ISI and other multinational Islamist organisations. Despite frontal attacks by the ISI sponsored jehadists on its core values India surely is not passing through the critical phase of civilisational conflict. The historical conflict has, however, reached a critical stage that can be defeated by deft manipulation of bilateral and multilateral diplomacy and Indian solidarity with the global and regional strategic forces. Exploitation of the existing and emerging fault lines in Pakistan is another weapon to contain the enemy inside its side of the fence. India should be seen as being capable of launching pre-emptive strikes against the Pakistani 'circles of evil' and making good friends out of the plural civil society of that country.

India has neglected its inherited fault lines and has allowed new fault lines to emerge. Police and military measures alone cannot fight the threats emerging from internal security fault lines and geo-strategic machinations. It requires deep political insight and national sacrifices to repair these fault lines. The Pakistani establishment and its 'third estate', the ISI, can be better fought if they are denied the pleasure of exploiting these socio-economic, ethnic, religious and political fissures. Tending the fault lines is as important as keeping the powders dry for the eventual thrust against the 'circles of evil' that have been bleeding India since the days of transfer of power. The ISI just happens to be a major part of that 'circles of evil.' It cannot be destroyed in isolation.

6

Threats to Security

Prashant Dikshit

The nation state of Pakistan is going through convolutions of a major change. A path charted by the military regime of Zia-ul-Haq is being altered by yet another military regime–that of Musharraf. In both the endeavours, coalitions of nation states were principal players led by the United States of America propelling the change. As the sobriquets of the "withering state" or the "failed state" are being hurled at this entity of a nation envisioned by the Quaid-e-Azam Mohammed Ali Jinnah, there are serious anxieties whether Pakistan is in control of its destiny.

I have a feeling that Pakistan's own fault lines- in Sindh, Baluchistan, NWFP, Tribal Areas, Gilgit Agency- are required to be brought out, in addition to Sunni-Shia fighting. The MQM factor requires more attention. Pakistan is better described as "a nation in search of nationalism and nationality."

With the unleashing of the war on terrorism by the US led coalition, after Afghanistan, the most potent impact has been seen in Pakistan. Most reluctantly, it had to divest itself of the burden of the Taliban fraternity and a deeply entrenched Afghan connection. The historical legacy of these adventures, however, remains embedded in the psyche and the polity of Pakistan. The present threats to the security of Pakistan emanate from the intertwined influences of sectarian divides, religious terrorism and a deep-rooted societal weaponisation. The drug culture, cultivated over the years, has led the society on a criminal path. Addressing a *darbar* of Punjab Police, with a tinge of sadness, President Pervez Musharraf went on to acknowledge that "Pakistan is a soft state. Here in Pakistan lawbreaking is considered a prestige point".[1]

All states emerging from the colonial yoke had inherited some of these aberrations in their nationhood; the task of grappling with the traumas of insecure infanthood remained with the founding fathers. But in the case of Pakistan, the protective arm of institutional governance seemed to disappear for good with intervention by the Pakistan Army; it was in fact a joint venture by the Bureaucracy and Military in the democratic process of the country. The troika of the army, the bureaucracy and the elite in the country rules Pakistan. Although, there have been sporadic democratic governments, these in reality have been masquerades functioning under the military yoke. The matters of defence decision-making and as a sequel, foreign policy matters, remained an unencroachable military turf at all times.[2] It is fair to assume that the Punjabi dominated troika mentioned earlier had an elitist construct as a group. It was thus denied the benefits of a government by the people and for the people. Zulfikar Ali Bhutto in his wisdom had moaned that "(India) survives through the chaos of its democracy"; a process he himself had been known to have subverted on having denied a rightful place to the eastern wing of the country. He would have been pained to see the might of an illicit drugs industry marginalising the economy of Pakistan. He had the opportunity of correcting this after 1971. He did not.

On Handling Afghanistan

Round 1979

The threats of today trace their origins to the thought processes and policies pursued by Pakistan's ruling classes. This is most evident in respect to Afghanistan. The regimes in Pakistan always had a great fascination with a self-assumed "Frontline State Syndrome" for their country. "The politics of aiding the Afghan mujahideen was largely linked with the geo-political objectives of the Pakistani ruling elite"[3] In their vision it was a rightful role for Pakistan, the contours of which went much beyond Afghanistan and included even the Central Asian Republics of the former Soviet Union. Pakistan's involvement in Afghanistan as an interventionist scheme was seen as far back as in 1974, much before the communist coup in April 1978, and Soviet intervention in 1979. For Zia's government the Soviet adventure was a godsend. Although, within the Pakistani military establishment the centrality of threats revolved around Moscow instigating ethnic separatist movements in Baluchistan and the North West Frontier Province (NWFP). Selig Harrison in his amplification stated that, "As for the security threat posed by the presence next door, many foreign observers felt, as I did, that there was a more serious possibility of Soviet support for separatist movement in Pakistan than that of a direct military aggression. Zia, however depicted direct aggression as a clear .and present danger. He skillfully used the Soviet menace to rally support for his regime. At the same time he was quick to perceive that the Soviet presence gave him a new rationale for American military aid."[4] Zia would have found it extremely difficult to last with his regime without the war in Afghanistan and the attendant international assistance it facilitated, especially from the US. "Zia also intended to use the war, and Pakistan's role as a frontline state, to project Pakistan as the defender of Islam against Soviet sponsored communism."[5] The military regime had envisioned several plans with this singular endeavour of meddling in Afghanistan. They hoped to resolve the Pashoonistan issue definitively and then try to establish a Muslim belt south of the Soviet Union, under Pakistani influence. It therefore, dealt directly with the Mujahideen west of the Durand Line and interacted extensively with the Pakistani Pashtoon elite, both civilian and military, to deal with the Afghan issue. Above all "Pakistan's generals also nurtured a more ambitious project—to establish, through a federation between Pakistan and Afghanistan, a Sunni Muslim belt that would have given Pakistan the strategic depth it lacks in front of India".[6] Zia had irrevocably Islamised Pakistan. His motive is required to be analysed.

"The crucible amalgamating these perceived advantages did not seem to take into account the Afghan polity and nearer, the influence of the inhabitants of the NWFP. The fact that forays and incursions into Afghan territory would have to essentially traverse through the NWFP was not considered serious enough".

Hitherto, Pakistan has been pursuing, for all practical purposes, a 'close border policy' in NWFP, where objectives were merely to monitor and manipulate land and people, as distinct from a 'forward policy', which was to administer and assimilate the area and its people. The choice of pursuing this policy evidently stemmed from an inability to engage in serious governance of these lands.

James W. Spain puts across a well reasoned rationale thus, "Put into the hands of his people enough weapons to provide a rifle to every adult male and several small but efficient arms factories of their own; make smuggling, especially of arms and ammunition, an ancient and honourable profession; endow them to a man with a simple and militant form of world's most martial religion, and you have a very volatile mixture.... Throw in a tradition of never having been fully conquered, a barren and infertile physical environment offering minimum opportunities for progress by peaceful pursuits but affording almost ideal conditions for armed resistance to authority, a sovereign neighbour with many historical and cultural ties which opposes integration of the frontier with the rest of the sub-continent and finally a long history of power rivalry in the area. It is not difficult to see why, quite apart from any specific, political, economic, or social issue, the frontier has been difficult to govern".

Even the British, during the Raj, 'avowedly followed a policy of not seeking dominion or political integration but rather suzerainty'. A direct administration did not seem feasible and a peripheral containment of the region could only be aimed at.

An amicable settlement with the regions of the NWFP and that also temporarily perhaps, came about only in 1986. The elapsed inclement years, since the Soviet invasion, had contributed enough to the warlords in the region to emerge as drug lords and smuggling kingpins. The northern and eastern regions of Afghanistan bordering Pakistan are widely termed as the 'Pushtoon' region and the inhabitants have strong affinities and linkages with the NWFP. Pakistan used the radical fundamentalists of the Pushtoon ethnic groups settled on both sides of Afghanistan as its tools.

The Pak-Afghan border extending through nearly 2,500 km, was extremely porous. Trans-border smuggling and drug trade were quite rampant. The cultivation of poppy in most of the regions of Afghanistan and the western regions of Pakistan had received a fresh impetus with the crackdown on, and closure of poppy cultivation in Turkey. It was as if a vacuum was being filled.

Arms for insurgents were to be ingested into Afghanistan through societies and cultures whose life cycles and prosperity depended very largely on the illicit poppy trade. They had already tasted the enormous financial gains and would have had a great stake in preservation and continuation of the trade. Any clandestine activity, relying on demands of regional support, had to take place with the connivance and active support of rural landlords, ruling blossoming drug empires.

The choice and selection of weapons had to be kept to the 'small arms' variety to fulfil the requirements of an insurgent war. The weaponry was to meet the demands of 'guerilla warfare'. Strong possibilities existed that a fair share of the weapons would find their way into private armies as a stockpiling programme. Also, a possible retrieval of the arsenal would have been impossible at a future date.

The pertinent question, which now emerges, is whether the Zia regime in power, had perceived a long-term scenario and had evolved a *modus operandi* to counter such developments at a later date. Also, after having entered the fray, would the instrumentalities of audit and control function as planned? Or take it to a basic level of planning, were there any instrumentalities envisaged? The post-Soviet-Afghan war scene however, pointed to the contrary. The drugs and arms syndrome was to rampage Pakistan in the ensuing years, as nowhere else in the world.

Marvin G. Weinbaum points out that, "Pakistan never had anything approaching a national consensus on how to bring the war to an end most quickly and favourably to the country's interests. Moreover, neither in aiding the Afghan resistance nor in pursuing a settlement, did officials in Islamabad ever manage to square Pakistan's covert and overt policies. What Islamabad professed publicly was often at considerable variance with its behind the scenes role".

In this atmosphere of policy bewilderment, "Six billion dollars worth of arms were assessed to have been pumped in by the US and Saudi Arabia alone". The most sophisticated small arms reached the fractious Mujahideen groups after a usual 'rake off' in the Pakistani military depots. Even after the Soviet withdrawal, the arms supplies continued, as in the perception of the Pakistani military, a complete victory over the Najibullah regime was an essential prerequisite for a political solution. The regime in Saudi Arabia it would seem had for many years acted as a restraint on those policy makers willing to press the Mujahideen towards a diplomatic settlement. The Saudis firmly supported a decisive military victory and particularly the ascendance of Wahabi-Sunni groups."[7]

Pakistan emerged as the second biggest victim of its own policy choices. The current problems trace their origins to insecure methodologies and a total lack of control over its apparatus, engaged in the application of policies. It was assessed that the country's drug problem was deeply linked to the Afghan war. The criminalisation of the Pakistani society, and collusion of highly placed members of various regimes in power with the drug barons, both in Afghanistan and Pakistan, pointed to an ominous direction towards which the polity was being led.[8]

The chagrin of the Pakistani society was truly reflected by D. Shah Khan, when he wrote, "the scenario has wholly changed with the western promoters of jehad losing interest in the country after the withdrawal of Soviet troops. They were merely using the resistance as a cat's paw to fight a proxy war with the Soviet Union......"[9]

Round 1994 - The Taliban

After the exit of the Soviets, Islamabad failed to bring all warring factions into a government of national reconciliation. Several attempts and accords broke down. Pakistan's refugee problem assumed monumental proportions and so did the upsurge in drugs and arms smuggling. Sectarian and ethnic violence spread throughout Pakistan. With the second return of Benazir Bhutto to power a strange dichotomy rose to the surface in the management of the Afghan imbroglio. In the choice of selecting a nominee to be installed as head of a pliant regime in Afghanistan, Gulbudin Hekmatyar was being nurtured by the Inter-Services Intelligence (ISI) of Pakistan. The Bhutto regime chose to unseat Hekmatyar from this pedestal. Several reasons are being cited, but not one of them clearly for a government of consensus, which could bring stability to Afghanistan. The Bhutto government considered Hekmatyar inimical to its interests, as the radical Jamat Islam Party supporting him was hostile to the Prime Minister. The West and Saudi Arabia in particular did not approve of him either. The Americans insisted on distancing themselves from Hizbe-I-Islami, the Hekmatyar group. But at the operational level the ISI maintained its loyalty to the Hizbe-I-Islami and other fundamentalist parties. In the midst of a rather grey scenario the Taliban was discovered.

It would seem that in the middle of the Afghan civil war Pakistan's strategic designs came into play. This was one more extension of its initiative as a front-line state. "In 1994 itself, Pakistan embarked on an ambitious project to repair the most damaged sections of the Herat highway in Afghanistan."[10] There was tremendous excitement over securing of this land route as it provided a major land access to the natural gas fields of Turkmenistan. The warlords and henchmen of ISI, recruited to provide a security cover for this venture, were decimated by a Mujahideen turned religious students who led a vigilante group. This movement apparently snowballed and caught the attention of the ISI. These were to emerge as Taliban, an alternate power group to the Hekmatyar faction. Sreedhar has clarified that " the majority of the Taliban activists were drawn up from the madarsas (religious schools or seminaries) operated by the JUI (Jamiat Ulema-I-Islam) in NWFP and Baluchistan provinces of Pakistan."[11] These were mostly Sunni Pashtoons who were earlier displaced from Afghanistan. However, the noteworthy point is that this over 40,000 strong force at the outset had Pakistani identity cards, and had canvassed for the JUI candidate during the general elections in Pakistan. And in the initial phase the Taliban did operate from Pakistani soil with full knowledge of the government in Islamabad.

The choice of the Taliban as a possible contender to the seat of power, till today resounds as an incredulous decision. The answers to this riddle can only be discerned from the historical emergence of Pakistan as an Islamist state perennially buffeted by the 'politics of religion'. These pressures emanated both from within and beyond from powerful and rich Islamist nations like Saudi Arabia. There was also a strategic fear of Shiite cultural and religious influences from Iran making incursions into the Pakistani sphere of influence. The Saudi path was already chosen by the Zia regime in the 1980s and thus the ultra conservatives in the Sunni sect of Islam were to be promoted. This in substance meant funding from the Saudi source, inasfar as selecting an appropriate hue of the Sunni sect. In the perceptions of the Pakistani regime, the puritanical zealotry demonstrated by the Taliban clearly identified the Taliban as a replacement for the Hizbe-I-Islami of Hekmatyar. Ajay Darshan Behara elaborates thus, "In Pakistan a large amount of money goes into funding the institutions of madrasas and other religious organisations. General Zia's Islamist policies in the 1980s had opened the floodgates for this funding to come in. Channels were further opened with the intensification of the Afghan civil war. The sudden withdrawal of funding from the West for Pakistan after the departure of Soviet troops from Afghanistan was more than compensated by the Saudi's who kept the funding going on for the former frontline state. The funding which earlier used to be for the Jamat Islami headed by Qazi Hussain Ahmed has now shifted to Deobandis represented by JUI headed by Maulana Fazlur Rahman. The Deobandis are inspired by the Wahabi (Sunni) version of Islam enforced in Saudi Arabia.... Most of the madarsas where the Taliban grew up and received education are controlled and run by the JUI belonging to the Deobandi school of thought."[12] It has been reported that the arrangement worked in the early 1980s to fight the Soviets, continued in creating and sustaining the Taliban in the 1990s also. The US, Pakistan and the Saudi conglomerate continued.

Even if the plan was to puppeteer this entity to do the Pakistani bidding, the quality of this human resource lacked the awareness needed for such tasks. " Pakistan used the cement of Islamic extremism to knit together a force of disparate Pushtoons into a large size conventional army."[13] In fact, they could only be trained for strong-arm forays but always to be kept on a tight leash. According to Anthony Cordesman, a regional security specialist at the Centre for Strategic and International Studies in Washington, "Spawned in war, the Taliban has no experience in governing and no plans to modernise. Revolutionary societies are never a source of stability, although they are invariably a source of exaggerated short term hope"[14] The groups were trained as fighters by the Frontier Corps and the army commandos of Pakistan to fight the troops of Rabaani and Masood till their supremacy was established. Beyond that point, the process of governance, it is presumed, was to have moved to a more enlightened system. But this was not to be, because enriched by power and substantial financial aid the Taliban were to emerge highly independent in thought and action. It was also reported that the drug barons contributed liberally to the Taliban to essentially neutralise the drug enforcement authorities of Pakistan and US operating in the region.[15]

Eminent Muslim scholars had found grave deficiencies in the Islamic theological tenets pursued by the Taliban. They had in their zeal misread that the Deobandi school sought to teach students how to interpret the Sharia with the events and values of the contemporary world. And therefore, the Taliban's excruciatingly oppressive attitude towards women spread a wave of great universal revulsion, including in the Islamic world. In a way, under pressure from 'Human Rights' groups, this was the beginning of US estrangement with the Taliban. The sanctuary to Osama bin Laden by the Taliban was gravely disliked by the Saudi regime, as he was being treated as an undesirable person of sorts. Although he was universally identified as a global promoter of terrorism and the supremo of the infamous al-Qaida, "it was Pakistan (which was) accused of paying the Taliban for hosting the training camps for Islamic militants."[16] From the Indian perspective, this human resource was for a nefarious application on the Indian soil, although religious militancy was on the rise in all of the Central Asian

Regions, Russia, China and even in Pakistan. Despite the strategy of stemming the cries for an independent Pakhtoonistan, the Pushtoon dominated NWFP passed a bill in 1997 for renaming the province as Pakhtoonwa. Then General Musharraf acquiesced. "The Taliban administration represents the majority Pashtoon population in Afghanistan and it is in our interest to support them", and also that it " would be most imprudent to confront or have differences with the Pakhtoons of Afghanistan".[17]

Eventually, the catalyst for the end of the Taliban regime was Osama bin Laden a creation of his benefactors. During their seven-year reign, the Taliban attempts to finance the war and the prolonged period of conflict in Afghanistan led to a black market and extensive smuggling across the Pakistan-Afghan border of consumer goods, drugs and arms. Some reports claim that the Taliban gained about $100-200 million a year through their 20 per cent tax levied on the trade.[18] Pakistan lost substantial revenue as a sequel and tried to close several illegal markets along the border with Afghanistan. Primarily the Pashtoon traders protested.[19] The border issue with respect to the Durand Line rose to the surface between the governments. And much to the detriment of Pakistan the work on the strategic pipeline from Pakistan to Turkmenistan was stopped due to the threats from Muslim hardliners in Pakistan and Afghanistan against the US interests, protesting against the US bombing of terrorist training camps in Afghanistan in August 1998. The Taliban were not there to prevent it.[20]

Perils to Internal Security

Traditionally, security has been perceived in terms of ability and capacity to preserve the minimum core values of state such as territorial integrity, independence and sovereignty. For most developing states however, the problem is from within, due to fragmentation along ethnic, religious and linguistic lines. The cohesiveness of these entities is crucial, essentially in the initial steps to nation building. An absence of this process on the contrary could threaten the very existence of a state in making. The demands for political participation, welfare, as well as for more equitable distribution of economic resources by the general populace, further complicate the process of state making, which leads to conflicts. There is erosion in the legitimacy of the state when political institutions are unable to provide the minimum order, and when the state is unable to provide security to its citizens who may no longer perceive the central governments as the manager of conflicts. In such circumstances, groups perceiving deprivation tend to resort to violent solutions to their grievances. A diffusion of small arms and light weapons at this stage can promote the process of state breakdown due to violent internal strife. The small arms diffusion is a transnational phenomenon energised by proximity of conflicts. Global experience reveals, that the diffusion combines with drug trafficking, smuggling and other tentacles of organised crime including money laundering.[21]

Weaponisation of Pakistani Society

The Pakistani paradigm fits with this scenario. If at all, a fillip was provided by an uncontrolled pushing of weapons into Afghanistan with Pakistan as a conduit. A survey of the Pakistani scene of those years was illustrative of the looming scourge. For example, Swedish engineers were captured by the Muslim Jaanbaaz Force (MJF) of Kashmir in May 1991. The abductions were carried out by college students armed with Kalashnikov rifles. The Afghan Mujahideen trained the students and provided the weapons.[22] Three Chinese engineers were kidnapped by dacoits in Dadu district in Pakistan.[23] The Sindh Director General of Health was kidnapped.[24] A kidnapped judge was killed in the crossfire with Sindh dacoits in Mirpurkhas.[25] A Dutch diplomat in Islamabad escaped an abduction attempt.[26] In a tribal clash in Pishin between two groups of a tribe, both factions freely used mortar shells, rocket-propelled grenades and Kalashnikov rifles.[27] The Sipah-Sahaba leader was killed by assailants armed with sophisticated weapons.[28] These incidents were only a few from the hundred odd incidents in which sophisticated small arms were used to settle scores.

The regime in power did not act in consonance with their own professions. They relaxed the ban on issuing arms licenses;[29] and this despite the 12,000 arms licenses had already been issued for Kalashnikov rifles.[30] There was no regard for the well-known fact that there were hundreds of thousands of Kalashnikov rifles in Pakistan illegally and an attempt at stemming the proliferation would have sent a strong signal to the people. The alarmist crescendo of the media and the political groups went unheeded. Smuggling of weapons spurted with this impetus. Arms smuggling boomed into a domestic industry in which families, women and children freely participated. Arms dealers, purportedly in collusion with the police, turned "the area from Niazi Chowk to Azadi Chowk in Lahore where at least 25 arms shops were operating, into Dera Adam Khel gradually".[31] The traditional routes from the tribal areas "were Peshawar from North Punjab (Sargodha, Faislabad, Lahore and Gujranwala divisions) and via Dera Ghazi Khan for Southern Punjab. Southern Punjab also received its supply of arms from Baloochistan, again via Dera Ghazi Khan; the stuff arriving from the tribal areas reached via Mianwali and Bhakkar for onward transmission."[32] The most sensational news on weaponisation came from Dera Adam Khel, where the provincial governor is known to have unearthed an arsenal of nearly 300,000 Kalashnikov rifles along with hundreds of automatic weapons, rocket launchers and anti-aircraft and anti-tank rockets.[33] What was most ominous was the total blackout on this news under mysterious circumstances. Bazaars like Jamrud, Landi Kotal and the Bara Bazaar, were thus able to offer the latest thing in infantry weapons, and distribution networks all over the country were built up.[34]

The weapons within the political groups reached through loyal student factions and the hostels and colleges. Ethnic movements like the Mohajir Quami Movement (MQM) and Jiye Sindh flourished, as well as Jamaat Islami and its student wing, the JIT, an openly violent and fundamentalist party. "Students were encouraged to believe that the person living in the neighbourhood colony and speaking in a different accent is the real reason for everything wrong with our lives....[35] At a prominent university in Sindh, a six-hour running battle over the control of a hostel underlined just how much student politics had degenerated into an orgy of violence and crime.... hostels became the control rooms for major kidnapping as the young activists took the inevitable route into organised/politically motivated crime.

The student wing of Jamaat Islami was the first to introduce automatic weapons to campus politics. At Jamsheroo, the heartland of Sindhi nationalism, the newly created wing of Pakistan Peoples Party (PPP) was to arm itself and followed later by Jiye Sindh. The Baloch Students Organisation also went the same way. It was estimated that nearly 20,000 highly trained militants remained in the fold of three political parties.[36]

Regimes in Pakistan never seriously addressed the task of de-weaponisation. Contrarily, it has been alleged that "even during General Musharraf's rule, the de-weaponisation programme of the federal interior minister was deliberately hindered by the ISI that it might have a negative impact on the Jehadi organisations in Pakistan."[37] Recent estimates of unaccounted small arms in Pakistan indicate that Punjab has 800,000, Sindh 500,000, Baluchistan 250,000 and the NWFP more than 500,000 weapons. Further, there are probably more than two million small arms circulating in Pakistan today and another three million in clandestine stockpiles, part of which goes to arm any militant group that is desirous of acquiring them. The small arms trade in the NWFP markets has been quantified at nearly one billion dollars per annum.[38]

The Drug Culture

The drugs came along with the weapons and have been the sustaining factor since then. Ironically, it was the instruments of the regime which had participated in spurring the malaise. It would be recalled that during the Afghan war the vehicles of the army controlled 'National Logistics Cell', which used to supply arms to the Mujahideen, were used as drug carriers.[39] The nefarious relationship eventually burgeoned into a drug baron-politician nexus. And, "names of various prominent political leaders like the former Prime Minister Nawaz Sharif, President Ghulam Ishaq Khan, the late President Zia-ul-Haq and even Benazir Bhutto have been linked with one drug syndicate or the other".[40] A report published by the United States Central Intelligence Agency (CIA) in 1993 titled "Heroin in Pakistan: Sowing the Wind" claimed that Pakistan was run by drugs and that heroin is becoming the lifeblood of Pakistan's economy and politics.[41] According to a Pakistani periodical *Newsline*, the multibillion-dollar business which fetches for its dealers a revenue of over $8 billion, almost double Pakistan's annual budget, is wrecking Pakistan's social fabric.[42] The drug money had corrupted the law enforcement agencies and turned them into puppets in the hands of powerful drug barons. There was also an exponential rise in the number of drug addicts in the country from zero in 1979 to 1.2 million in 1993. Historically, the seed of the drug empire in Pakistan was sown during the Afghan war; the ISI of Pakistan propped up most of the tribes in the region and gave them a free hand to indulge in various activities ranging from gun running to drug trafficking. After the disintegration of the Soviet Union and the emergence of new Central Asian States, new lucrative land routes opened for smuggling of heroin into Europe. Tajikistan and Uzbekistan were already getting infected.

In the post-Taliban period, the drug menace truly went on to acquire a transnational dimension. The assessment that the efforts of the Taliban curbed the drug trade, does not appear to be rational. The process of clamping down encouraged stockpiling and pushed the prices up.

The Taliban earnings went up from the fixed levy. As has been stated earlier the Taliban used to generate revenue. This was in reality an illustration of accepting the illicit trade. Both the Taliban and the al-Qaida were involved in the drug trade. But what is of importance is the sizable terrorist constituency raised by them which is now permeating into the Central Asian States. Michel Chussdovsky, Professor of Economics, University of Ottawa, in his recent article, has brought out that the production of opium in Afghanistan in 1998-99 coincided with the build up of armed insurgencies in the former Soviet Republics and reached a record high of 4,600 tons. The CIA continued to support the Islamic jehad out of Pakistan. Meanwhile, Islamic missionaries of the Wahabi sect established themselves in the Muslim republics...despite its anti-American ideology, the Islamic fundamentalism was largely serving Washington's strategic interests in the former Soviet Union. The most damaging revelation has been made by the weekly *Independent* in Pakistan that the CIA revived its old links with the traders in Afghanistan and then allowed them to offload their stocks as a *quid pro quo* for providing crucial information on the Taliban militia.[43]

It is a complex situation for Pakistan as a state. The drug empire grows like an epidemic, deep within Pakistan and flowering beyond, engulfing most of Afghanistan and all Central Asian States. There are powerful terrorist and drug forces intertwined. According to a study, Afghan drug mafias constitute the first line of buyers in the international opiate trade. "The second group of actors are the transnational criminal organisations who successfully took advantage of the post-cold war environment in Afghanistan and the Central Asian Republics to establish their role in the lucrative opiate market."[44] Groups' operations take place beyond Afghanistan and they use Iran, Pakistan and the Central Asian Republics as the operational bases. In the widespread industry, between the groups and the narcotics trade, the lateral participation spawns through an unholy spectrum of warlords, militants and the terrorists. All fundamentalist militant religious movements in the region were enmeshed in the trade. The al-Qaida and Islamic Movement of Uzbekistan (IMU) were definitely players in the field.

Despite the well-established visible linkages between the terrorists and the narco trade, "members of the international coalition have already turned their backs on discussions of how to strategically disrupt the illicit trade in opiates".[45] This apparently myopic view is perhaps due to a plan on focussing on terrorism only and exploiting the drug infrastructure towards this objective. Pakistan's vulnerabilities are enhanced as according to the eminent daily *Dawn*, "Pakistan has one of the highest opiate addiction rates in the world and smugglers are increasingly using the country for trafficking in drugs after the launch of war against terrorism in Afghanistan"[46] Thomas Ziendl, an official of the UN drug control programme, had expressed deep fears on the development.[47] "The number of narcotics addicts in Pakistan rose from 10,000 in 1979 to around 3-4 million in 1999."[48]

The Violent Sectarian Conflict

The fact that religious extremism and sectarian militancy got closely identified with proliferation of seminaries across Pakistan is noteworthy. So is the acknowledgement by the history of Pakistan since the planting of the seed of activist conservative Islam by Zia-ul-Haq. Delving into an account of Pakistan of those times, Christina Lamb records, "Condemned internationally for the hanging (of Bhutto), Zia launched a stern Islamisation programme to make Pakistan a theocracy, in the start of painful search for legitimacy of his regime"[49] At a superficial plane, several commentators ascribed the decision of the General to him being the son of a cleric, although the concept may have appealed to the army as a means to neutralise strong sectarian divisions within the Islamic state. There is no palpable historical evidence of a societal debate though, advocating this profound social change. Neither in the portals of the government machinery was a theosophical examination undertaken. This was totally at variance with the views of Pakistan's founding fathers. The Quaid-e-Azam in his first speech as elected President of Pakistan's constituent assembly in Karachi on 11 August, 1947, had said, "in course of time Hindus will cease to be Hindus and Muslims will cease to be Muslims, not in a religious sense because that is the personal faith of each individual, but in a political sense as citizens of a nation".[50] This was a liberal statement fıom a leader of an Islamic State. Zia had thus altered the course of not only Pakistan but of the whole region. The difficulties of Pakistan till then were a strong ethnic allegiance of the populace based on the regional belonging and a linguistic divide. Like in undivided India, there were sectoral differences between the Shia and Sunni sects of Islam having grown out of different religious schools. Shia-Sunni clearage is also a reflection of struggle between Iran and Iraq. Both the countries funded the Pak Shias and Sunnis. Antagonisms of a somewhat stronger nature used to surface against the Bihari migrants (the Mohajirs) and the migrant movement was striving for an identity. It was an economic issue sought to be resolved by a political process. The Bangla faction had already separated, being branded as the 'inferior breed' by Ayub Khan.[51] In the absence of a national consensus however, the political parties, in their narrow visions, accentuated the ethnic chasms and violent skirmishes broke through. Given time, the patiently moving wheel of democracy would have aligned itself and over an extended period a resolution could have been politically achieved.

Various regimes who sat at the helm of affairs of Pakistan after that never seriously examined or moderated the Islamisation regimen as to its social relevance for a modern Pakistan. The seminaries multiplied manifold. From a motley number of 563 in 1979 in Pakistan, by 1996 Punjab alone had recorded 2,500 seminaries with a combined strength of over 200,000 students. Of these, 750 institutions were identified as actively engaged in military training while 1,700 were receiving funds from foreign sources. Currently, according to government estimates there are around 2,715 seminaries in Punjab with 250,000 students. Reflecting on the scourge of religious militancy Azmat Abbas thus wrote in the *Herald,* "Seminary students have become increasingly active in not only local and national politics but militant movements all over the world. The Taliban in Afghanistan, the Harkatul Mujahideen in Kashmir, the Sunni Jammat Tulaba, Sawd Azam Ahle Sunnat, Ramzi Yousaf's International Islamic Movement, the Sipah-Sahaba of Pakistan are just some of the organisations that were born in and around the country's religious seminaries and recruited from among students."[52] This was the madarsa culture referred to earlier which had a direct linkage with the Afghan war. The communist threat had prompted the Middle East countries to support activities to strengthen Islamic identity in Pakistan. These funds were channeled into the seminaries and over the years became a great attraction.

The cardinal problem to grow out of the madarsa regime was the increasing inadequacy of scientific temper in the Pakistani milieu whilst militant conservative religiosity received enormous boost. There are several generations of this product which threaten the social construct of the society. The efforts of the Musharraf regime in trying to remedy this aberration have met with strong opposition. The religious heads are terming the step as an encroachment of their freedom and religious liberty. Of greater difficulty is the task of converting the poor families who with conviction believe "that (if the child) grows up to be a prayer leader and (then) even death (for) some version of Jehad is considered a special blessing".[53]

To blame it only on the madarsas, for the phenomenon of the breeding grounds of terrorism, we will not be able to relate to the problem in totality. The ISI promoted these groups for their nefarious ends not merely in the management of the conflict in Afghanistan, but also in the incursions in Jammu and Kashmir in India and several insurgencies in the Central Asian States. The 'Talibanisation' of Pakistani society has been an issue of concern in many quarters in the country. An increasing number of sectarian killings were a pointer to this phenomenon. The most telling comment came at a debate in the National Assembly at which Siddique, a leader of the opposition party MQM, argued that *"over* five million trained religious extremists, equalling the number of regular Pakistan Army is a potential threat to the region".[54] He claimed that the Pakistan military intelligence organization ISI created, sponsored and armed the Taliban. The provincial government in NWFP on the other hand disbursed a sum of rupees 1.3 million to representatives of various seminaries and promised another rupees ten million over the years to ensure the smooth functioning of these institutions. The government did not insist on changing the curriculum as decided by the federal government nor did they ask the seminaries to divulge the source of the funds.[55] There is also an inherent subversion within the education department itself with the presence of seminary graduates as Arabic teachers. This practice had commenced at the instance of Zia-ul-Haq in 1984-85.

War on Taliban and al-Qaida and The Tussle Within

The US led war on the al-Qaida-Taliban combine, unleashed new pressures on the Musharraf regime. It was faced with a contradiction between Pakistan's external and internal policies with respect to the stability and security of Pakistan. The Afghan policy was pivotal to the riddle. The prospects of dumping the Taliban under severe American pressures would have also meant doing away with the prospects of an amenable government in Afghanistan. Pakistan would also have had to deviate from its long-term goals of nurturing the Pakhtoon constituency both in Pakistan and in Afghanistan. In the process the well-entrenched campaign of promoting an ultra conservative Sunni doctrine in Islamic theology would have to be given a go by. And thus benefits of strategic inroads into the Muslim societies in the Central Asian States could not easily be accrued. As this was linked with a strategic depth against India, a loss of material gain was to be reconciled. On the domestic front, a fully blossomed theocratic regime had to be contended with.

It was a tightrope walk for the regime. According to media reports the decision to go along with the American requests was made for the Pakistani government as they had no option. "The US had stated that it would feel free to attack Pakistan's strategic facilities including its nuclear installations, if it did not get the desired reaction from Pakistan. Also, the ISI chief Lt General Mahmood who was in the US when the terrorist strike occurred was apparently told in no uncertain terms what the US stand on the issue was"[56] A charter of seven demands was sent through the Lt General which was eventually accepted by Musharraf albeit, positively. The demands were:

- not allowing al-Qaida operatives to cross the border, stopping arms shipments from going through Pakistan,
- giving the US overflight and landing rights,
- allowing access to naval bases, airbases and borders,
- providing intelligence reports,
- condemnation of the 11 September attack and curbing domestic support for terrorism,

- stopping fuel supply and Pakistani supporters of the Taliban from going to Afghanistan, and
- breaking diplomatic ties with the Taliban if it was proved that the al-Qaida network was involved and if the Taliban continued to harbour Osama bin Laden.[57]

The reaction to the strategic turnabout of the Afghan policy was mixed. The approach was well received by liberal elements and the actions were supported by mainstream political parties. The developments were referred to as the "the greatest national security challenge facing since 1971", and de-linking from the Afghan connection was expected to greatly ameliorate the conditions.[58] The utterances notwithstanding, the actions of the political parties were seen as growing out of a desire to gain maximum political mileage from the situation. Also, in the absence of heavyweight political leaders like Benazir Bhutto and Nawaz Sharif, the overall credibility of the political segment remained in doubt. The PML (N), had in any case, not gone along with the Musharraf regime.

The religious fundamentalist groups on the other hand, reacted in a very hostile manner. There were violent street protests and they tried to come together as a group under the banner Pak-Afghan Defense Council (PADC). "Though these organisations indulged in several violent demonstrations their campaign came to an end with the fall of the Taliban in Afghanistan".[59] However, the statement of Maulana Sami-ul-Haq indicated the tone of the quality of the opposition when he said that "Musharraf should step down and be sent into exile, and the Pakistan

Army and people of Pakistan should take over the government" [60] The hatred and the anger against the US was expressed in several attacks against foreign nationals and Christian minority institutions in parts of Pakistan. The killing of 18 Christians in a church in Bahawalpur in October 2001, is a case in point. Sectarian massacres took place in Karachi. Activities of the Tehrike-i-Nifaz-i-Shariat-i-Mohammadi (TNSM) came to notice. It blocked parts of Swat, Dir and the Karakoram highway protesting against the US forces operating in Afghanistan. The weekly *Independent* commenting on the military regime's co-operation with the US for nabbing Osama wrote, "The Taliban influence has been on the rise for some time. A Taliban like movement, the TNSM has been raging in the Malakhand division for at least seven years.[61] The government planned a major crackdown to cleanse the student hostels and the refugee camps in the Malakhand division. Heavily armed TNSM activists were to be tackled. It was a joint operation between the rangers and the police personnel to recover arms.[62] New armed groups emerged; for example an armed group calling itself the 'Al Saiqa', attacked a frontier constabulary troops outpost with rocket launchers and submachine guns at Thalkol-Bata gram. It claimed to pursue a doctrine of 'Darul Harab' i.e. home of war."[63]

Most dangerously, the opposition from the ISI simmered at a sub surface level. Because doubts were raised as to whether Pakistan was playing a double game in continuing to provide support to the Taliban whilst overtly appearing to be participating in the war as coalition partner. The US Ambassador to Pakistan raised the point that the Taliban were continuing to receive armed men and ammunition in Pakistan[64] This was a telling comment on the ISI which had been the instrument of the Pakistani state pursuing its policies in Afghanistan. Several other instances came to notice during the conduct of the anti-Taliban campaign in which ISI operatives were suspected to have connived in allowing the Taliban fighters to escape, and that it was averse to sharing information with the US about the Taliban, Osama bin Laden and the al-Qaida network.[65]

A sudden quantum change in the attitude of the ISI as an organisation could not be expected. Being a part of the Pakistan Army's infrastructure, it had burgeoned into a very institutionalised apparatus of clandestine linkages all around. Its operatives had dabbled in, from gun running to promoting jehadi fighters. There was great emphasis on religious militancy under its tutelage, especially in the task of nurturing fundamentalist groups throughout Pakistan. It is difficult to eradicate this legacy. And in the history of its evolution it had reaped substantial financial benefits in the drugs and weapons deals. Like all intelligence outfits, it had cultivated several relations beyond the direct cadres of the organisation. Therefore, in removing the head of the organisation i.e. Lt General Mahmood, a mere salutary message was being conveyed. There was no hierarchical purge and nor was a cleansing exercise undertaken. There is a view that a strong backlash would have surfaced had these steps been taken. Above all, the institution is still perceived to have its utility in the war against the Taliban and the like. In fact, the military went greatly out of its way in persuading the US authorities to extricate the ISI operatives from war ravaged Afghanistan, specially, to save them from the wrath of the Taliban. The ideological underpinnings of the ISI nevertheless, continue to remain.[66]

In the drive against the terrorist groups a selective approach has been adopted by the regime. The axe has fallen essentially on organisations nominated by the US intelligence; the Sipah Sahaba, Jaish-e-Mohammed and Lashkar-e-Toyba are to name a few. A few additions have been made purely on the basis of inclemental relationships. Although there is a general ban imposed on collection of funds by religious organisations, there is no special structure created to monitor its implementation. The slush funding system of the 'Hawala Route' remained vigorous as ever. It continued servicing the funding channels. Pakistan's then Finance Minister Shaukat Aziz, a former executive vice-president of Citibank in New York, said that from $ 2 billion to $ 5 billion moved annually through the 'Hawala System', in Pakistan, more than the amount of foreign transfers.[67] After 11 September 2001, US authorities believe that millions of US dollars were sent through Hawala by Al-Qaida to Dubai.[68]

Managing Change

Emboldened by the support of the American Administration in spirit and letter, the military regime has been reasonably successful in containing the immediate problems to the stability of Pakistan. It has been able to keep in check the country's powerful elite and specially the army's top brass by a series of transfers of generals and important police and administration officials. There was no doubt a fear that the hardliners on adherence to Afghan policy, within the army, might rise against Musharraf, although there was visible unanimity that the US request must be acceded to.

The war on the al-Qaida and the Taliban, on the other hand, has not kept pace with the timetable planned for the task. The terrorist fighters have fled to Pakistan and are submerged in Pakistan society, largely in the NWFP region. The most plausible explanation for this situation is that the fighters are part of a homogeneous group of the ultra conservative militant variety. They largely belong to a similar stock and have strong affinities with the people of NWFP. Most important of all, as a concept, they subscribed to the jehadi tenet and looked up to Osama for guidance. The leaders are being identified periodically in various towns of Pakistan by the American intelligence and captured in raids jointly conducted with Pakistani security teams. The grassroots cadres are not easily distinguishable in the milieu of the country and are therefore moving freely. The same would apply to the Taliban. The crucial point is that this intensely indoctrinated community could regroup on appropriate summons.

The campaign to reshape the theological construct of the Madarsa education system embarked with a reining in process of the system and insistence on the madarsas registering with the government. The streamlining policy includes a revision of the teaching curriculum to include mathematics and science apart from Urdu. Textbooks in these subjects are being centrally coordinated. Computers are being introduced with a plan to provide 100 computers every year.[69] The effort could only be considered a symbolic beginning, considering the enormity of the change. It drew a positive response from the American Administration. The Secretary of State, General Colin Powell, as a sequel to his visit to Pakistan, said to the International Relations Committee of the US

Senate that, "General Musharraf wants to put in place a public education system. He is so interested in getting debt relief and other aid not to bu eapons but to put in place schools that will teach kids and prepare them for the 21st century".[70] The whole policy of the systemic change in the educational ethos seems to be spearheaded by the Ministry of Interior in the Pakistan government and therefore indicates a security orientation to the drive. Such an approach can only be seen as a short-term impetus to reform. In the view of experts, educationists must oversee the overhaul, for tangible long-term contributions. A review of the religious indoctrination, per se, can only bring about a reversal of deep fundamentalist underpinnings. This may be at formidable costs to the acceptance of the regime as a perceived protector of Islam. Not merely within the milieu of Pakistan, but also by the substantial constituency providing financial support from outside Pakistan.

The result of the October 2002 elections in Pakistan are assessed as a setback in the country's movement towards a liberal state and a modern society. The impressive showing of the Muttahida Majlis-e-Amal Pakistan (MMA), a party with a strong fundamentalist orientation, can be an obstruction to the President's efforts in neutralising the ultra conservative ethos. The MMA has a thumping majority in the NWFP and has come to this position by the dint of its anti-US stance and is hawkish on all existing religious leanings including the core issue of Afghanistan. In view of the hung Parliament, the prospects of Maulana Fazlur Rehman, the head of the MMA, assuming the position of a principal player in the political scene is imminent. The US administration although has already indicated its opposition to accept him in a pivotal political appointment.

A Prognosis

The US has established a substantial presence in Pakistan; not only are the activities in Afghanistan monitored through Pakistan, but the American Administration has negotiated for a long term lease for a 60,000 acres military base in Baluchistan. As the lease is for a 30-year period, the speculation is that the US presence, in all probability, would be for a long period. The assumption that this strategic step has been taken in pursuit of the war on the al-Qaida-Taliban does not appear to be entirely appropriate. On the face of it, these are indicative of long-term geopolitical objectives. Economic issues of controlling and tapping the formidable hydrocarbon resources of the Central Asian Region, appear to be the core factor pushing the strategy. There would be a great desire to keep both Pakistan and Afghanistan under their tutelage to, thus, obviate the growth of Iranian influence in the region. The development of the oil pipeline linking Pakistan to Turkmenistan, for primarily American conglomerates, had provided an inkling of the emerging game plan. In the American perception, there would be several attendant advantages. The nuclear flashpoint scenarios between India and Pakistan could be contained within manageable limits; and also the growth of militant fundamentalism stemmed. The moot point is whether long-term American presence would be in the interest of the stability and security of Pakistan.

In the current situation therefore, regime stability in Pakistan appears to be a factor common to all interests, wanting to benefit from Pakistan. The military regime would flourish in the *status quo*. Amongst the American people and the members of the legislature, the cry for a democratic process in Pakistan, was an impediment to the US policies in the region. The Pakistani military regime's manipulation towards a democracy, to a large extent, moderates the voice of dissent in the US. For the moment, the concept of a guided democracy, put in place by the military, is largely accepted even in Pakistan. With no political group of substance visible in the domestic environment, the ultra conservative group like the MMA is the only organisation which could emerge as the point of strong opposition. In fact, the MMA appears to be the only entity capable of rallying all likeminded splinter religious bodies for countering the military regime. It may be able to influence sections of the military establishment including the cadres of the ISI. The MMA has already given a call for the resolution of the Kashmir issue, a subject of enormous emotive content in the psyche of the masses in Pakistan.[71] The military regime may resort to some adventure of the Kargil variety to whet domestic appetite. In that situation an Indian response would be extremely damaging to Pakistan. The US would invariably intervene.

The sectarian friction in Pakistan, will now find a catalyst in the fundamentalist provocation. The military regime will be at odds to deal with the situation. A solution for the strong sectarian syndrome lies only in a democratic process.

An anti-drug industry drive will remain the baby of governments in power. With deep tentacles within Pakistan and even stronger outside, no success is foreseen in the near future. The prospects of getting out of the economic and social quagmire are therefore bleak. The lovers of democracy in Pakistan are going to be disappointed for a long period of tomorrow.

Notes:

1. *The News,* 31 January, 2001.
2. For an elaboration of this logic please see Smruti Pattanayak, "Civil-Military and Coordination and Defence Decision-Making in Pakistan", *Strategic Analysis,* 2000.
3. This concept is explained by Ajay Darshan Behara in his article on "The Battle for Kabul", *Strategic Analysis,* January-February 1997. A discussion with the author revealed a deep-rooted desire amongst the Pakistani elite to spread the Pakistani sphere of influence west and northwestwards.
4. Quoted from "Pakistan's Goals and Strategies in Afghanistan", by Sumita Kumar, *Strategic Analysis,* January-February 1997. Primary source: Diego Cordovez and Selig S. Harrison, *Out of Afghanistan: The Inside Story of Soviet Withdrawal,* New York: Oxford University Press, 1995.
5. Sumita Kumar, n.4 ibid.
6. Oliver Roy, "The Lessons of Soviet – Afghan War", Adelphi Paper No 259, summer 1991, as quoted by Sumita Kumar, n.4 ibid.
7. This is an extract of the study conducted by the author. Please see "(Pakistan's) Afghanistan Policy", Prashant Dikshit, *Strategic Analysis,* November 1993.
8. Prashant Dikshit, n.7 ibid.
9. D. Shah Khan, "The New Afghanistan", *The Herald,* April 1990.
10. G.D. Bakshi, "The Military Dimension", *Strategic Analysis,* January-February 1997.

11. Sreedhar, "The Taliban Factor in the Ongoing Afghan Civil War" *Strategic Analysis*, January-February 1997.
12. Khaled Ahmed, in "A Frontline State Falls Apart", *The Friday Times*, 7-13 November 1996 and Rahimullah Yusufzai, in "Here come the Taliban", *Newsline*, February 1995.
13. G. D. Bakshi, n10 ibid.
14. Quoted in n10 ibid.
15. Sreedhar, in n11 ibid.
16. Quoted in the, *Scientific Report*, February 2002.
17. n16 ibid.
18. Rubin Barnett quoted in n16 ibid.
19. Report of the UN Secretary General on the situation in Afghanistan, June 2000 quoted in n16 ibid.
20. Ahady Anwar-ul-Haq quoted in n16 ibid.
21. For an analysis of the impact of diffusion of light weapons syndrome, please see Ajay Darshan Behara in "Light Weapons Diffusion and Security", *Strategic Analysis*, July 2001.
22. *Peoples' Opinions Trends*, No 94, 3 May 1991.
23. *Jasaarat*, 9 May, 1991.
24. *News*, 22 May, 1991.
25. *Dawn*, 25 February, 1991.
26. *Nation*, 22 May, 1991.
27. *Dawn*, 31 May, 1991.
28. *Muslim*, 10 April, 1991.
29. *News*, 21 May, 1992.
30. *Viewpoint*, 9 January, 1992.
31. *Frontier Post*, 30 June, 1992. Dera Adam Khel in the NWFP is the legendary arms bazar.
32. n31, ibid.

33. Tara Kartha, "The Spread of Arms", *Strategic Analysis*, November 1993.

34. n33, ibid.

35. *Newsline*, October 1989, as quoted by Tara Kartha in n33 ibid.

36. n33, ibid.

37. Khan Aamer Ahmed, "The End of Jehad", *The Herald*, December 2001.

38. This data has been gleaned from "The Supporting Structures for Pakistan's Proxy War in Jammu & Kashmir" by Ajay Darshan Behara, 2001.

39. *Newsline*, December, 1989.

40. Ruchita Beri in "Poppy Culture", *Starategic Analysis*, November, 1993.

41. CIA Report on " Heroin in Pakistan: Sowing the Wind", *The Friday Times*, September, 1993.

42. *Newsline*, December, 1993.

43. CIA'S ROLE IN THE DRUG TRADE: ANALYSIS, *Peoples' Opinion Trends*, 23 November, 2001.

44. Tamara Makarenko "Systematic Transnational Crime", *Janes International Review*, May, 2002.

45. N 42, ibid.

46. *Dawn*, Karachi, 8 March, 2002.

47. *Dawn*, Karachi, 28 February, 2002.

48. See Larry P. Goodson as quoted in n16, ibid.

49. Christina Lamb in *Waiting for Allah*, London: Hamish Hamilton, 1991.

50. Quoted by Christina Lamb in n49 ibid.

51. n49, ibid.

52. Azmat Abbas, *The Herald*, November 2001.

53. n49, ibid.

54. View obtained from the *Scientific Report*, February 2002.

55. n49, ibid.

56. Abbas Zaffar, "Pakistan's Great Gamble", *The Herald*, October 2001.

57. These charter of demands were carried by the *Dawn* Karachi, on 30 January, 2002. Although this text is reproduced from Sumita Kumar, " Politics in Pakistan Post-September 11, 2001", *Strategic Analysis*, April- June 2002, for the original see, Dan Baltz, Bob Woodward and Jeff Himmelman, *Washington Post*, 29 January, 2002.

58. Hasan Syed Ali Dayan, "No Pain No Gain", *The Herald* 2001.

59. Sumita Kumar in n57 ibid.

60. n57 ibid.

61. Aimal Khan writing in the *Independent*, 21-27 September, 2001.

62. *The News*, 16 December, 2001.

63. *The News*, 31 January, 2001.

64. n37, ibid.

65. n57, ibid.

66. This analysis was arrived at after discussions with experts.

67. Douglas Frantz, "The Financing: Ancient secret system moves money globally", *The New York Times*, 3 October, 2001 as quoted by N. S. Jamwal in "Hawala - The Invisible Financing System of Terrorism", *Strategic Analysis*, April-June 2002.

68. Douglas Farah "Qaeda's: Following the trail to Dubai", *The International Herald Tribune*, February, 18 2002.

69. Azmat Abbas in *The Herald*, November 2001.

70. For this statement, see n69 ibid.

71. See the report of the 'Strategic Foresight Group', *The Times of India*, 11 November, 2002.

7

Dealing With 'Big Brother'

Mahendra Ved

Forever active in the South Asian region and in the international arena, the India-Pakistan rivalry has been at its competitive best in the situation that developed after the terror attacks in the United States on 11 September, 2001. The attacks took place in the Western Hemisphere, but the source was located in the South Asian neighbourhood in the form of Osama bin Laden and his al-Qaida terror network. This made the Indo-Pak angle to the upcoming crisis inevitable. The spillover of the 'Nine/Eleven', to use the American term to indicate the terror attacks, to Kashmir, "the world's most dangerous spot" as former US President Bill Clinton put it, has hogged a significant part of the international community's attention.

India and Pakistan came dangerously close to an actual war twice during the year 2002. This, even as the region witnessed a million soldiers, armed to the teeth and on the highest battle alert, one of the highest and the most alarming since World War II, for ten long months. The demobilisation along the International Border–the wintertime build-up continues along the Line of Control in Jammu and Kashmir–has only served to throw the ball back in the diplomatic court. This, even as daily 'incidents' on the border continue. The low intensity conflict has only taken a new dimension.

On the one hand, the May 1998 nuclear tests by India and Pakistan have only added a nuclear dimension to the rivalry, making it more fierce and inviting world concern at the slightest of provocations. Pakistan perceives that it has used its 'nuclear blackmail' tactics with a fair amount of success, to 'internationalise' the Kashmir issue. The major powers find this threat credible because while India sticks to the no-first-use promise, Pakistan uses this very commitment to say that it would not exercise any such restraint. The world is prepared to accept the Indian case of cross-border infiltration being sponsored from Pakistan and have asked the latter to curb it and respect the sanctity of the LoC. On the nuclear issue, they started separating India and Pakistan with the latter acquiring the image of a "nuclearised bad boy".

If, on the other hand, holding of elections was seen as a political exercise leading at some stage to political resolution of the Indo-Pak disputes, then elections in Jammu and Kashmir and the simultaneous exercise that General Pervez Musharaf conducted in Pakistan, have served only marginally to lower the tensions. Indeed, Pakistan did its utmost to muddy the waters in Jammu and Kashmir to thwart smooth elections. Musharaf called them "farcical" even as the poll process began, debarring the All Party Hurriyat Conference and other separatists from contesting the elections and signalling a hike in infiltration and pre poll violence. Yet, the elections won nearly unanimous approval from international observers and the media as being fair and transparent.

The same quarters, however, refused to sanctify Pakistan's poll exercise, which was seen as flawed, having been preceded by constitutional and political changes. It is quite another matter that the US and the major powers applauded Musharaf for keeping his promise as per the schedule and taking the country back on the road to democracy. The US's applause stands in stark contrast to its insistence on democracy in Iraq – a subject that has been oft-commented on, but has not brought about a change in the US attitude.

Post-9/11, India and Pakistan seem more like the two sides of the South Asian coin with less and less meeting ground. Pakistan will not rest in peace till it gets Kashmir and India simply will not give it. Denied the 'strategic depth' in Afghanistan, Pakistan feels compelled to keep the Kashmir pot boiling with the hope that international pressures will at some stage force India to come to the negotiating table without laying any preconditions.

In response, India is resisting a dialogue till it can get some concessions. It is an uphill task. The carrot-and-stick approach is working but not as well as it should. The demobilisation from the international border without securing tangible gains has somewhat limited India's options to lay any preconditions. A clear example is the fact that India began its campaign in January 2002 by demanding that Pakistan hand over 20 wanted criminals. Pakistan denied and prevaricated and finally said it would not work on that line at all. After ten months, nobody is talking of the 20 wanted persons.

In a clear signal that Pakistan's Kashmir policy would remain unchanged, irrespective of which party or group forms the governments – in Srinagar and Islamabad – the Musharaf regime has asserted its "complete solidarity" with the people of Kashmir and its "unwavering resolve" to support them in their "legitimate struggle against Indian occupation[1]." Obviously, the message was intended for India and for the international community. Minister of State for Foreign Affairs, Inam-ul-Haq, referred to the "recent sham elections" in Jammu and Kashmir, which was a rejection of the popular government of Mufti Mohammed Sayeed and a signal to the separatists who began to make a beeline for the Pakistan High Commission in New Delhi the moment the poll results were out.

Viewed from the US angle, or that of the European Union up to a point, terrorism and violence in the name of Kashmir, combined with the nuclear threat, is the central point on which India and Pakistan can clash. While strengthening bilateral ties with both countries, they want the two to talk and sort out their problems. Russians do join in on the diplomatic front, while leaning towards India, just as the Chinese do, supporting Pakistan tactically. It is cold war in a different incarnation, but the trump card of disciplining Pakistan remains with the US and China.

That is how the post-9/11 developments in South Asia need to be viewed. Churlish as it may seem, but the completion of the elections and the beginning of the process of de-escalation by the two neighbours that followed, could best be viewed as a success of the US' short and medium term plans in South West Asia.

This is because, their denials notwithstanding, the two adversaries have been under constant US pressure, particularly since they went nuclear in May 1998. This process is destined to continue in the situation that has accrued since 9/11. Since the agenda is sought to be set by the US, its success, or otherwise, is bound to make a deep impact on South Asia.

The urgency and intensity of the US effort could be gauged from the fact that even before the respective legislatures had chosen their chiefs and popular governments installed, and within a day of the announcements of demobilisation – a process that is bound to take weeks – pressures began to mount for a bilateral dialogue. The pace caught Pakistan breathless, as it emerged as a client state of the US. On its part, India politely told the US officials – Secretary of State Colin Powell, National Security Advisor Condoleezza Rice and the ambassador in New Delhi, Robert Blackwill – that it would not engage in a dialogue till it saw concrete results of General Pervez Musharaf's promise to end cross-border infiltration.

The almost simultaneous poll exercises did provide a democratic veneer to what must be seen as the US game plan, supported by major powers – chiefly Germany, France, Britain, the European Union as a whole, China and Japan. But the extent of its success or otherwise would perforce have to be over a period. And during that period, some questions would need to be answered.

In raising these questions or seeking answers, the idea is not to run down the widespread appeals for resolution through talks for restoring peace and normalcy in South and South-West Asia. It goes without saying that the concerns of the world community need to be addressed.

But questions do arise because of South Asia's complex history and its current geopolitical situation. South Asia is witnessing a clash of two opposing ideologies. They have arisen almost simultaneously – the "Hindutva" forces in India with the justification that India is being "surrounded" by "jehadis" and communists. The 'Rath Yatra' that gave political voice to this sentiment took place in 1989, at the same time as the Afghan War ended and insurgency began in Jammu and Kashmir. The break-up of the Soviet Union which represented a secular, even if irreligious ideology, also lent justification and strength to the rise of religious conservatism and even antagonism. With 9/11, the US, representing in a sense the Christian "onslaught", hitherto confined to the Gulf region, moved into South-West and Central Asia in a big way. The terror attack in Indonesia and the hostage crisis in the Philippines in 2002 are perceived as the South-East Asian extension of this epicenter.

Musharaf raised the issue of Gujarat's communal riots and violence against Christians in India at the UN General Assembly. There can be no condonation for these acts. But the Indian polity has shown enormous amount of resilience and its institutions are strong enough to provide checks and balances against these trends. Opposition parties rule in more states than the ruling coalition at the Centre. And despite a decade of insurgency degenerating into a proxy, war and terrorism fully supported by Pakistan, the elections in Jammu and Kashmir have indicated that the people, tired of violence and political and economic instability, want to move on. They forced a change of government and are still raising questions that need answers.

The 9/11 took place in the other hemisphere but it is this region that has emerged as the epicenter of what is being described as the "Clash of Civilisations". It is a clash in which India and its "Hindutva" forces, along with Israel, are viewed by a section of Islamic protagonists as allies of the Christians. They perceive that if India is projected to be in the "Christian-Jewish camp", then peace with Pakistan becomes that much difficult. Even though a part of the international alliance against terrorism, Pakistan remains politically (its population and Saudi Arabian support) and militarily (because of being the only Muslim nuclear nation) a key member of the Islamic side of the "clash." Neither India, nor Pakistan is thus free to decide its national course in isolation to what is happening around it, near or far. At least that is how Pak-Islamists want to project the Indian subcontinent.

That being the situation, the question is: Is a dialogue between India and Pakistan, whether or not there is a meeting point, adequate to meet the challenge? A meeting ground has not so far been identified and India has resisted the "talk-talk" talk so far. Assuming at some point, India would agree to a dialogue shedding its seeming inflexibility, the process, undoubtedly would be long-drawn, and intially it may lead to nowhere. India could go back, just as Musharaf has done, on curbing the activities of the jehadi groups on Pakistan's territory. Such a dialogue would come to naught.

Secondly, how does the US want to tackle the consolidation of forces in Pakistan that are inimical to its presence? Is the demand of the new winners that the US troops should leave Pakistani soil, merely a pressure point? The US unwillingness to accept changes in the Islamic world after the Islamic Revolution in Iran in 1979, is at the root of the sudden rise of radical Islamic groups. In post 9/11 a section of the intelligentsia is asking-Have the crusaders come to South Asia? If so, what will be its impact on a secular India?

Thirdly, Is "civilianisation" of Pakistan, minus the mainstream political leadership, seen as an answer to the problem of combating terrorism? Earlier military dictators attempted selective democracy, introducing distortions in the country's body politic that have rarely been corrected. Musharaf has conveniently used the copybooks bequeathed by his predecessors, and to meet the current challenges, has gone beyond them. He has successfully kept out the principal players, allowing their parties to contest. Does the outcome of such an election spell, as he claimed before the elections, loosening of the hold of the feudals and the families on Pakistan politics?

Musharaf publicly said last year that religious extremists constituted no more than five to ten per cent of the electorate. The aerial bombing of Afghanistan in post 9/11 has changed all that. Elections have shown that their percentage is much higher. This strong emergence of *Islam-pasand* parties at the national level and in Baluchistan and North West Frontier Province (NWFP), the two provinces bordering Afghanistan, and the near-inevitability of their alliance with the Pakistan

Muslim League (Qaid-e-Azam), a creation of Musharaf, should have sent alarm signals to the US. But the world's sole superpower has reacted cautiously. The CIA is too well entrenched in Pakistan not to have foreseen the consolidation of the pro-Taliban forces in electoral terms. Apparently, it had calculated this setback to its plans to fight radical Islam in South-West Asia.

The Pakistan Muslim League (Qaid-e-Azam), the 'king's party', has now to coalesce with the Islamist conglomerate, Muttahida Majlis-e-Amal, (invoking Jinnah while naming the political party should place Musharaf a few notches above the wily Zia-ul Haq in political gall and grit.) Past dictators could make and unmake prime ministers at will. But Musharaf may not find it so easy to deal with a civilian prime minister because of the network of madrasas, and their leaders can call the shots now. The post-October 10, 2002, election verdict can work both ways. How far the constitutional safeguards Musharaf adopted before the polls might need to be resorted to if any political challenge to his position is posed, is anyone's guess now.

"Civilianising" of the government by Musharaf is bound to generate its own dynamics. There is bound to be friction between the civil and the military "wings" of the government. If that has been taken into calculation, it would be reasonable to assume that the US might seek to establish a rapport with the new civilian entities. The latter would become that much stronger, directly at the cost of Musharaf. Is the US looking for alternatives, military or civilian, to Musharaf? Is the Pakistani establishment, composed mainly of the armed forces, the civil bureaucracy, dominant business classes and willing politicians, about to open itself to a formal entry of the jehadis?

In theory, the US should be happy with the election outcome. It will not be a fully civilian government and yet, with an element of transparency, Musharaf would find it difficult to back the militants. That, perhaps, explains why ignoring charges of electoral malpractice leveled by international observers, the major powers are prepared to applaud his political feat.

Media reports say the results took everybody by surprise. It is plausible that India too had calculated this outcome prior to or after Pakistan's tenth general election, dubbed "General's election". That these forces are at once anti-America and anti-India is all too well-known. For India, which went through a difficult election in Jammu and Kashmir almost simultaneously, the concern is immediate and in close proximity. How the jehadi groups, active on both sides of the Line of Control (LoC), react to the poll results in Pakistan is bound to influence the thinking of the winners and losers in Jammu and Kashmir. And on the national and international plane, it will determine how New Delhi approaches the dialogue with various political groups in the state and at some stage or the other, with Islamabad.

The winners in Pakistan invoked the "India factor", comparing themselves with the "Hindutva" forces that are supposed to be in power in India. In this comparison lies an inherent justification of their traditionally anti-India policies that have been compounded by the fact that India is part of the international alliance against a cause with which they have been sympathetic and willing participants.

Same Side: Differing Agenda

The South Asian paradox in the world as it exists post-9/11 is that India and Musharaf's Pakistan find themselves on the same side of the fence in the global fight against terrorism. Overtly both are part of the same international alliance that took shape in the aftermath of the terror attacks of September 2001. Pakistan became a place from where the US led alliance is launching a war against radical Islamic groups. India, on the other hand, remained a subtle partner in the alliance, refusing to get dragged into head hunting. But each has joined the alliance with a different agenda–an agenda that conflicts violently.

India sees the alliance and its subtle participation in it as vindication of its standpoint on what it has been suffering earlier in Punjab and later in Jammu and Kashmir, namely, militancy by separatist elements actively helped by Pakistan. For Pakistan, utterly mindful of its geopolitical importance, the U-turn in the Afghanistan policy – turning a hunter from a gamekeeper – it is the question of joining the right side in the fight. While India is bleeding in Kashmir and is looking for allies who will support its cause, Pakistan has been made a party to the war.

Born in adversity and forever opposing each other, as neighbours and in every conceivable forum, the two South Asian giants have clashed to further their respective – and conflicting – viewpoints in the midst of the fight against terrorism. If the world is concerned at the South Asian flashpoint, there is also the not-so-mute voice of the smaller nations in the region who say the conflict in the region impedes development. By no means a sideshow of the global war, the Indo-Pak tussle has often tended to influence the main thrust, even if there are developments in West Asia or the terror attacks in South East Asia (The Philippines, Indonesia).

South-West Asia has emerged as the epicenter of global terrorism, and Pakistan its principal hub, making the Indo-Pak cleavage deeper. In his report to the United Nations General Assembly, Secretary General Kofi Annan has recorded that the Taliban and al-Qaida fighters, ousted from Kabul, are regrouping on the Afghan-Pak border and deep inside Pakistan's North-West Frontier Province and the Northern Areas. The hideouts include even Punjab from where Osama bin Laden was reported to have escaped. Their coordination with the jehadi groups in Pakistan, which remain active and effective through their own efficient networking despite the ban imposed by General Musharaf, is a matter of record with the UN, the United States and anyone watching this region.

In the post-9/11 situation, hostile forces surround India more than ever before. India finds itself at the receiving end of a terror onslaught from its northwest that is spreading surreptitiously to other neighbours having weak security structures. The deterioration is not only in security terms, but is also political. There are serious strains in bilateral relations and even regional dealings (in particular SAARC) are adversely affected. Thus, even as relations with China, Myanmar, Bhutan, Sri Lanka and the Maldives have been good and even recorded improvement in recent years, those with Pakistan, Bangladesh and up to a point, Nepal, have witnessed convulsions.

Take Pakistan first. After keeping the main political players out through constitutional and political measures, Musharaf conducted an election through a "king's party" that will do business with the fundamentalist alliance of Muttahida Majlis-e-Amal (MMA). In any case, Musharaf would continue to call the shots like his peers – Ayub Khan, Yahya Khan and Zia-ul Haq. It is a negative signal considering the fact that successive military regimes in Pakistan have nurtured a culture that terms friendship with India as anti-Pakistani and 1990's milieu unIslamic. Over five decades, this has coloured the views and actions of even those who are not votaries of jehad. For India, the task of dealing with Pakistan becomes more difficult even if it wants to hold bilateral talks.

The "Pakistan factor" has bedeviled India's relations with other neighbours. India suspects that the respective neighbouring governments are unable, or unwilling to control elements within their territories having links with Pakistan's ISI.

Nepal is a case in point. Destabilised after the royal family's killings in June 2001, its situation is worsened by the growing Maoist insurgency. India finds Nepal a weak neighbour that occasionally plays the China card, but usually allows its soil and the sky to be misused by interests inimical to India. Pakistan has used Kathmandu as the bridge not only for its route to South-East Asia, but its ISI has nurtured it as a route for smuggling as a drug route for movement of insurgents and for gangsters who are fugitives from Indian law. Indian efforts to persuade Nepal to tighten its security apparatus in the wake of the December 1999 hijack have succeeded only partially.

Similar is the case with Bangladesh, which too has time and again allowed sanctuary to insurgents from the India's northeast. The spread of its migrant population, a phenomenon that began during the British era, has continued, causing demographic changes well beyond the borders with India. It has been harsh on its religious minorities, forcing migration each time there is political turmoil. The India factor heavily influences not only its politics, but also its economic activity. The politicisation of the issue of export of natural gas is an example.

But the real problem in Indo-Bangladesh relations is the spread of Islamist ideology that thrives on activities inimical to India. The last decade has witnessed constant rise in this and even the Sheikh Hasina government, perceived – and maligned at home – as being friendly to India, was unable to curb it for fear of antagonising the public.

The process has accelerated since the advent of the Khaleda Zia regime wherein the Islamic Oikya Jote (a conglomerate of Islamist forces including the Jamaat-e-Islami that opposed the birth of Bangladesh) shares power with Zia's Bangladesh Nationalist Party. The Pakistan factor in the politics of this erstwhile East Pakistan is too obvious to miss. Stray Bangladeshi groups are known to be active with al-Qaida and had joined the Taliban. In the aftermath of 9/11, thanks to the strong Saudi influence, the Bangladeshi political stance, in the name of Islamic solidarity, has been distinctly anti-US and sympathetic to the Taliban. The *Time* magazine report (PTI, 14 October, 2002, since disputed by both *Time* and the Bangladesh Government) about the planned relocation of al-Qaida and Taliban fighters ousted from

Kabul and Kunduz to Bangladesh and the activities of Harkat-ul-Jihad Islami (HUJI), provide succinct confirmation of this phenomenon.

Nuclear Blackmail

India is often criticised at home and outside, with a measure of justification, for thinking excessively Pakistan-specific and tailoring its domestic and foreign relations accordingly. Meeting the Indian delegation led by Prime Minister Atal Bihari Vajpayee at Copenhagen in the second week of October 2002, the European Union suggested that India should not look at the world from a "Pakistan prism" and should not shy away from a dialogue with Pakistan, especially on the Kashmir issue. The Indian side retorted by saying that it is the world that should stop looking at India through such a prism. There was no reference to India-Pakistan dialogue and on the question of cross-border terrorism in the joint declaration.

Behind the EU's concern, and the general insistence of the world community that India and Pakistan must talk to resolve their disputes is the fear of a nuclear war. Even before 9/11, the fact that both countries went openly nuclear in May 1998, alarmed the world community. While this is not the forum for discussing whether the decision to go nuclear was right or not, the fact remains that it has ever since heightened tensions in South Asia. India cited China as the potential threat, which angered China, prompting it to further forge closer military ties with Pakistan. India faced the world community's anger and sanctions from Japan, and the US, which it surmounted with its inbuilt resilience over a period till they were lifted. But Pakistan went nearly bankrupt. Kargil was a natural corollary pursued by Pakistan to deny India whatever advantage it acquired by going nuclear. And equally natural to the debacle in Kargil was removal of the Sharif government and takeover by Musharaf.

The advent of Musharaf did not change things radically on the economic front. But there is enough evidence to suggest that the US, bracing itself to meet the long-term challenge of Islamist terrorism after the attacks on its embassies in Africa and then the attack on *USS Cole*, did move in to prop up the withering state held desperately together by Musharaf. A political pariah and a militarily suspect (because of the support to the Taliban regime) although Pakistan was, it had to be kept on the economic drip. The US sought to impress upon India, with adequate justification, that an economically desperate Pakistan was a military risk to its neighbours. All along, however, Islamabad continued to nurture the regime in Kabul and consolidate its "strategic depth". This charade went on till 9/11.

In the post-9/11 phase, the world community's concern reached great heights after India upped the ante in December-end 2001. Following the terror attack on its Parliament on 13 December, India deployed its forces on the border, placing them on the highest alert. Pakistan responded likewise. The international security managers perceived that the Indian subcontinent was "close to a conflict" that sent chilling reminders of 1971 – that there was much more manpower, more ammunition and technology and the nuclear arsenal now than thirty years ago.

The numerous peace missions to South Asia, the global shuttling and the meetings did not seem to help beyond a point. Musharaf committed, in his 12 January, 2002, speech that he would stop infiltration "permanently". He reiterated his commitment later in the year to the US and the British interlocutors, but within days went back on it or according to same observers was not able to implement it.

In the months that followed, amidst shelling from both sides of the Indo-Pak border and especially, along the Line of Control (LoC), it was feared that any small thing could spark a full-fledged conflict – a conventional one that could escalate into the first nuclear war since World War II. It was Pakistan that gave a fillip to these fears by repeated assertions by Musharaf and other leaders and officials that Pakistan will not hesitate to use nuclear weapons as a last resort.

Such assertions and the Indian rhetorical response only caused exaggerated fears compelling some of the major powers to hold the warring nations on an international leash in the summer of 2002. Stern travel advisories were issued and some embassies in New Delhi and Islamabad evacuated their spare staff and their families. It is significant that while the US, the British, the Canadians and some others evacuated surplus staff or sent them away home on holiday, the Russians, Germans, French and others did not do so. All this affected tourism and kept away business investors for some weeks. While this ploy provided some elbowroom to the peace emissaries, it failed to bring the two sides to the negotiation table.

In the post-9/11 scenario, the world is treated to a bizarre situation wherein both India and Pakistan at times use identical language to say different things. The UN General Assembly session in September 2002, witnessed speeches and furious diplomatic drives by both sides. Both condemn terrorism, but while India talks of cross-border terrorism, Pakistan simply denies it. "There is nothing happening on the LoC," Musharaf repeatedly told the US media while in New York. Having earlier called the impending Jammu and Kashmir elections "farcical" and prevented any possibility of the separatists participating in them, Musharaf descended to the level of bringing in the Gujarat riots in his UNGA speech.

In the post-9/11 scenario, however, Pakistan's case that what is happening in Jammu and Kashmir is a "freedom struggle" has been rejected by the Great powers. India, on its part, has been able to gain wide acceptance for its term "cross-border terrorism". It is a definite gain for India in that these countries found these terms were difficult to digest till the 1999 Kargil conflict. It has taken India tremendous diplomatic effort–that included the "coercive" element of deployment of its armed forces–to achieve this.

Apart from acceptance or otherwise of terms and descriptions, however, the bottom line is that India has met with only limited success on the ground. Cross-border infiltration stopped only briefly during the winter months of 2002, only to go up during the summer as weather conditions permitted such an exercise. The ground reality is that infiltration continued throughout 2002, and through the elections in Jammu and Kashmir, despite heavy Indian deployment, the US pressures, and clear calls from other influential nations. This shows that while taking a complete U-turn in the Afghanistan policy, Musharaf was able to continue with the same Kashmir policy.

Kashmir: Root Cause, But Not Core Issue

India's chief problem has been that it is bleeding in Kashmir without respite. Thanks to the insurgency that began in 1989, and turned into a proxy-war after the ISI replaced the Kashmiris. Its troops are on the Siachen Glacier, the world's highest battlefield, since 1984. The deployment of the armed forces on high alert on the LoC since December-end 2001 cost India economically and in terms of goodwill—globally and regionally. During the period 1990 to 2001, Indian economy was able to get out of Hindu growth rate of 3-4 percent and reach 6-7 percent levels.

When it took the path of economic reforms in 1990, some perceive that the move came as a reaction to the disintegration of its closest ally, the Soviet Union. The Russians had withdrawn from Afghanistan a year earlier, which enabled Pakistan to divert a number of Afghan war veterans to Kashmir. What was essentially a separatist political movement became a foreign-funded and armed insurgency movement. There was disillusionment among the ranks of the insurgents by the mid-1990s and the leadership went into the hands of foreign mercenaries and this converted the movement into organised terrorism.

The break-up of the USSR and the resultant emergence of a number of new Central Asian nations provided a psychological fillip to the separatists in Jammu and Kashmir, who had been bitter about the rigging of the assembly polls in 1987. By entering into an alliance with the National Conference and sharing power with it, the Congress had left a political vacuum in the opposition ranks, but had not allowed the local forces, including the separatists who had contested the polls, to fill it. The late 1980s were a period when Pakistan was in turmoil because of the sudden exit from the scene of Zia-ul Haq and India could have applied the correctives. Instead, it allowed this political vacuum in Jammu and Kashmir, which was totally taken advantage of by Pakistan.

The "democratic" decade in Pakistan (1989-99) affected India-Pakistan relations only marginally. This was mainly because the Kashmir policy was not with the civilian political leadership but remained effectively with the army, or in a larger sense, with the military-civil bureaucracy. The political class made up for this handicap by deriving political mileage – more so the two Nawaz Sharif regimes than the two headed by Benazir Bhutto. Out of power, Benazir even rued the Kashmir policy that was pursued when she was the political boss, and blamed it on the army. Both politicians, however, remained creatures of the army and rather than nurture democratic institutions, used them, even bent them or broke them, for their narrow ends.

Throughout this decade, Pakistan tried to continue its arms race with India, bolstered as it was with the "strategic depth" that Afghanistan provided. Seeing itself as a natural leader of the Islamic world (with Iran and Iraq in the US doghouse and with willing help from Saudi Arabia) Pakistan sought to utilise this period to expand its influence to Central Asia, but with limited success.

The second Bhutto regime made a success of the Afghan policy by creating the Taliban and eventually installing them in power in September 1996.

Armed with a "heavy" mandate gained from a poor voters' turnout, Sharif continued this policy, deriving political mileage and allowing the military-civil establishment its own way. His turning point came when India surprised the world by going openly nuclear in May 1998. Sharif had no choice but to follow suit. The rapprochement was attempted at Lahore amidst international fanfare, but Sharif was clearly out of favour with the army when Sharif asked the army to create "*chotasa gadbed*" in Kashmir to have a better bargaining in his post-Lahore summit visit to India, the latter went berserk and started a war. The army top brass in GHQ Rawalpindi thought that Kargil was the natural corollary to the nuclear race and the political "adventure" at Lahore. A withdrawal from Kargil under the US pressure eventually cost Sharif his job.

The India-Pakistan rivalry sharpened greatly after General Musharaf ousted Sharif and took over as the Chief Executive. The Vajpayee Government wanted to have no truck with a man it knew as the architect of Kargil and one with known sympathies to the jehadi groups. His being a Mohajir was yet another negative point, the general Indian perception being that a Mohajir military man is anti-India by his professional compulsion of being part of a Punjabi-dominated Pakistan Army. Unlike Zia-ul Haq, who made avid efforts to win friends in India and succeeded considerably, Musharaf's efforts to win support in India or in the world community met with very limited success.

Ironically, India provided the first major dose of respectability to Musharaf by inviting him to Agra in mid 2001. The invitation and the respectability both came under international pressures to get two adversaries to talk, and that too, at the highest level. Musharaf made himself the country's president, all but pushing out the incumbent, citing protocol reasons. From a pariah military dictator, he became a Head of state to whom the principal adversary was willing to talk.

Musharaf also managed his home constituency well by talking to the army, the ISI, the intelligentsia and the media and a broad section of politicians. Thanks to this mandate and the media blitz, he had already acquired a larger-than-life image when he reached Agra.

The talks, set without an agenda and preparations, were doomed to failure and they did. But not without Musharaf virtually hijacking the summit with the help of a pliant media, both national and international, which saw him as a great peace maker and fell in love with his "body language." He painted Vajpayee as someone who was a virtual prisoner of the hardliners in his government and the BJP. But what Vajpayee later told his cabinet colleagues, Musharaf tried to do a diplomatic gung-ho, whipping out a draft joint declaration from his pocket and urging Vajpayee to sign on the dotted line. Vajpayee did not oblige.

Post-9/11, under totally changed circumstances in the wake of 12/13 – the terror attack on Indian Parliament – India has shown no inclination for repeating a Lahore, nor an Agra. Vajpayee shook the hand dramatically extended by Musharaf at the Kathmandu SAARC Summit in January 2002, but reiterated that there could be no talks till cross-border infiltration ended. They met again at Almaty, Kazakhstan, but despite best efforts by Vladimir Putin and Noorsultan Nazarbayev, the host, and with Jiang Zemin by the Pakistani side, the ice could not be broken.

9\11 And After

If Zia-ul Haq's hour of glory was the rejection as "peanuts" the first big packet that the Carter Administration offered on becoming the "frontline state" in the fight against the Soviets in Afghanistan, it was Afghanistan again that provided Musharaf with both a challenge and an opportunity. Twenty-two years apart, the two were widely different, but the common point was Pakistan's geo-strategic position and its willingness to play the US ally.

India was among the first few nations to offer the US its support in the fight against terrorism. This was later specified as one on the land, sea and air – meaning political, military and logistic support. The Vajpayee Government was criticised in some political quarters, but there is little doubt that there was a measure of understanding with the non-communist opposition, particularly the Congress.

It would be a matter of informed assessment, and that too by hindsight, on the extent to which the Indian move prompted Pakistan to join the international coalition, rather than oppose it or drag its feet. The widespread assumption at that time was that Pakistan would not be able to snap its umbilical chord with the jehadis and its over-weaning interest in supporting the Taliban. But Musharaf took one grim week to act and to prove India wrong. He even earned from New Delhi a grudging no-objection support. In his 19 September, 2001, speech, that of a very tense person, he said he was joining the international coalition. He said he had tried to persuade the Taliban to hand over Osama bin Laden. (Some days later, he sacked the ISI chief, Lt. Gen. Mehmood Ahmed, who had opposed his policy and rather than persuade the Taliban, had egged them on to act tough).

Significantly, but not surprisingly, Musharaf devoted more than half of his speech to India-bashing with a "hands-off-Pakistan" call. This was meant for the home audience. To the world community, he justified his U-turn with the emphasis that he was saving his country's sovereignty, its nuclear arsenal and keeping intact the policy of supporting the "freedom struggle" in Kashmir.

While deciding on this difficult course, Musharaf carried his corps commanders with him. Those opposing the change were silenced and later removed. It is difficult to guess how he sold his plan to his colleagues. But the Pakistan Army was under the impression that the US would go for the al-Qaida and probably also bomb Osama hideouts, but spare the Taliban. Effort was indeed made to draw this line with the US, but the latter did not agree. But this did delay the US action as it looked for "moderate" Taliban and waited to break their ranks. Simultaneously, Musharaf launched a diatribe against the Northern Alliance, opposing it vehemently and projecting them as lackeys of India, Iran and Russia who could not be trusted and who had a bad human rights record. (The human rights violations in the form of ethnic cleansing of the minorities by the Pushtuns, incidentally, were supposed to have been carried out in the early months after the Mujahideen won, right under the benign presence of Pakistanis).

The Pakistani gambit managed to delay the involvement of the Northern Alliance by over three weeks. It was only in the end of October 2001 that the ground operations took off in a major way, after the US's air operations had failed to change the ground situation.

For obvious reasons of logistics, the US did not utilise the Indian offer, but operated from Pakistan and from Central Asia. The US depended heavily on the ground intelligence, at times deliberately misleading, available from the ISI. With Pakistani personnel already in Afghanistan, the US found it easy to fall back on an old ally used to Western armaments, communications and intelligence gathering techniques. It was, therefore, not surprising that at Kunduz, Musharaf was able to rescue key Pakistani personnel, along with Taliban leaders and even al-Qaida operatives, in a deal that the US continues to deny it with Pakistan.

Musharaf deserves full marks for making the best of a grim situation confronting his regime. By comparison, Zia was already on the US side, but Musharaf had to do a complete U-turn in his Afghanistan policy. He ditched the Taliban after having supported them to the hilt. He risked personal security tremendously and annoyed the jehadi groups, again one of his constituencies, by this change. He has received close to a billion dollars and has been able to lease out three air bases to the US for a fat amount. He has been able to explain away the killing of *Wall Street Journal* journalist Daniel Pearl and the French submarine technicians, conveniently, but not convincingly,.

Musharaf has kept unrelenting pressure on India on the Kashmir front and on the diplomatic plane, making the neighbour as an inflexible entity unwilling to see reason from the world community. If India thought it would utilise the Afghanistan changes to advantage on the Kashmir front, Musharaf has thwarted it successfully. Under pressure, he committed to ending the jehadi groups' activities and even issued formal ban orders, but the jehadis were allowed to go underground. Only some of the main leaders were placed under benign house arrest. The bank accounts were frozen, but before that, they were emptied out, according to reports in the Pakistani media.

The Indian score card as a result of an unrelenting campaign and "coercive diplomacy" of placing its forces on a high alert on the border has been that none of the major powers is ready to accept the Pakistani version of what is happening in Kashmir. In the post-9/11 situation, and with the September 2001 UN resolution in place, it is all terrorism. India is happy with this situation as the way the US led war on terrorism started unfolding.

One year after it launched its operations in Afghanistan, the US has made it clear that it is here to stay. It is involving itself in Pakistan heavily and in Pakistan, it is Musharaf only, as long as he delivers. Concessions and gestures to India would be made to the extent that they do not affect Musharaf's scope of action. Overtly it appears, Musharaf's "after me, the Jehad" line has worked with the US and because of the US, the world community in general. The US would not allow India or anyone else to infringe on Musharaf's "sovereignty." The bottom line is that the US needs

Musharaf for the sake of stability in the region and for the operations against al-Qaida to continue. And these operations have to be restricted to Afghanistan.

Under Zia-ul Haq during the earlier Afghan war, Pakistan was called a "frontline state." The Bush Administration, and President Bush himself, have been profuse in their praise of Musharaf. The chemistry at work is different, but it is working under more complex circumstances. The American media as also many Congressmen and think tanks, though, have been circumspect about the role of Pakistan and with Musharaf at its helm. But the bottom line is that the chemistry at work under more complex circumstances when compared to the 1980s, has helped Musharaf to drag his country out from a failing state with a near-bankrupt economy to being "a valiant fighter" in the war against terrorism.

On one score, however, the US has not been fully successful; Musharaf remains at risk of being attacked. The attack on his person could come from any of the jehadi groups or some disgruntled army men, serving or retired. There have been two reported attempts on his life. One was in May 2002, another in September 2002 was talked about, but not widely reported. The surmise is that the attempts did not succeed because in neither case, was the higher echelons of the ISI involved. Musharaf has since been avoiding too many public functions for security reasons.

At home, he held a referendum on his presidency, which earned him full five years more and a congratulatory telephone from US Secretary of State Colin Powell. His ability to seize any opportunity seems formidable in that immediately after this congratulatory message, he denied making any commitment to Richard Armitage or any other US official or British Foreign Secretary Jack Straw that he would end "permanently" the cross-border infiltration into Jammu and Kashmir.

Musharaf kept his election schedule after ensuring that neither Benazir Bhutto, nor Nawaz Sharif were able to contest. The two main parties fielded their B teams. The role of the third big party, the MQM, also remained marginal. The conducting of the elections and the results strongly indicate that rigging had been done to ensure that PML (Qaid-e-Azam) emerged the largest and that Parliament would remain a fragmented one. An excessively calibrated elections might have earned more seats for the PML (QA), but these would have become unacceptable.

The bottom line here is that the victory for the pro-Taliban MMA may have been higher than calculated. This can work both for and against Musharaf. He can use their presence to tell the US that he is helpless. But to remain in the US good books, he will still have to battle them carefully as they will work to further slow down the hunt for the Taliban and al-Qaida remnants hiding in Baluchistan, NWFP and the Northern Areas.

After the elections, Musharaf can safely be perceived as a weaker person. His political control over his territory stands considerably exposed. The era of rejecting American "peanuts" may be over for Musharaf. His continuance as the Army Chief is bound to cause heartburn among other generals with ambitions. The pro-Taliban lobby within the armed forces, which he has kept at bay for a year after 9/11, may become stronger and cause him problems in future. More so since even retired armed forces officers are also powerful in Pakistan.

There seems no immediate threat to Musharaf's position,. He may gain in stature as Head of a state with a democratic regime. But he would certainly enter a new era of having to deal with politicians who have earned legitimacy through elections. The civilian government will take sometime to settle down and till then, even the US is unlikely to unsettle or ruffle up Musharaf.

Mobilisation On Indo-Pak Border

Hardly had the Taliban been ousted from Kabul and mopping up operations were on in Afghanistan, with Pakistan licking the wounds of a political and military debacle, the Indo-Pak border charged up. Things became really hot in South Asia after the terror attack on Indian Parliament. Along with mobilisation of forces on the border, recalling of the High Commissioner from Islamabad, canceling overflights and ending the run of Samjhauta Express, India mounted a calibrated diplomatic offensive. Pakistan was forced to respond.

Through the ten months that followed, India and Pakistan were perceived by the major powers as being dangerously close to a conflict. Peace missions moved in and out of South Asia, the smaller neighbours in the sub-continent also lent their voices of concern and in the process, often equating both adversaries.

And through these ten months, except for a brief period of about a month, the flow of infiltration remained high as compared to previous years. It needs to be noted that in the ding-dong battle for superiority on the ground, the Indian security forces were able to eliminate a larger number of militants and foreign mercenaries.

Mounted on a massive scale, the largest since India and Pakistan became separate entities, the mobilisation by the Indian side, however, stopped having its impact from June 2002 onwards. Pakistan was able to continue with the flow of infiltrators, even as it sought to draw political mileage on the Kashmir issue. Musharaf, who began with his "hands off Pakistan" threat on 19 September, 2001, sang a different tune on 12 January, (2002) promising to curb infiltration. His later rhetoric turned to Kashmir repeatedly, the most bizarre one being: "Kashmir is in my blood."

India announced demobilisation on the international border (IB) mid-October (2002), retaining high vigil along the Line of Control, once the Jammu and Kashmir elections were over. Pakistan responded likewise. The new scenario requires a report card.

India responded to the 13 December attack on Parliament on a scale that left no higher option. From there to climb down became difficult. After a few weeks of "we shall teach a lesson" mood, reality sank in that it was going to be a long standoff. The armed forces waited for orders to act, which never came. Being on a high alert, without action, without a forward movement, it became untenable.

It would be churlish to say that India should have never mobilised in December 2001. The circumstances demanded stern action and India acted to send a message across the border and to the world community. It worked. Pakistan was forced to re-deploy its forces from its western border and amass on the one with India at a time when Afghanistan was in turmoil and the Taliban-al-Qaida fighters, not to speak of Pakistani ex-servicemen-turned-mercenaries, were on the move. There is little doubt that Pakistan felt extremely vulnerable and was forced to use the nuclear threat. This was the period when India successfully garnered support and sympathy of the world community. Post-9/11, there were few takers for Pakistan's line that there was no infiltration and that Jammu and Kashmir was facing little else but freedom struggle.

For the Indian armed forces and the country as a whole, it was being on the brink, waiting for action. The political decision did not come about. India came under tremendous pressure from major powers not to retaliate to 12/13 with force. Still recovering from 9/11 barely three months past, the world community was horrified at the prospects of a war next door to Afghanistan. India utilised the military build up as part of its "coercive diplomacy" with some positive results. But on the ground, infiltration in Jammu and Kashmir never really stopped ten months down the line. India got nothing in response to the list of 20 wanted criminals supposed to be hiding in Pakistan. After some attempts at "locating" them and some prevarication, Pakistan refused to cooperate.

Losses in economic terms are not fully estimated. Indo-Pak trade has gone entirely to third-country transactions. Divided families have rued the stoppage of air and rail links. This stoppage along with the no-talks stance has cost India in terms of public goodwill at home and outside. The PIA closed down its operations in India and simply sent the staff home without salaries or compensation.

On the military front, a lack of political will on the part of India prevented tougher action. India failed to open up another front during the Kargil conflict and once again, under pressure, sought to keep the tension with Pakistan localised to the LoC, even while staying fully mobilised along the entire border.

The outcome of a war would be difficult to predict, considering that highly professional armies are pitted on both sides. But in the heat of the psychological moment, India could have conducted some incursions across the border and hit at the militants' camps in POK – and got away with it. This is but an academic question now.

Once demobilisation takes place along the international border, a bulk of the Indian force stationed along the international border could return to their training and normal operations. Tensions can be expected to be lowered and so also casualties. India now assesses that its armed forces can be mobilised at short notice when needed.

As for the Pakistani armed forces that have been relieved from the Indian border, notionally, they would be available to guard the Afghan frontier as well. The US could use them in special operations against the al-Qaida and Taliban cadres. But this is bound to be a sop, a continuing low-key operation, with occasional spurts of actions that will be publicised to show results. The US-Pak cooperation on this front has been a bit of a myth, and may remain as such. The US does not have high expectations from the Pakistani armed forces on this score. The emergence of pro-Taliban regimes in NWFP and Baluchistan would further lessen local cooperation and is bound to make such operations even more untenable.

Status Quo

After the de-escalation that began along the international border of India and Pakistan, the situation accruing in the sub-continent once again lends itself to a continuation of the no-war-no-peace situation. In more sense than one, it is '*jaise the*', a status quo with which the region and the world are familiar. As far as immediate future is concerned, neither the elections in Pakistan, nor the one in Jammu and Kashmir are likely to make any material change so far as Indo-Pak relations are concerned. Both India and Pakistan are most likely to get back to sabre-rattling–mutually, and in the international fora.

So far as the larger region is concerned, for the US, there is a definite change in the focus away from South Asia towards West Asia. Iraq is the new focal point. After demobilisation, the US would have less reasons to worry about South Asia. But it would retain its presence in the region, reducing it but marginally for operational reasons.

More importantly, the "Afghan fatigue" has set in and the US is giving lower priority to Afghanistan. It can be expected to continue with special operations against the al-Qaida/Taliban. Occasional headline-grabbing news about Osama bin Laden and Mullah Omar are in store. The US would continue to provide security to President Hamid Karzai and support his administration.

Participation in nation building including training and equipping of the armed forces and the police can be expected to continue. But Afghanistan may cease to be a hot spot, at least for the US–unless the Taliban/al-Qaida fighters mount operations from neighbouring Pakistan's difficult-to-govern areas, threatening Kabul's stability.

This is mainly because the US realises that Afghanistan is a no-win situation. There is little chance of Osama or Omar being nabbed, given their ability to hide in inaccessible areas on the Pak-Afghan border, where they enjoy tremendous support and sympathy. In stark terms, the US and other allies have drawn the maximum mileage out of Afghanistan and would now be content with monitoring it closely and participate in its reconstruction.

The Indo-Pak relations lend themselves to some possible scenarios:

Scenario 1: No Meaningful Dialogue

Both India and Pakistan would pick up respective threads of development in timeless taxing. For Pakistan, the survival game resumes. Putting it starkly, it would live to fight another day such has been the Pakistani psyche since its birth. The loss of its erstwhile east wing, now Bangladesh, has made the Pakistani establishment paranoid. Each soldier commissioned after the 1971 war takes an oath that this humiliation would be avenged.

Apart from dramatic handshakes and pleasantries on the sidelines of international conferences, particularly SAARC, there is unlikely to be a meaningful dialogue for some time to come, despite pressures. Major powers, particularly the US, have made a virtue of these pressure tactics. They conveniently forget how long the US itself took to talk to the Vietnamese.

A "civilian" government is likely to seek dialogue on more meaningful terms with India. If it lessens its diatribe on Kashmir, India may readily respond by resuming over-flights and land and rail services. It is a measure that would be welcomed by the people in the region and by the world community. If this works, trade may follow. India's problem in furthering this interaction is that it is faced with a failing state, born and living in adversity, for which Kashmir-or-nothing-else line overrides everything. Its successive governments have rejected Indian attempts at cultural exchange as "cultural invasion" and scoffed at offers for economic cooperation as overtures from "Hindu shopkeepers."

A dialogue on the Kashmir issue would depend upon the course of events in Jammu and Kashmir. The presence of a government with a "Hindutva" agenda in India and the resurgence of Islamist forces in Pakistan should, theoretically at least, prevent a sustained dialogue on this vexed issue. This is where the outside pressures could work. But *realpolitik* – assuming that neither New Delhi, nor Islamabad wants to allow *Azadi* to the Kashmiris – on both sides might dictate a lot of hemming and hawing on the Kashmir issue, but no serious attempt at a dialogue. If the situation remains "under control", meaning no escalation on the border, then outside pressures, aimed mainly at defusing a tense situation, may not come into play.

However, the entire Asian region is very much under the Osama spell. This is evident from the terror attack in Indonesia. Closer home, a serious incident like 12/13 could spark tension between India and Pakistan. The role of Pakistan's ISI in other neighbouring countries, particularly Nepal and Bangladesh, could spark trouble among neighbours.

In Jammu and Kashmir, the electoral gains of the Peoples Democratic Party (PDP) indicate that this regional party, given a share of power, may press for a dialogue among various Kashmiri groups. It wants an unconditional dialogue covering the separatists, to be followed by a dialogue with Pakistan to which those demanding *Azadi* are a party.

India needs to chalk out a clear Kashmir policy shorn of sentiment and ideology - and implement it without spelling it out publicly. This is easier said than done, but needs doing. There are no instant solutions that many within the Indian establishment are looking for. At the same time, there is no point in dragging its feet on Kashmir -- not after the political momentum that the elections have provided. A deft and diligent dialogue with the separatists could help arrive at a solution. Every single move gets hyped up by the media and loses track: Lahore and Agra, particularly the latter, are good examples of this. Despite being a media person, this writer suggests that if the two sides are sincere, they will have to learn to work without seeking/allowing media glare.

A solution to the Kashmir problem is necessary so that the future generations can live in relative peace.

What exists now is passing on of the legacy of hostility from one generation to another, with justifications and rationale articulated. The Indian political scene was relatively free from an anti-Pakistan phobia but its being bled in Kashmir in the last decade has thrown up or strengthened forces that advocate an eye-for-an-eye approach. In a country with 150 million Muslim population – the second largest in the world, this is impacting on the domestic situation.

As for Pakistan, no matter who is in power in Islamabad, cross-border infiltration is bound to continue. To counter it, New Delhi will have to deploy security forces and this in turn will continue to have its repercussions. The vicious cycle will continue. It is time other options are explored.

India needs to set its own house in order. The internal security of the country as a whole needs to be strengthened. The ISI charge, albeit truthful, when repeated for every administrative and security lapse, has degenerated into a bogey.

Scenario 2: Dealing With Terrorism

South Asia has turned into the theatre of the absurd– only terrorism is too serious and dangerous a business to laugh away. It is bound to continue in one form or the other. The regrouping of al-Qaida and Taliban is bound to keep Pakistan and Afghanistan on the boil–with direct repercussions for Jammu and Kashmir. There are enough mercenaries of various nationalities, and enough jobless Pakistanis, to keep the terrorists' pot boiling. While Musharaf has been going through the charade of curbing jehadi groups, there have been absolutely no curbs on the madrasas, at one time estimated at 200,000 that produce these highly motivated militants. The emergence of Maulana Fazlur Rahman, on the political scene; who was instrumental in establishing a large number of them in the last two decades, should point to more madrasas and more jehadis. South Asia promises to be the battleground for the "clash of civilisations."

Whether or not the US moves from Afghanistan to what it calls the "nexus of evil"–Iran, Iraq and North Korea–terrorism is bound to thrive. To counter terrorism, the US is in for a long stay in Asia–West, South, Central and South-East–and this presence itself will fuel terrorism. The vicious cyclical movement is inevitable.

As the Indian leadership has been repeatedly saying after being disillusioned with the US's inability/ unwillingness to tame Pakistan's promotion of jehad and jehadis, there is no alternative to fighting one's own war. Terrorism as a phenomenon which became global after 9/11 the response to it so far remains America-centric. India will have to fight its own war on terrorism, no matter what it costs.

Scenario 3: How To Deal With Pakistan

Having begun to demobilise its forces, India now needs to take a deep breath, pause and ponder over how to deal with Pakistan – a failing state that thrives on causing impediments. How to alter the world's view of India? India needs to look at the world not through Pakistan's prism and deal with the world differently. A detached approach to Pakistan would ensure more respect and better appreciation of India. If the blood ties have got to turn always bloody, it is time to move away from Pakistan.

Whatever the pressures and from whichever quarter, India needs to keep away from the temptation of doing another Lahore or Agra. Already twice bitten, India ought to be shy about 'summiteering'. Any dialogue with Pakistan must start at the lowest possible level and must move up, depending upon the success in identifying areas of dialogue and cooperation. The summiteering has failed and should not be repeated. Track II and other moves can be resorted to but only carefully. India needs to widen its spectrum.

Here again, there is an urgent need for restraint in talking. Everyone talks about Pakistan and Paki-bashing is a favourite pastime. Much of the talking is done for instant popularity and publicity. The talkers are at times officials or politicians who failed when they were occupying positions from where they had dealt with Pakistan. There is much wisdom of hindsight.

India has fast improving relations with the US and other major powers. The Pakistan factor has tended to bedevil these bilateral or multilateral relationships. Without appearing to be competitive, India needs to point out Pakistan's role as a state involved in terrorism, and leave it at that.

Addressing FICCI on 10 September, 2002, on the eve of the first anniversary of 9/11, Defence Minister George Fernandes summed up the Indian approach *vis-à-vis* India, Pakistan and the world, particularly the US: "We are aware that the US will act in consonance with its own perceived national interests, and to that extent, one does not expect Washington to pull our chestnuts out of the fire. What merits careful reflection is the manner in which the US defines its abiding interests, and the extent to which these interests are defined and shaped, by the liberal, plural values enshrined in the US Constitution. Hence, support for democracy and liberal values must be Holy Grail for US foreign and security policies, but realpolitik considerations are an inescapable reality. Thus, the current US security doctrine is that 'mission defines the coalition'. However, we can understand the utility and relevance of Pakistan–even though it is under a military ruler–in the US war against terrorism. The US also realises that–whether it is the brutal assassination of Daniel Pearl, or the manner in which the al-Qaida and Taliban cadres have 'disappeared'–Pakistan is part of the problem and of the solution. This may well explain the US ambivalence and discomfiture about General Musharaf".

Notes

(Report from Islamabad in *The Hindu*, 6 November, 2002).

8

Looking Into The Future

Sreedhar

Before analysing the future of Pakistan, three factors need to be taken into consideration. There is a widespread feeling among a section of the Indian intelligentsia that the US involvement in Pakistan since 9/11 is substantial, and this would result in the emergence of a moderate Islamic state. The US is not committing the mistakes it did during 1979-89, that is, giving a free hand to the Pakistani armed forces in dealing with the jehadis. According to a US journalist, unlike in the 1980s, this time they have the Pakistan armed forces firmly under control. If we go by the media reports, the US Federal Bureau of Investigation has opened more than 200 offices across Pakistan to monitor the jehadis' activities. Therefore, the US will ensure that Pakistan emerges as a leader of the Islamic world.

However, they ignore the fact that Pakistani liberals who benefit the most from the US involvement in Pakistan are not part of the power loop. Therefore, left to themselves, Pakistani liberals would not have allowed the country to be derailed as much as it happened during the past 55 years. The country went through chaotic conditions including a partition because the liberals were kept away from power.

Since 9/11 the Pakistani armed forces, allowed themselves to be used by the US on two conditions. The US must ensure a government that is not anti-Pakistan in Kabul. Now it is a known secret that at the US prodding only Hamid Karzai, the President of the interim government in Afghanistan, first visited Islamabad before visiting other countries in the neighbourhood. Similarly, at the US insistence, the Hamid Karzai government agreed to receive General Musharaff in 2002. Inspite of this coercion from the US, the progress in Pakistan-Afghanistan relations is not as smooth as Islamabad wanted it to be. In fact, the speeches made at Grand Loya jirga convened in June 2002, by various delegates clearly indicate the anti-Pakistani sentiment in Kabul. At another level, Pakistan wanted the US to play a major role in resolving the Kashmir dispute.. Again it is a known secret that the US capacity to mediate in Kashmir is extremely limited. No government in New Delhi can give up any territory to Pakistan. The manoeuvrability in this context is also extremely limited.

Since the progress on these two counts is rather limited Pakistan is keeping its bargaining point, catching the Taliban-al-Qaida leadership, but as vaguely as it can do so. Even after more than one year of war, the Taliban-al-Qaida leadership are still at large, thanks to Pakistani agencies and the armed forces. This is now a widely accepted fact.

Secondly, after more than two decades of Talibanisation of the Pakistani polity, many in Pakistan started believing that it is the only solution to eradicate the ills of Pakistani polity. The overwhelming mandate of MMA in the 10 October, 2002, elections, whether manipulated or accidental, shows that at least a large section of people in Pakistani polity, are in favour of the mentors of the Taliban movement.

Though initial noises being made by the MMA leadership are politically correct, once they assume power, they are bound to come into conflict with the pro-US groups in JUI and JI. Both these parties have more or less an identical stand on Kashmir and Indo-Pak relations and the war against Taliban-al-Qaida. Since a solution acceptable to them cannot be found, the clash of interests is bound to come up. Any amount of tightrope walking by Musharaf and the US cannot make them change their stance; and even if the leadership whittles it down the cadres will not allow them to do so.

Simultaneously, the assumption on which the Pakistani armed forces were nurtured for the last five decades - Hindus cannot fight a war with Muslim Pakistan - has to be demystified. In the process the Pakistani elite, General Musharraf included, have to accept that in 1971 their country was divided by India and they cannot do anything about it. The Pakistani ruling elite has also to abandon the policy of 'a thousand cuts to bleed India'. All this means that a lot of change has to be brought into the Pakistani mindset in the coming years. This means making Pakistanis accept geographical realities that they are neighbours to a country four times bigger than them; re-writing Pakistani history that the concept of two-nation theory based on the principle that Hindus and Muslims cannot coexist as one nation is not correct. Though from an Indian perspective, it is a desirable development, in the immediate future and in the medium term it is highly unlikely to happen.

Third, any effort by the Great Powers to bring in a change in the Pakistani perception of its worldview is bound to be resisted. At the popular level in Pakistan many perceive that their miseries are largely due to the exploitation of their resources by the West. Whether such a perception is right or wrong can be debated; but such a perception resulted in the radical Islam of Osama bin Laden variety becoming popular in the Pakistani polity. In fact, the first American soldier killed on the Indian sub-continent was in Pakistan way back in November 1979. The way Pakistan could hoodwink the world since October 2001, about the Taliban and al-Qaida convinced many in Pakistan, that like the former Soviet Union, the US too could be defeated.

The Pakistani experiment with various forms of governance, from democracy to authoritarian rule has not yielded the desired results in terms of socio-economic development. The political power struggle was always among the elite groups and the armed forces remained arbitrators sometimes in this struggle and quite often even usurpers of this power. In this process the politicians and the armed forces tried to discredit each other. The only model they have not tried as yet is theocracy; and with the present mandate, if put into force vigorously, we may be witnessing a highly Talibanised polity. Many in Pakistan talk in terms of the Taliban model of governance being required to pull the country out of the despair in which it is now. They argue that the Mujahideen were successful in defeating a superpower and bringing peace and stability to a war ravaged country like Afghanistan.

It is in this context, that one has also to look into Pakistani credibility as a nation state. From experience, India witnessed that every new regime that came into power ignored all past agreements. For instance, Zia-ul-Haq dishonoured every word of the Shimla Agreement of 1972, signed by his predecessor. Much worse even before the ink was dry, the Lahore Declaration was discarded by the Generals (with or without the knowledge of the civilian government). Similarly, in spite of all promises made to the West, Pakistan resorted to proliferation of its nuclear technology by making it available to North Korea. Though not conclusively proved as yet, Pakistan was about to transfer technology for manufacturing weapons of mass destruction even to regimes like the Taliban. All this means that the ruling elite in Pakistan can be adventurous. It can go to any extent in pursuing its perceived strategic objectives.

Lastly, the ruling elite always came from Punjab, and many argue that the Punjab province set Pakistan's national agenda. There are many reasons for this perception, including the fact that the majority of persons in the Pakistani armed forces come from Punjab, the most populated province in the country. The result is that there is considerable amount of resentment among the remaining three provinces. Added to this, the politics of consensus, generally accepted for 'governing a multi-ethnic society like Pakistan', is absent in that country.

All this makes Pakistan a fragile polity even after more than five decades of independence. Many thought that after the 1971 division of the country into two, what is left of Pakistan would emerge as a cohesive unit and the ruling elite would address itself to socio-economic development and building up political institutions for good governance. Instead the country got involved in an unending war in Afghanistan and another war with India. The idea of good governance ended with spells of civilian and military rule. This has unleashed a set of new socio-economic forces making the polity more fragile than ever before. No one knows who rules Pakistan in real terms.

Scenario One

Against this backdrop one can visualise four scenarios for Pakistan. Given the post 9/11 developments, Pakistan can emerge as a role model of moderate Islamic state in the coming years. The basis for this optimism is that the Pakistani people being considerably disillusioned with the existing ruling elite are looking for ways and means to evolve a new politico-social order based on the Holy Book, which will be acceptable to the rest of the neighbourhood.

In addition, there is an external factor too – the US, which is working towards this goal. After the Islamic Revolution in 1979 in Iran this role was assigned to Pakistan by the US and Saudi Arabia. They envisaged Pakistan could be an alternative model to Iran and discredit the Islamic Revolution in Iran.

However, the difficulty in achieving this role model of moderate Islamic state is not keyed into the Pakistani psyche. The entire country's perception has to undergo a radical transformation – from a military power that can produce quick results to peaceful co-existence. It has to sink into the minds of the ruling elite that transformation is necessary for the survival of the nation state. For such a drastic change in the nation's psyche can come only if there is a charismatic leadership at the top; only such a leadership can bring about the structural changes in the polity. Unfortunately, one cannot see such a charismatic leader anywhere on the horizon in Pakistan at this point of time.

In addition, the ruling elite's conviction that a low intensity conflict has paid dividends in the past and will also pay dividends in the future needs to change. That requires repositioning of the armed forces in Pakistani polity. The armed forces, who emerged as the power brokers in the Pakistani polity during the last four decades are unlikely to accept any new arrangement which will undermine their predominant role in the body politic. As one commentator put it, how can Pakistani armed forces that never accepted civilian rule of people like Benazir Bhutto and Nawaz Sharif in the past, now take orders from people like Fazlur Rehman and Hussein Qazi. Until yesterday all these mullahs were taking orders from the Generals in GHQ in Rawalpindi. Pakistan is one place where the armed forces has a country and not a country with an armed forces.

Scenario Two

The second scenario could be Pakistan becoming a theocratic state, ruled by a group of mullahs (ilerics). A development in this direction is becoming a possibility because of disillusionment with other forms of governance, and the religious leadership having the resources and capabilities to confront the armed forces. More than two decades of collaboration in Pakistan's Afghan policy brought the two groups – the theocrats and armed forces together much more closely than at any time in the past. Though empirical evidence is lacking, many observers believe that Pakistani theocratic groups have made strong inroads into the armed forces. The rank and file in the country's armed forces look to the theocratic leadership for solutions to the country's problems. In fact, the way the armed forces ensured the victory of MMA in the elections held on 10 October, 2002, is an indication of this scenario. That the armed forces' continued collaboration with Taliban-Al-Qaida elements even after 9/11 is another indicator. The network of mosques and madrasas provide the ideal communication channel for the theocrats to mobilize masses. With ex-servicemen, former generals and jawans supporting, the theocrats can break the command structure of the armed forces.

The limitation of theocratic parties is that they are not broad based as yet. The bureaucracy and the urban population cannot reconcile themselves to a rule by mullahs. In all the elections held earlier, the percentage of votes polled by them was never in double digits. Even in the 10 October elections, their main area of strength is in the provinces bordering Afghanistan and Iran and not politically active Punjab or Sindh.

Equally important is that none of the leadership of the theocratic parties is charismatic like Zulfikar Ali Bhutto was in the early 1970s. During the two decades of long Pakistani Afghan involvement, most of these leaders have managed to build their own spheres of influence – that too in limited areas only. They have a large following, and the chain of mosques and madrasas across the country provide them with an effective organisational structure. But none of them are of the stature of Ayatollah Khomeini in the neighbouring Iran who managed to bring in an Islamic Revolution.

Again, the US may like to apply brakes to any such development. The Pakistani economy continues to be in a vulnerable position and to get it out of the woods substantial economic aid from outside is required. The Pakistani theocratic leadership is in no position to mobilise such aid. However, the pro-theocratic parties argue that like Afghanistan under Taliban, they can also survive on a subsistence level economy without much difficulty.

Scenario Three

The third model that is likely to emerge is the Turkish model of governance. Already the predominance of the armed forces in the Pakistani polity is a well-established fact and General Musharraf on more than one occasion has expressed his preference for the Turkish model. His plans to create a National Security Council-a sort of a super cabinet-dominated by the armed forces is seen as a step in that direction.

After the 10 October elections, whether this will be acceptable to other political groups, especially the theocratic parties, is debatable. By all available standards the Turkish model of governance has not brought the desired results in the governance of that state. No doubt

Turkey is not allowed to become another theocratic state, but a double-digit inflation, low level of socio-economic development and a permanent client state of the West, make many wonder how long this arrangement will continue. In governance of the state, Turkey had three constitutions in the last 42 years and innumerable politicians and political parties were banned on one pretext or the other. In the beginning of the 21st century, how can the Pakistani armed forces, who almost legitimised terrorism globally, be given a permanent role in governance of a state? Many feel it is a dangerous proposition. Contemporary history tells us that if anyone is to be blamed for Pakistan reaching this impasse, it is largely the armed forces of that country.

Therefore, the Turkish model may provide a temporary respite only. It cannot be a permanent solution for the governance of Pakistan.

Scenario Four

Lastly is the disintegration of Pakistan into three distinct regions. The successful completion of elections in the adjacent Jammu and Kashmir of the Indian Union and the coming of a popular government in Srinagar is bound to raise questions in Pakistan occupied Kashmir (POK). With everyone accepting them as free and fair elections, questions are bound to be asked about similar elections in POK. Added to it, the entire militant movement in the name of liberation of Kashmir by the Pakistani armed forces, shifting to POK, may find it difficult to sustain themselves when the people across the border start leading a normal life. Already there are signs that the locals are finding it difficult to support violence in any form. Even organisations like Hizb-ul Mujahideen and JKLF see no reason to stay away from mainstream politics of J&K and the Indian Union. The hardcore among them feel that General Musharraf having disowned the Taliban can also disown them if sufficient incentives are given by the West.

At another level, the coming of MMA in the bordering provinces of Afghanistan and Iran, that is NWFP and Baluchistan, signals two things: in these areas Talibanised version of rule is accepted by the majority of the people. The MMA leadership has already made a demand that the US war against Taliban-al-Qaida must be stopped. This majority support to MMA also indicates a process of polarisation in NWFP and Baluchistan on ethnic and tribal lines. Given the existing power equations in the Pakistan polity at this particular point of time in history, General Musharraf is in no position to repeat what his predecessor General Tikka Khan did in the early 1970s in these two provinces.

In this rather abnormal situation theocratic parties came close to capturing political power, but were not able to get it. There is every possibility of these provinces distancing themselves from Punjabi rulers in Islamabad. Will it result in creation of a new independent state like Greater Pukhtoonistan and Greater Baluchistan? This is a development that needs to be looked into.

Notes:

Index

Notes:

Notes: